D0903133

Religious Controversies
of the Elizabethan Age

Peter Milward

Religious Controversies of the Elizabethan Age
A Survey of Printed Sources

With a Foreword by G. R. Elton

Z
7778
.E5
M54
1977

London
The Scolar Press   1977

Printed and published in Great Britain by
The Scolar Press Limited, Ilkley, Yorkshire,
and 39 Great Russell Street, London WC1B 3PH

ISBN 0 85967 356 1

Copyright © Peter Milward, 1977

CONTENTS

37331

Foreword

BY G. R. ELTON

THERE are few more useful things a scholar can do than guide his fellows to the historical evidence. Since the only sound principle of research insists that everything available and conceivably relevant should be read, any enterprise that makes that awesome task more possible is highly welcome. The need is perhaps greatest for those who study the sixteenth and seventeenth centuries. Medievalists have long possessed the means to survey their relatively restricted sources, while those concerned with recent centuries are sufficiently aware of the problems that superabundance brings. Historians of early modern England, on the other hand, have for too long supposed that they knew all about their sources when they have in fact been operating with quite a small selection from them. This is particularly true for the history of intellectual and political discourse. All the debates and controversies analyzed in this volume are thoroughly familiar themes of Tudor history, from the debate engendered by the Elizabethan Settlement of 1559, through the Puritan and Catholic attacks on it, to the violent conflicts within both Protestant and Papist camps. But while the themes are familiar, the sources from which they must be studied are not; or rather, historians have been quite content to describe these conflicts from an often small selection of writings which turn up time and again, to the detriment of that comprehensive coverage which alone can reveal the truth.

And that truth matters. The history of Elizabethan England – of its Church and its religion – is one of loud debate. It may not always have been a very edifying debate – indeed, it rarely was that – but the heated and bitter arguments provided a main preoccupation for contemporaries and a main setting for the politics of the day. In this half-century, printing in English came of age. Technology supplied the means; pride and fear (disguised as religious faith) supplied the drive; the consequent outpouring both demands attention and by its sheer mass repels it. It has been extremely difficult to dig out the relevant works from such general catalogues as exist, catalogues which moreover quite often err in both the descriptions and distinctions. Here, at last, we have the key to open that door.

There is certainly something either awe-inspiring or frightening (or both) about these urgent, passionate and invariably partisan contributions, frequently repetitive, of course, but none the less varied. To look only at the outstanding writers and productions is to miss the general involvement and also quite often to overestimate the level of debate; it is to deprive oneself of any chance of judging this history dispassionately and in the round. The debate between Jewel and Harding, or that between Whitgift and Cartwright, without the contributions of the many others who rushed into the fray, becomes attenuated, esoteric and unreal. Only thus has it been possible for so long to overlook the strong theological strain in Puritan writing, usually treated as though it was concerned only with government and manners, and to discount the strong political strain in the work of Catholic controversialists who have been seen too regularly as purely men of the faith. Partial knowledge and the constant re-use of a familiar sample have hampered proper historical investigation and encouraged partisanship.

Now, however, there can no longer be any excuse for such dubious short-cuts. Father Milward's well-organized catalogue of 630 entries (a few of them duplicated because some writings bear on more than one controversy) at last enables the student to follow the dictates of the correct historical method by reading comprehensively. His descriptions are full, which matters greatly if confusion is to be avoided between different items similarly entitled and dealing so repetitively with a relatively restricted number of topics. This catalogue really enables one correctly to identify books and pamphlets found in libraries, as well as to seek them out in the first place. One word of warning: print does not exhaust the materials in existence, and it is hoped that historians will not overlook the drafts of finished work or (even more important) the treatises which remained in manuscript. But hitherto it has not been possible to place these more recondite materials in relation to what was printed, another valuable service performed by this book. Whatever one may think of two generations of intelligent men who spent so much time, thought and ink on lambasting one another in the cause of the Prince of Peace, a vital part of the age's experience flowed in those channels. Scholars' gratitude for the splendid help here offered will, one hopes, be some recompense to the compiler for what must often have been painful and tiresome labours. To have had that burden borne by another gladdens the unrepentant heart and calls for unstinted respect and acknowledgment.

Preface

A SURVEY of this kind is not so easy to categorize as it may appear on first sight. Since it professes to deal with the religious controversies of the Elizabethan Age, one's first instinct may be to place it under the heading of Theology or Church History. It certainly falls into both these categories; but it is by no means circumscribed by them. It may claim to have no less important bearings on the political history and philosophy of the period; for this was an age when politics and religion were even more than usually interlocked. Hooker's *Laws*, for instance, takes its immediate rise out of the religious controversies; and yet it is a document of fundamental importance in the history of English political thought. Behind this book stands the whole Puritan movement, as it developed out of the religious controversies and subsequently entered into the political structure of English life and thought. Or take Persons' *Conference about the Next Succession*: it belongs at least as much to the political as to the ecclesiastical history of the period, but hardly touches the theological issues at all.

Nor are the religious controversies unrelated to the philosophical movements that played so important a part in forming the intellectual climate of the seventeenth and eighteenth centuries. It is not just that the issues they dealt with were theological, and therefore raised the perennial question of the relation between faith and reason. What is of more far-reaching consequence is that the controversialists on either side called in question the fundamental presuppositions of their opponents, and thus indirectly encouraged many thinkers to look elsewhere for a common basis of thought — if not in theology, at least in ethics and natural philosophy — on which at least men might agree.

There is, moreover, a deep but much neglected connection between the religious controversies and the secular literature of the Elizabethan Age. At most, histories of English literature will refer to the controversies by way of explaining the literary gap of fifty years between the rise of humanism under the early Tudor kings and the renaissance of poetry and drama that took place in the later years of Elizabeth's reign. Yet these controversies were but gathering momentum during the period of this gap, roughly between 1530 and 1580; and they reached their full growth almost concurrently with that of the Elizabethan Renaissance in poetry and drama. Nor did they remain unrelated to that poetry and drama – witness the connection between Martin Marprelate and the 'university wits', between the Jesuits and John Donne (to mention only one poet), between the Jacobean divines and the metaphysical poets. As for Shakespeare himself, there is more than one point of contact (if hidden from the casual observer) between his plays and these controversies, which after all continued unabated during the whole period of his theatrical career.

It was, in fact, mainly with a view to exploring this sadly neglected aspect of Shakespeare's background that I was originally led to undertake this survey. Once I had entered into this field of research, I soon felt a strange perplexity growing upon me. Not only was the subject exceedingly intricate, with ramifications extending into almost every aspect of Elizabethan life and thought; but I was astonished – if not scandalised – to find that it was largely virgin territory, and that through it I must make my way alone. There exist, of course, detailed studies of this and that controversy. The bibliography of the Harding–Jewel controversy has been ably dealt with by A. C. Southern in his *Elizabethan Recusant Prose* – though he deflected much of his attention to mere considerations of style. On the early Puritan side, we have A. F. Scott Pearson's authoritative treatment of the life and writings of Thomas Cartwright. On the coming of the Jesuits and the Seminary Priests, we have competent biographies of both Allen and Campion, though the failure of Father Leo Hicks to publish his much desired life of Persons still leaves a yawning gap to be filled. The political–religious controversies have been ably studied in Father Thomas Clancy's *Papist Pamphleteers*. The Puritan movement of the late '80s has been more thoroughly investigated. The Marprelate controversy is, of course, particularly rich in scholarly researches. The separatist movement, beginning with Browne and Harrison and continuing with Barrow and Greenwood, has been minutely examined by Albert Peel and Leland Carlson in their valuable editions of Puritan texts. And, of course, the *Laws* of Hooker has attracted many specialist studies. As for the Appellants, they have been competently – though not always objectively – presented by T. G. Law in his study of *The Archpriest Controversy*. Nevertheless, with all these substantial studies, it remains true that large areas of the controversial literature of the age have hardly been examined; and in any case the field as a whole has been left uncharted, both in its general proportions and in its various ramifications and interconnections.

Hitherto specialist studies have, for understandable reasons, tended to follow confessional lines and confessional interests. Anglican scholars have naturally preferred to devote their attention to such divines as Jewel, Whitgift, Bancroft and Hooker. Non-conformist scholars have been more interested in the origins of Non-conformism – in Cartwright, Browne, Penry, Barrow and Greenwood. Catholic scholars have in their turn concentrated on recusant studies, with special reference to Allen, Campion and Persons. All this has obscured the fact that the controversies were closely interwoven throughout the period under consideration; so that a full understanding of any one book or author or controversy calls for some knowledge of its or his relation to other books or authors or controversies, each of them in turn linked with others in almost unending ramification. The more deeply I have delved into these writings, the more I have found myself led on from one to another, and to many of whose existence I had not previously known. Gradually I have come to recognise in them all together a certain pattern or network of inter-relationship that reaches back to the establishment of the Protestant religion at the beginning of Elizabeth's reign and carries on into the reign of James I, if not into that of Charles I, till it comes to a climax in the Puritan Rebellion.

What I have tried to do in the present volume is to trace this network with as much accuracy as possible: beginning with Jewel's challenge to the Catholics in 1559–60; then going on to the rise of Puritanism out of the Vestiarian disputes of 1566 and the *Admonition to Parliament* of 1572; then turning to the counter-challenge of Campion to the Anglican Church in 1580 and the immense literature this evoked at the time; then tracing the further development of the Presbyterian discipline in the '80s, culminating in the challenge of Martin Marprelate to the bishops and the judicious response of Hooker to the Puritans; then considering the disaffection of certain Seminary Priests towards the Jesuits, which led to the scandalous outburst of Appellant writings towards the end of the reign; and finally attempting to gather the scattered controversies of the last ten years of the reign into some kind of order. These movements, and the controversies which are at once their written expression and further provocation, are all inter-related. The general pattern emerging from them may perhaps be compared with that of a pendulum swinging now to the right, now to the left, according to the varying challenge of each decade.

I have therefore followed the development of these controversies not so much in a chronological as in a logical order — 'like as the waves make towards the pebbled shore' — now pursuing a particular controversy to its ultimate development, now returning to pick up the general thread of my argument and to pursue the next controversy that offers itself. In this way my survey is far from being a mere catalogue of bibliographical items in alphabetical order — such as one finds in standard works of reference like the indispensable *Short Title Catalogue* (here referred to as *STC*) or Allison and Rogers' *Catalogue of Catholic Books* (referred to as *AR*). Nor is it a chronological series of entries, such as one finds in several large libraries, in which each controversy would inevitably become confused with others in progress at the same time. Rather, it may be termed an analytical catalogue of all printed books that feature in these controversies given in their logical order of succession, so far as I have been able to work it out. It is at the same time more than a catalogue, as I have added a commentary explaining the context of each controversy and even each book, interspersed among the various items; though I have tried to keep this commentary as brief and factual as possible.

In recording the bibliographical items I have not been content to give only the short title, as one may find it in the *STC* or *AR*, considering that its brevity tells one little about the contents or context of the book. I have therefore preferred to transcribe the full title, however long it may be; though some of them, as will be seen, are often exceedingly long and sometimes no less tedious. In this way there is much valuable information to be gleaned not only about the book itself, but also about the general course of the controversy in which it occurs, and about the spirit (often mutually abusive) in which the controversy was conducted. In order to obtain these full titles, and to determine their implications with regard to contents and context, I have aimed at examining each item in this survey for myself — so far as possible in its first edition and any subsequent variant. This has entailed a kind of bibliographical pilgrimage from library to library, and from country to country; for I considered that recourse to the Ann Arbor Microfilms in such a project would be nothing short of ruinous to my eyesight. Beginning, therefore, with the Huntington Library in San Marino, California, I have visited the Folger Shakespeare Library in Washington, D.C., the Bodleian Library in Oxford, the Cambridge University Library, the Lambeth Palace Library, the Doctor Williams's Library in London, and the British Museum Library, as well as private collections of recusant literature at Ampleforth College, Stonyhurst College, Mount St. Mary's College, Oscott College, and Farm Street Church. It has been a fascinating voyage of exploration; and I am deeply indebted to the librarians and staff of all these libraries who have to a greater or lesser extent assisted me in my researches.

I have even come to feel a personal familiarity with all the books mentioned in this survey and with their authors. As I examine each book, I come to regard it with affection as a new specimen added to my growing collection; though my deepest affection remains with the earliest specimens, the writings of Jewel and Harding. However much their authors may have been at loggerheads with each other, I have learnt to feel, not just kindly or patronisingly disposed to them (as an indulgent uncle might feel to a wayward nephew), but even sympathetic to their respective viewpoints, however different they may be (in formal statement) from my own Catholic viewpoint. In all of them I feel I have discerned some precious aspect of that Christian truth which each author was convinced he fully possessed, and which he sincerely endeavoured to convey, if not to his opponents (of whose conversion he usually despaired), at least to his wavering supporters. For the purpose of this survey my emphasis has, it is true, been primarily bibliographical. But the human and religious interest of its several items cannot, after all, be kept out of sight for long. Here and there it gleams through the crevices of this volume, and will (I hope) be allowed to shine forth in full splendour from the pages of another volume of a more interpretative and readable nature.

As it is, what I have here provided is rather a work of reference, a tool of research for historians of the Elizabethan Age — whether political or ecclesiastical or philosophical or literary historians. In studying this period at first hand (rather than through secondary works) one comes across frequent mention of one or other of the books mentioned in this survey, and possibly conceives a desire to follow up such a mention and find out more of its bibliographical context. Here this context may be found in detail, and (I dare to claim) nowhere else — unless one prefers to go through the laborious process (though for me a loving one) that lies behind this book. For the process has indeed been a laborious one, not only because the books involved are scattered round the world in different libraries, and are in some cases exceedingly rare, but also because, even when tracked down and opened up, they often reveal little of their true identity on first inspection. The circumstances of their composition — particularly when they were opposed to the established Church, which in Elizabethan times was practically identified with the State — were often such as to require secrecy. Hence the names of author and printer are in many cases withheld, or only partly revealed in the form of initials (sometimes inverted), which have to be deciphered. Even the date of publication, if given at all, is at times falsified; and even when correctly given, it usually (but not always) follows the old calendar with the old year carrying on till March. As for the contents, some authors assume a knowledge of the context in their readers and never once explain the state of the question; and they may write against one or more books without once specifying either the title or the name of the author. Sometimes, too, when they name a book, it may be one that has not withstood the vicissitudes of time, or one that even then existed only in manuscript.

A difficulty of a more practical kind has been to determine the limits of this survey, as to place and time, nationality and language. It is easy enough to say 'the controversies that took place during the reign of Queen Elizabeth in matters of religion'. But in that age where precisely can one say that religion ends and politics or philosophy or literature begin? And what about books written not in English, but in French or Latin; and what about books written by foreigners, whether in English or French or Latin, provided they are related to the controversies in England? The *STC* excludes from its pages all books written in Latin and published abroad, though by English authors; and so it ignores Sanders' *De Visibili Monarchia Ecclesiae*, which is one of the most important works in Elizabethan controversy. Sometimes, moreover, a book written in Latin and published in England is countered by a book written in English and published abroad, and vice versa. *AR* excludes all Latin books (or almost all), though published by English recusants and contributing to English controversies. And what about foreign theologians, like

Robert Bellarmine, who though an Italian, living and writing in Rome, came to take a leading part in the English controversies (those conducted in Latin) from the '80s onwards? Whenever such questions have arisen, it has been my general policy to be all-inclusive, even at the risk of extending my quest to apparent endlessness – though here and there I have uttered a reluctant 'No'.

As for the time limits of this survey, it is simple enough to begin with the accession of Queen Elizabeth; for that important event, which may well be called the main turning-point of English history, was in fact the starting-point of all the controversies recorded in this volume. But when the Queen died in 1603, the controversies did not all die with her, though many of them, like the Appellant controversy, did, and the new reign of James I certainly brought in a new approach to religion. There are not a few controversies that linger on into the new reign, and others that had their beginnings in the closing years of Elizabeth but their full development under James. Still, I have done my best to round off the various controversies as best I could with the death of Queen Elizabeth, though in one or two cases I have ventured to trespass into the new reign. In any case, I have found both my studies of these religious controversies and my previous interest in Shakespearian drama combining to demand the preparation of a sequel to this volume under the parallel title of *Religious Controversies of the Jacobean Age.*

Finally, I must acknowledge my indebtedness, not only to the librarians and staff of the various libraries I have visited in the course of my pilgrimage, but also to the authorities of Sophia University for granting me a sabbatical year in which to bring my researches to their (comparative) completion, and to those who have afforded me hospitality in the various places I have stopped at on my pilgrim's route: Mgr. James Hourihan, of Saint Andrew's Church, Pasadena; the Rector of Georgetown University, Washington; Canon Raymund Hammer, of the Queen's College, Birmingham; Dr. Anthony Dyson, Principal of Ripon Hall, Oxford; Canon Paul Taylor, pastor of the Church of Our Lady and the English Martyrs, Cambridge; the Master of Campion Hall, Oxford; the Rectors of Stonyhurst, Mount St. Mary's and Oscott; the Superior of the Jesuit residence at Mount Street, London; the Abbot of Ampleforth; and, above all, my own family in Wimbledon. I am also particularly indebted to my publisher, Mr. John Commander of The Scolar Press, to his predecessor, Dr. Robin Alston, to the Editor of the *English Recusant Literature* series of facsimiles, Dr. David Rogers, and to Mr. Sean Magee of The Scolar Press, who have all encouraged and assisted me in a variety of ways. I hope that with the publication of this volume I may do something to repay my debt.

Sophia University, Tokyo   Peter Milward, S.J.
1 May 1975

ABBREVIATIONS

AR *A Catalogue of Catholic Books in English Printed Abroad or Secretly in England,*
1558–1640,
by A. F. Allison and D. M. Rogers (Bognor Regis, 1956)

ERL *English Recusant Literature, 1558–1640,*
edited by D. M. Rogers: series of facsimile reprints
(The Scolar Press, London and Ilkley)

GS *General Series* of Scolar Press facsimiles
(London and Ilkley)

STC *A Short-Title Catalogue of Books Printed in England, Scotland, & Ireland and of*
English Books Printed Abroad, 1475–1640,
compiled by A. W. Pollard and G. R. Redgrave (London, 1926)

Wing *Short-Title Catalogue of Books Printed in England, Scotland, Ireland, Wales, and*
British America and of English Books Printed in Other Countries, 1641–1700,
compiled by Donald Wing (3 vols.; New York, 1945)

NOTE *In the bibliographical entries*
only the first editions are noticed,
except where special mention is made in the text
of other editions varying from the first.
Fuller bibliographical information
may be found in the STC *and* AR.

CHAPTER 1

Anglican Challenge

a) *The Jewel–Harding controversy*

THE ACCESSION of Elizabeth to the English throne in 1558, and the consequent religious settlement in favour of the Protestant party, inevitably gave rise to a series of religious controversies that came to provide Elizabethan printers and publishers with an unfailing source of 'copy'. The first of these controversies, termed 'The Great Controversy' by A. C. Southern in view no less of the number of its printed items than of the importance of its theological issues, was initiated by the victorious Protestants towards the end of 1559. Its occasion was a sermon preached by the bishop-elect of Salisbury, John Jewel, at Paul's Cross on 26 November 1559, and repeated by him at court on 17 March, and again at Paul's Cross on 31 March 1560. In it he challenged the Catholics to justify certain of their beliefs and practices, listed in twenty-seven articles, from the writings of Scripture and the Church Fathers of the first six centuries after Christ. This 'Challenge Sermon' (as it came to be called) produced a sensation at the time; but the Catholic response was at first slow and surreptitious, as the Catholic theologians were either in confinement and bound to silence or else in exile and disarray. The first reaction took the form of a private correspondence between the deposed Dean of St. Paul's, Dr. Henry Cole, and the Bishop of Salisbury. This was shortly afterwards published by the latter, as a further vindication of his position, together with the sermon that had given rise to the correspondence.

1. *The copie of a Sermon pronounced by the Byshop of Salisburie at Paules Crosse the second Sondaye before Ester in the yere of our Lord, 1560. wherupon D. Cole first sought occasion to encounter, shortly set forthe as nere as the authour could call it to rembraunce, without any alteration or addition.* 1560   (STC 14599a)

2. *The True Copies of the Letters betwene the reverend father in God Iohn Bisshop of Sarum and D. Cole, upon occasion of a Sermon that the said Bishop preached before the Quenes Maiestie, and hyr most honorable Counsayle.* 1560   (STC 14612)

(The items of this correspondence were set forth in the following order:

a) 'The Copie of a letter sente from D. Cole to the Bishop of Sarum, upon occasion of a Sermon that the saide Bishop had preached in the Courte before the Quenes Maiestie.' 18 March

b) 'The Bishop of Salisburies answere unto the letter afore written.' 20 March

c) 'D. Coles seconde Letter to the Bishop of Sarum.' 24 March

d) 'The answere of Io. Bishop of Sarum unto D. Coles seconde Letter.' 29 March

e) 'Doctour Coles answere to certaine parcelles of the seconde Letter of the Bishop of Sarum, set forthe in such sorte as it came from the Authour.' 8 April

f) 'A Letter sent from the Bishoppe of Sarum to Doctour Cole, wherin he requireth of him a true and ful Copie of the former answere.' 22 July

g) 'The Replie of the Bishoppe of Sarum to the Letter above written, which D. Cole contrarie to even dealing had geven out and sent abroade, not to the said Bishop to whome he wrote it, but prively and secretly unto certaine of his owne frendes.' 18 May)

Not long after the publication of this correspondence there appeared an anonymous Catholic answer in manuscript, dealing with the first of Jewel's twenty-seven articles on the subject of 'private Mass'. It was passed from hand to hand and eagerly copied out by the Catholics. Eventually it came to the attention of an Oxford scholar, Thomas Cooper, who later became Bishop of Lincoln, and then of Winchester. He published the Catholic manuscript, together with a reply of his own, without giving his name; but he was later identified as author by Edward Cradocke in 1572, in his book, *The Shippe of assumed safetie*, and by William Fulke in 1580, in his book against *T. Stapleton and Martiall* (36, 67) and in *A Retentive* (47, 154).

There were three issues of this book in the same year, 1562, each bearing an altered title, because the Catholics (as the publisher complained in his preface to the third issue) bought it up and separated the confutation from the *Apologie*, saying 'that it was now published in defence of their masse, by the alowance of the reverend father in God Bishop of London'.

3. *An Apologie of private Masse, spred abroade in writing without name of the authour: as it seemeth, against the offer and protestacion made in certayne Sermons by the reverent father Bisshop of Salsburie: with an answer to the same Apologie, set foorth for the maintenance and defence of the trueth. Perused and allowed, by the reverent father in God Edmonde Bisshop of London, accordynge to the order appoincted in the Queenes maiestes Iniunctions.* 1562 (STC 14615)

The other two editions were variously entitled:

A Lewde Apologie of pryvate Masse, sedyciously spred abroade in wrytinge without name of the authour: as it seemeth, against the offer and protestacion made in certaine Sermons by the reverende father Bishop of Salesburie: With a learned and godly answere to the same Apologie, set foorth for the maintenance and defence of the trueth. 1562 (STC 14617)

An Apologie of private Masse sediciously spredde abroade in writyng without name of the authour: as it semeth, against the offer and pro-testacion made in certain sermons by the reverende father Bishop of Salesburie. With an answere and confutacion of the same, set forth for the defence and maintenance of the trueth. 1562 (STC 14616)

Three years later, when the Catholic response to Jewel was at last getting under way among the exiles at Louvain, Cooper's answer was in turn answered by a young scholar, John Rastell.

4. *A Replie against an answer (falslie intitled) in Defence of the truth, made by Iohn Rastell: M. of Art, and student in divinitie.* 1565 (STC 20728, AR 707, ERL 14)

The main counter-attack, when it came, was led by a mature scholar and doctor of divinity, Thomas Harding, who had formerly been Regius Pro-fessor of Hebrew at Oxford and Warden-elect of New College. His path had already crossed that of Jewel in various ways. They were both Devon men and Oxford scholars, and they had both followed the new ideas under Henry VIII and Edward VI; but Harding had retracted his Protestantism under Mary, and had received a benefice in the diocese of Salisbury, only to be ejected under Elizabeth by the new bishop, John Jewel. He now emerged as the leading Catholic controversialist against the English Protestants, and has a good claim to be regarded as the greatest writer on his side for his clear argumentation and vigorous style. The first of his writings, which greatly heartened the Catholics, came out in two editions in successive years, one at Louvain in 1564, the other 'augmented with certaine quotations and addi-tions' at Antwerp in 1565.

5. *An Answere to Maister Iuelles Chalenge, by Doctor Harding.* 1564, 1565 (STC 12758−9, AR 372−3, ERL 229)

Jewel was now faced with the formidable task of replying to this answer; and to it he devoted much of his time with the assistance of a team of helpers. Before his *Replie* had come from the press, he expressed criticism of Harding's book in an unpublished sermon at Paul's Cross on 27 May 1565. To this Harding responded with an open letter, 'To Maister Iohn Iewell', printed in the form of a broadsheet at Antwerp on 12 June, requiring a true copy of Jewel's sermon − ironically echoing Jewel's similar demand of Cole five years before. Instead of complying with his request, Jewel preached another sermon on 8 July, repeating his criticism; and to this Harding replied in a small pamphlet, entitled *A Briefe Answere*.

6. *A Briefe Answere of Thomas Harding Doctor of Divinitie, touching certaine untruthes, with which Maister Iohn Iuell charged him in his late Sermon at Paules Cross the viii of Iuly, Anno 1565.* 1565   (not in STC, AR 374, ERL 309)

The following month Jewel's lengthy *Replie* was published, with yet another issue in 1566.

7. *A Replie unto M. Hardinges Answeare: By perusing whereof the discrete, and diligent Reader may easily see, the weake, and unstable groundes of the Romaine Religion, whiche of late hath been accompted Catholique. By Iohn Iewel Bishoppe of Sarisburie.* 1565, 1566 (STC 14606—7)

To this reply Harding responded with surprising rapidity in two successive and substantial volumes, each entitled *A Reioindre*. The first, which he published the following May, dealt only with the first of Jewel's articles, on 'private Mass' (a term to which he objected). The second, which came out a year later in 1567, dealt with three other articles on the Mass. Fuller replies to further articles Harding left to his colleagues at Louvain.

8. *A Reioindre to M. Iewels Replie. By perusing wherof the discrete and diligent Reader may easily see, the Answer to parte of his insolent Chalenge iustified, and his Obiections against the Masse, whereat the Priest sometime receiveth the holy Mysteries without present companie to receive with him, for that cause by Luthers Schoole called Private Masse, clearely confuted. By Thomas Harding Doctor of Divinitie.* 1566   (STC 12760, AR 377, ERL 303)

9. *A Reioindre to M. Iewels Replie against the Sacrifice of the Masse. In which the doctrine of the Answere to the xvii Article of his Chalenge is defended, and further proved, and al that his Replie conteineth against the Sacrifice, is clearly confuted and disproved. By Thomas Harding Doctor of Divinitie.* 1567   (STC 12761, AR 378, ERL 38)

Jewel himself was apparently too busy to reply to these two rejoinders, and he left the task to a Puritan minister, Edward Dering, who was gaining a reputation for his preaching. The latter brought out his *Sparing Restraint* of Harding in 1568.

10. *A Sparing Restraint, of many lavishe Untruthes, which M. Doctor dothe chalenge, in the first Article of my Lorde of Sarisburies Replie. By Edward Dering Student in Divinitie. With an answere unto that long, and uncourteous Epistle, entituled to M. Iuel, and set before M. Hardings Reioinder.* 1568   (STC 6725)

Meanwhile, Jewel and Harding were also protagonists in a parallel, and wider-ranging, controversy arising out of the former's *Apologie* for the Church of England, which appeared two years after his Challenge Sermon. This was originally published in Latin for the benefit of continental readers, and then translated into English in two separate versions. The second version, of 1564, which became the accepted one, bore the initials A. B. — for Lady Anne Bacon, the wife of the Lord Keeper, Sir Nicholas Bacon, and mother of Sir Francis Bacon. Both in Latin and in English the author's name was withheld, as an indication of the official nature of the work; but in it Harding easily recognized the style of Jewel; and when it was reissued after his death in both languages, it invariably carried his name.

11. *Apologia Ecclesiae Anglicanae*. 1562   (STC 14581)

12. *An Apologie, or aunswer in defence of the Church of England, concerninge the state of Religion used in the same. Newly set forth in Latine, and nowe translated into Englishe.* 1562   (STC 14590, GS 15)

13. *An Apologie, or answere in defence of the Churche of Englande, with a briefe and plaine declaration of the true Religion professed and used in the same.* 1564   (STC 14591)

    (anr. trans.)

To this work Harding again turned his critical attention and, using the 1564 translation, came out in the following year with his *Confutation*, which may be regarded as his controversial masterpiece. Once again a battle of books ensued. Jewel produced his *Defence* in 1567, and Harding replied with *A Detection of Errors* in 1568. By way of rejoinder Jewel brought out a second, augmented edition of his *Defence* in 1570, adding special notes where necessary to the first edition.

14. *A Confutation of a Booke Intituled An Apologie of the Church of England, by Thomas Harding Doctor of Divinitie.* 1565   (STC 12762, AR 375, ERL 310)

15. *A Defence of the Apologie of the Churche of Englande, Conteininge an Answeare to a certaine Booke lately set foorthe by M. Hardinge, and Entituled, A Confutation of &c. By Iohn Iewel Bishop of Sarisburie.* 1567.   (STC 14600)

16. *A Detection of sundrie foule errours, lies, sclaunders, corruptions, and other false dealinges, touching Doctrine, and other matters, uttered and practized by M. Iewel, in a Booke lately by him set foorth entituled, A Defence of the Apologie, &c. By Thomas Harding Doctor of Divinitie.* 1568   (STC 12763, AR 376, ERL 202)

17. *A Defense of the Apologie of the Churche of Englande. Conteininge*

> an *Answeare to a certaine Booke lately set foorthe by M. Hardinge, and Entituled, A Confutation of &c. Whereunto there is also newly added an Answeare unto an other like Booke, written by the saide M. Hardinge, Entituled, A Detection of sundrie foule Errours &c. Printed at Lovaine, Anno 1568, and inserted into the foremer Answeare, as occasion, and place required, as by special Notes added to the Margine it maie appeare. By Iohn Bishop of Sarisburie.* 1570 (STC 14601)

(anr. ed. of 15)

b) *Subordinate controversies*

This contest between Jewel and Harding was brought to an end by the death first of Jewel in 1571, and then of Harding in the following year. But other scholars had meanwhile come to the support of one or other protagonist, and many lesser skirmishes arose. One of the earliest and most prolific of the Catholic writers was John Rastell, whose defence of the *Apologie of private Masse* has already been noticed. He also wrote an answer to Jewel's Challenge Sermon in the very year of its delivery, but was unable to get it published till four years later in 1564, when the Catholic counter-attack at length began. This contained a counter-challenge to Jewel, which was separately published early in the following year.

> 18. *A confutation of a sermon, pronounced by M. Iuell, at Paules Crosse, the second Sondaie before Easter (which Catholikes doe call Passion Sondaie) Anno Dni. MDLX. By Iohn Rastell M. of Art, and student in divinitie.* 1564   (STC 20726, AR 705, ERL 13)

> 19. *A Copie of a challenge, taken owt of the confutation of M. Iuells sermon made by Iohn Rastell.* 1565   (STC 20727, AR 706)

On the appearance of Jewel's *Replie* to Harding's *Answere*, Rastell further undertook to expose the fraudulent dealings of the former in a treatise comprising three books, of which the first two were published together in the spring of 1566 and the third separately towards the end of that year.

> 20. *A Treatise intitled, Beware of M. Iewel. By Iohn Rastel Master of Arte and Student of Divinitie.* 1566   (STC 20729, AR 709, ERL 255)

> 21. *The Third Booke, Declaring by Examples out of Auncient Councels, Fathers, and Later writers, that it is time to Beware of M. Iewel. By Iohn Rastel Master of Art and Student of Divinitie.* 1566   (Not in STC, AR 708, ERL 332)

Finally, before withdrawing from the arena of controversy to join the Society of Jesus, he published *A Briefe Shew* in 1567 in support of Harding's *Confutation* of Jewel's *Apologie.*

22. *A Briefe Shew of the false Wares packt together in the named, Apology of the Churche of England. By Iohn Rastell M. of Art and student of Divinitie.* 1567   (STC 20725, AR 704)

All his writings were, however, ignored by the Protestants, until many years later his *Confutation* of Jewel was answered by William Fulke, Master of Pembroke Hall, Cambridge. This was not because it had acquired any new relevance in 1579, when Fulke published his 'Refutation', but because it was the abstract policy of the latter to leave no Catholic work of controversy unanswered, if he could help it. Even so, Rastell's work failed to receive Fulke's undivided attention, being the third of three works which were dealt with together.

23. [= 46, 63] 'A Refutation of Maister Iohn Rastels Confutation as he calleth it of maister Iewels sermon' in *D. Heskins, D. Sanders, and M. Rastel, accounted (among their faction) three pillers and Arch-patriarches of the Popish Synagogue, (utter enemies to the truth of Christes Gospell, and all that syncerely professe the same) overthrowne, and detected of their severall blasphemous heresies. By D. Fulke, Maister of Pembroke Hall in Cambridge.* 1579   (STC 11433)

Another of Harding's supporters, also from New College, was Thomas Dorman. He undertook to defend four of the articles challenged by Jewel: those dealing with the Papal claims and the sacrifice of the Mass, as being of more fundamental importance than the others.

24. *A Proufe of Certeyne Articles in Religion, denied by M. Iuell, sett furth in defence of the Catholyke beleef therein, by Thomas Dorman, Bachiler in Divinite. Whereunto is added in the end, a conclusion, conteinyng xii Causes, whereby the Author acknowlegeth hym self to have byn stayd in hys olde Catholyke fayth that he was baptized in, wysshyng the same to be made common to many for the lyke stay in these perilouse tymes.* 1564   (STC 7062, AR 275, ERL 321)

The Protestant reply to Dorman was undertaken by the Dean of St. Paul's, Alexander Nowell, beginning with a detailed criticism of Dorman's Preface. This criticism was published separately and went into two editions in 1565. The following year he published a continuation, limiting his criticism to Dorman's first article, on the headship of the Church.

25. *A Reproufe, written by Alexander Nowell, of a booke entituled, A Proufe of Certayne Articles in Religion denied by M. Iuell, set furth by Thomas Dorman, Bachiler of Divinitie; and Imprinted at Antwerpe by Iohn Latius. Anno 1564.* 1565 (30 May and 13 July) (STC 18740–41)

26. *The Reproufe of M. Dorman his proufe of certaine Articles in Religion*

> *&c. continued by Alexander Nowell. With a defense of the chief author-*
> *itie and government of Christian Princes as well in causes Ecclesiasticall,*
> *as civill, within their owne dominions, by M. Dorman malitiouslie*
> *oppugned.* 1566   (STC 18742)

Before the latter book was published, Dorman replied to Nowell's criticism of his Preface; and this reply was eventually answered by Nowell two years later in a composite work of refutation.

> 27. *A Disproufe of M. Nowelles Reproufe. By Thomas Dorman Bachiler of*
> *Divinitie.* 1565 (3 December)   (STC 7061, AR 274, ERL 234)

> 28. [= 42] *A Confutation as wel of M. Dormans last Boke entituled A*
> *Disproufe &c. as also of D. Sander his causes of Transubstantiation, by*
> *Alexander Nowel. Whereby our Countreymen (specially the simple and*
> *unlerned) may understand, howe shamefully they are abused by those*
> *and like Bokes, pretended to be written for their instruction.* 1567
> (STC 18739)

Dorman also published a challenge to a sermon preached by Jewel at Paul's Cross on 15 June 1567, in which Jewel defended his *Replie* to Harding. But his challenge remained unanswered either by Jewel or by Nowell, or even by Fulke later on.

> 29. *A Request To M. Iewell. That he kepe his promise, made by solemne*
> *protestation in his late sermon at Pauls Cross the 15. of Iune. Anno.*
> *1567. By Thomas Dorman, Bacheler of Divinitie.* 1567   (STC 7063,
> AR 276, ERL 148)

c) *Stapleton, Sanders, Allen*

The work of Nicholas Sanders dealt with in the second half of Nowell's *Confutation* is his *Supper of our Lord* (1565), which will be recorded in due time (41). Meanwhile, we have first to notice the writings of another young scholar from New College among the Catholic exiles at Louvain: Thomas Stapleton. He subsequently emerged as the most eminent of English Catholic theologians, though by then he had come to confine his controversial writings to Latin. He now appeared mainly as a translator of books chosen for the support they gave to the Catholic position in the 'challenge' controversy. The books he translated into English at this time were: the *Apologia* of Frederick Staphylus, an eminent convert to the Catholic Church from Lutheranism (1562); the *Ecclesiastica Historia* of the Venerable Bede, which was also published in its original Latin at Louvain in 1566; and (probably) the treatise *De Expresso Dei Verbo* of Cardinal Hosius, the leading Catholic theologian of the time (1558). To these translations he also added some original discourses of his own against the Protestants. In his discourse appended to the *Apologie*, besides taking issue with the leading reformers on the continent, he also criticised a recent sermon by the Bishop of London, Edmund Grindal, for his attack on the Catholic doctrine of Purgatory. The discourse appended to his translation of Bede's *History* was also published separately under the title, *A Fortresse of the Faith*. Thus he gradually came to appear as a leading controversialist in his own right.

30. *The Apologie of Fridericus Staphylus Counseller to the late Emperour Ferdinandus, &c. Intreating Of the true and right understanding of holy Scripture, Of the translation of the Bible in to the vulgar tongue, Of disagreement amonge the protestants, Translated out of Latin in to English by Thomas Stapleton, Student in Divinite. Also a discourse of the Translatour uppon the doctrine of the protestants which he trieth by the three first founders and fathers thereof, Martin Luther, Philip Melanchthon, and especially Iohn Calvin.* 1565 (STC 23230, AR 794, ERL 268)

31. *A Sermon, at the funeral solemnitie of the most high and mighty Prince Ferdinandus, the late Emperour of most famous memorye, holden in the Cathedrall Churche of saint Paule in London, the third of October, 1564. Made by the reverend father in God, Edmund Grindall, bishop of London.* 1564 (STC 12377)

32. *The History of the Church of Englande. Compiled by Venerable Bede, Englishman. Translated out of Latin in to English by Thomas Stapleton Student in Divinite.* 1565 (STC 1778, AR 82, ERL 162)

33. *A Fortresse of the Faith, First planted amonge us englishmen, and continued hitherto in the universall Church of Christ, The faith of which time Protestants call, Papistry. By Thomas Student in Divinite.* 1565 (STC 23232, AR 797, ERL 163)

34. *Of the Expresse Worde of God. A shorte, but a most excellent treatyse and very necessary for this tyme. Written in Latin, by the right Reverend, Lerned, and vertuous Father Stanislaus Hosius, Bisshop of Warmia, Cardinal of the Holy Apostolyke See of Rome, and one of the Presidents in the late General Councel holden at Trent. Newly translated in to English.* 1567 (STC 13889, AR 404, ERL 73)

In none of these books does the author directly attack Jewel, concerned as he is with presenting the positive proofs for the Catholic position; but an implicit reference to the challenge of Jewel is everywhere apparent. Only in one book does he take open part in the controversy, with a criticism of Jewel's *Replie* (7) to Harding's *Answere* entitled *A Returne of Untruthes*. For this he was particularly commended both by Harding himself at the time and later by Robert Persons. Yet though his name is given on the title-page, and though there was only one book with this title, there appears a strange confusion concerning its authorship. In his 'Catalogue of Popish Books' pre-fixed to his refutation of *T. Stapleton and Martiall* (1580) (36), William Fulke mentions it twice, first as 'Rastel's Return of untruths, answered by M. Iewel' (though no book by Rastell, nor of this name, was answered by Jewel), and then as a book by Stapleton awaiting an answer (which was indeed the case). Later, when commending the book in his *Relation of the Triall* (1604), Persons attributes it to Harding himself.

> 35. *A Returne of Untruthes upon M. Iewelles Replie. Partly of such, as he hath Slaunderously charged D. Harding withal; Partly of such other, as he hath committed about the triall thereof, in the Text of the foure first Articles of his Replie. With a Reioyndre upon the Principall Matters of the Replie, treated in the Thirde and Fourthe Articles. By Thomas Stapleton student in Divinite.* 1566 (STC 23234, AR 799, ERL 308)

For the time being these writings were ignored by the Protestant side, until William Fulke came to deal with the *Fortresse of the Faith* in con-junction with a book by Martial. The work of Hosius was also refuted by Fulke in Latin, without any reference to the English translation.

> 36. [= 67] 'An Overthrow By W. Fulke Doctor of Divinitie, and Master of Pembroke Hall in Cambridge: to the feeble Fortresse of Popish faith received from Rome, and lately advaunced by Thomas Stapleton Student in Divinitie.' in *T. Stapleton and Martiall (two Popish Here-tikes) confuted, and of their particular heresies detected. By D. Fulke, Master of Pembrooke hall in Cambridge.* 1580 (STC 11456)

> 37. *Gulielmi Fulconis Angli, ad epistolam Stanislai Hosii Varmiensis episcopi de expresso Dei verbo Responsio.* 1578 (STC 11417)

Another related controversy in which Stapleton became involved at this time was with the newly appointed Bishop of Winchester, Robert Horne. Horne has undertaken to refute an unpublished manuscript of John Fecken-ham, the imprisoned Abbot of Westminster, in which the latter declared his scruples about taking the Oath of Supremacy. Horne now published the Abbot's declaration together with his own sharp criticisms; but as Feckenham was in no position to defend himself, Stapleton took up the matter with the help of material sent to him from England either by the Abbot himself or by another of the imprisoned Catholic leaders, Nicholas Harpsfield.

> 38. *An Answeare Made by Rob. Bishoppe of Wynchester, to a Booke entituled, The Declaration of suche Scruples, and staies of Conscience, touchinge the Othe of Supremacy, as M. Iohn Fekenham, by wrytinge did deliver unto the L. Bishop of Winchester, with his Resolutions made thereunto.* 1566 (STC 13818)

39. *A Counterblast to M. Hornes Vayne Blaste against M. Fekenham,*
    touching, The Othe of Supremacy. By perusing whereof shall appeare,
    besides the holy Scriptures, as it were a Chronicle of the Continual
    Practise of Christes Churche in al ages and Countries, from the time of
    Constantin the Great, until our daies: Proving the Popes and Bishops
    Supremacy in Ecclesiastical causes: and Disproving the Princes Sup-
    remacy in the same Causes. By Thomas Stapleton Student in Divinitie.
    1567 (STC 23231, AR 796, ERL 311)

This important work of Stapleton, dealing as it did with the fundamental
issue of ecclesiastical or royal supremacy, remained unanswered for six years,
when the Dean of Salisbury, John Bridges, at last undertook to refute
Book I, in his *Supremacie of Christian Princes*. In the same work he also
dealt with a part of Sanders' Latin treatise, *De Visibili Monarchia* (50),
where this issue was also discussed.

40. [= 51] *The Supremacie of Christian Princes, over all persons*
    throughout their dominions, in all causes so wel Ecclesiastical as
    temporall, both against the Counterblast of Thomas Stapleton, replying
    on the Reverend father in Christe, Robert Bishop of Winchester, and
    also Against Nicolas Sanders his Visible Monarchie of the Romaine
    Church, touching this controversie of the Princes Supremacie.
    Answered by Iohn Bridges. 1573 (STC 3737)

Another prominent personality in the group of Catholic scholars at
Louvain was the above-mentioned Nicholas Sanders, who joined them in
1565 after having accompanied Cardinal Hosius to the Council of Trent and
on other missions. He now devoted his energy to the common task of res-
ponding to Jewel's challenge. His first work was a defence of the Mass and
the doctrine of transubstantiation, specifically against Jewel's *Apologie* (12),
but also in response to a fresh challenge on this point made by Nowell in his
Reproufe (25) of Dorman. Sanders set forth his case in six books, adding a
seventh at the last moment in answer to Jewel's recently published *Replie*
(7) to Harding. This work went into two editions in successive years, with a
revised title-page in the second edition incorporating the seventh book.

41. *The supper of our Lord set foorth in six Bookes, according to the truth*
    of the gospell, and the faith of the Catholike Churche. By Nicolas
    Saunder Doctor of Divinitie. 1565 (STC 21694, AR 752)

At the end of the volume is added the title of Book VII:

Here unto is added the seventh booke, conteining a confutation of the
fifth article of M. Iuels Reply against D. Harding, concerning the reall
presence of Christes body in the supper of our Lorde.

The second issue has the following title:

The supper of our Lord set foorth according to the truth of the Gospell and Catholike faith. By Nicolas Saunder, Doctor of Divinitie, with a confutation of such false doctrine as the Apologie of the Churche of England, M. Nowels chalenge, or M. Iuels Replie have uttered, touching the real presence of Christe in the Sacrament. 1566 (STC 21695, AR 753, ERL 199)

As Sanders had taken up Nowell's challenge to Dorman, it was natural for Nowell in turn to answer Sanders' arguments; and this he undertook in part in his *Confutation* of Dorman's *Disproufe*. In his 'Catalogue of Popish Books' appended both to his *Retentive* (1580) (47) and to his refutation of *T. Stapleton and Martiall* (1580) (36), William Fulke mentions 'Sanders on the Sacrament, in part answered by M. Nowel'; but he was evidently dissatisfied with Nowell's partial answer, and went on to provide a fuller answer himself in another of his composite works of refutation.

42. [= 28] *A Confutation as wel of M. Dormans last Boke entituled A Disproufe &c. as also of D. Sander his causes of Transubstantiation, by Alexander Nowel. Whereby our Countreymen (specially the simple, and unlerned) may understand, howe shamefully they are abused by those and like Bokes, pretended to be written for their instruction. 1567* (STC 18739)

43. [= 156] *A Reioynder to Bristows Replie in defence of Allens scroll of Articles and Booke of Purgatorie. Also the cavils of Nicholas Sander D. in Divinitie about the Supper of our Lord, and the Apologie of the Church of England, touching the doctrine thereof, Confuted by William Fulke, Doctor in Divinitie, and Master of Pembroke Hall in Cambridge. 1581* (STC 11448)

Two more works of controversy came from Sanders' pen in 1567 on the other important issues of the Papal primacy and devotion to the Saints and their images – both of them in answer to Jewel, but the latter more explicitly in response to Jewel's *Replie* to Harding (7). Both works were later republished in 1624.

44. *The Rocke of the Churche Wherein the Primacy of S. Peter and of his Successours the Bishops of Rome is proved out of Gods Worde. By Nicolas Sander D. of divinity. 1567* (STC 21692, AR 750, ERL 328)

45. *A Treatise of the Images of Christ, and of his Saints: and that it is unlaufull to breake them, and lauful to honour them. With a Confutation of such false doctrine as M. Iewel hath uttered in his Replie, concerning that matter. Made by Nicolas Sander, Doctor of Divinitie. 1567* (STC 21696, AR 754, ERL 282)

Neither of these books received any reply from the Protestant side at the time; but later on they were both dealt with by Fulke in his compendious manner of refutation, beginning with the latter.

46. [= 23, 63] 'A Confutation of an idolatrous Treatise of Nicolas Sander Doctor in Divinitie, which mainteyneth the making and honouring of Images, by W. F. Doctour in Divinitie', in *D. Heskins, D. Sanders, and M. Rastel, accounted (among their faction) three pillers, and Arch-patriarches of the Popish Synagogue, (utter enemies to the truth of Christes Gospell, and all that syncerely professe the same) overthrowne, and detected of their severall blasphemous heresies. By D. Fulke, Maister of Pembroke Hall in Cambridge.* 1579 (STC 11433)

47. [= 154] *A Retentive, to stay good Christians, in true faith and religion, against the motives of Richard Bristow. Also A Discoverie of the Daungerous Rocke of the Popish Church, commended by Nicholas Sander D. of Divinitie. Done by William Fulke Doctor of divinitie, and Maister of Pembroke hall in Cambridge.* 1580 (STC 11449)

In addition to his English works of controversy, Sanders was also lecturing and writing in Latin against his adversaries in England from his chair as Professor of Theology at Louvain. He published three lectures on various points of controversy concerning the Mass in 1566; a treatise in two books on the honour due to sacred images in 1569; and above all his magnum opus, *De Visibili Monarchia Ecclesiae*, in 1571. This was universally acclaimed by the Catholics, and all but won for its author a cardinal's hat. By the Protestants it was recognised as a serious threat to their intellectual position, and Sir William Cecil himself arranged for its refutation.

48. *Nicolai Sanderi Sacrae Theologiae Professoris Tres Orationes in Scholis Publicis Lovanii Habitae, 14.Cal.Ianuarii, An. Domini.1565. 1. De Transubstantiatione. 2. De linguis officiorum Ecclesiasticorum. 3. De pluribus missis in eodem templo celebrandis.* 1566

49. *De Typica et Honoraria Sacrarum Imaginum Adoratione Libri duo, Quorum prior in adorandis Sanctorum Imaginibus nullum esse idolo-latriae periculum: posterior docet, figuralem quandam adorationem illis deberi, & Naturali, & Gentium, & Divino, & Ecclesiastico iure. Auctore Nicolao Sandero Anglo, Sacrae Theologiae Professore.* 1569

50. *De Visibili Monarchia Ecclesiae, Libri octo. In quibus diligens insti-tuitur disputatio de certa & perpetua Ecclesiae Dei tum Successione, tum Gubernatione Monarchica ab ipso mundi initio usque ad finem. Deinde etiam Civitatis Diaboli persaepe interrupta progressio pro-ponitur, Sectaeque omnes & Haereses confutantur, quae unquam contra fidem emerserunt. Denique de Antichristo ipso & membris eius; deque*

> *vera Dei & adulterina Diaboli Ecclesia, copiose tractatur. Si quid prae-*
> *terea difficile & scopulosum vel in Pontificum Romanorum historia, vel*
> *in Conciliorum Generalium ratione accidit; idipsum ex proposito*
> *discutitur & examinatur. Auctore Nicolao Sandero, Sacrae Theologiae*
> *Professore.* 1571

The only reply in English to this last work was the above-mentioned book of John Bridges (40) against Stapleton's *Counterblast* (39); and that only dealt with four chapters in Book II, concerning the Prince's claim to supremacy over a national Church. In the same year, 1573, however, there appeared two replies in Latin, each of them dealing with only a part of Sanders' book. Bartholomew Clerke concentrated his attention on Book VII, in the form of an open letter to Sanders; while George Ackworth attacked Sanders' Preface in a longer but far from adequate reply. Ten years later, the Regius Professor of Divinity at Cambridge, William Whitaker, published a criticism of the eighth and final book of Sanders on the nature and identity of Antichrist, which became an important topic of controversy in the following years.

51. [= 40] *The Supremacie of Christian Princes, over all persons through-*
    out their dominions, in all causes so wel Ecclesiastical as temporall,
    both against the Counterblast of Thomas Stapleton, replying on the
    Reverend father in Christe, Robert Bishop of Winchester, and also
    Against Nicolas Sanders his Visible Monarchie of the Romaine Church,
    touching this controversie of the Princes Supremacie. Answered by
    Iohn Bridges. 1573   (STC 3737)

52. *Fidelis Servi, subdito Infideli Responsio, una cum errorum &*
    calumniarum quarundam examine quae continentur in septimo libro de
    visibili Ecclesiae Monarchia a Nicholao Sandero conscripta. 1573
    (STC 5407)

53. *De Visibili Romanarchia Contra Nich. Sanderi προλεγομενον Libri duo.*
    Georgio Acwortho Legum doctore Authore. 1573   (STC 99)

54. [= 171] *Ad Nicolai Sanderi Demonstrationes quadraginta, in octavo*
    libro visibilis Monarchiae positas, quibus Romanum Pontificem non esse
    Antichristum docere instituit, responsio Guilielmi Whitakeri, Theo-
    logiae in Academia Cantabrigiensi professoris Regii. Accessit eiusdem
    Thesis de Antichristo, defensae in Comitiis Cantabrigiensibus. 1583
    (STC 25357)

Sanders replied to his critics, and in particular to Bartholomew Clerke, in another Latin book, *De Clave David*, which he left in manuscript with a friend on embarking for Ireland, where he died in 1581. It was not published till 1588, under the care of this friend, Philip Sega, Bishop of Piacenza; and it was soon after reissued in conjunction with the 1592 edition of the *De Visibili Monarchia Ecclesiae.*

55. *De Clave David seu Regno Christi Libri sex, contra Calumnias Acleri pro visibili Ecclesiae Monarchia, Auctore Nicolao Sandero Anglo, sacrae Theologiae Professore.* 1588

    (In the 1592 edition of *De Visibili Monarchia* the title of *De Clave David* is incorporated into that of the whole work:

    De Visibili Monarchia Ecclesiae, Libri VIII . . . Auctore Nicolao Sandero, sacrae Theologiae Professore. Accesserunt eiusdem Auctoris de Clave David, seu de regno Christi, libri sex, quibus continetur huius de visibili Monarchia Ecclesiae operis contra quosdam oppugnatores necessaria defensio, Romae primum, nunc etiam in Germania excusi.)

Another notable contributor to the controversy against Jewel was William Allen, who rejoined the group of Catholic exiles in 1565, on his return from a three-year sojourn in England for the sake of his health. During this sojourn he had drawn up an important document entitled 'Certain Brief Reasons concerning the Catholick faith', which reappeared in other forms under such names as 'Allen's Scroll of Articles' and 'Rishton's Challenge' — both of them mentioned somewhat confusedly by William Fulke in his 'Catalogue of Popish Books'. Allen himself did not publish them for the time being, but he left them to be published later on by his friend and colleague, Richard Bristow, in the form first of *Motives* (146) and then of *Demaundes* (147). For the present, in response to Jewel's challenge, he composed two treatises on the relatively minor issues of purgatory and prayers for the dead, of the sacrament of penance and the use of indulgences, with a view rather to satisfying his friends than to attacking his adversaries. Hence they are not directly controversial.

56. *A Defense and Declaration of the Catholike Churchies Doctrine, touching Purgatory, and prayers for the soules departed. By William Allen Master of Arte and student in Divinitye.* 1565 (STC 371, AR 10, ERL 18)

57. *A Treatise made in defence of the lauful power and authoritie of Priesthod to remitte sinnes: Of the peoples duetie for confession of their sinnes to Gods ministers: And of the Churches meaning concerning Indulgences, commonlie called the Popes Pardons. By William Allen M. of Arte, and Student in Divinitie.* 1567 (STC 372, AR 11, ERL 99)

Both these books remained unanswered till William Fulke undertook the task of their refutation in view of the prominence of their author on the Catholic side.

58. [= 151] *Two Treatises written against the Papistes, the one being an answere of the Christian Protestant to the proud challenge of a Popish Catholicke: the other a confutation of the Popish Churches doctrine touching Purgatory & prayers for the dead.* 1577   (STC 11458)

59. *A Confutation of a Treatise made by William Allen in defence of the usurped power of Popish Priesthood to remit sinnes, of the necessity of Shrift, and of the Popes Pardons. By William Fulke.* 1586   (STC 5009)

(This book was bound with *A Treatise against the Defence of the Censure*, 1586 (203))

Meanwhile, as Regius Professor of Theology at Douai University, Allen devoted many of his lectures to the more central controversial issue of the sacrament and the sacrifice of the Eucharist; and these lectures were taken down by his students and published in their original Latin in 1576. But they elicited no refutation from the Protestant side.

60. *Gulielmi Alani Angli, Regii Sacrae Theologiae Professoris in Academia Duacensi. Libri Tres. Id est, De Sacramentis in genere, Lib. I. De Sacramento Eucharistiae, Lib. I. De Sacrificio Eucharistiae, Lib. I. E vivae vocis diligenti & accurata tractatione, quam idem his de rebus contra nostri temporis Haereticos in Schola Theologorum habuit.* 1576

d) *Related controversies*

During these years Allen became increasingly preoccupied with the more practically urgent tasks of founding and running the English Seminary at Douai, which was opened in 1568 and was later obliged to move to Rheims. The subsequent controversy with Fulke he left in the hands of Bristow, as will be seen in due course. Meanwhile, there were other, minor contributions to the Catholic defence of the Mass against Jewel's attacks by Robert Pointz and Thomas Heskyns. They both set forth an impressive array of testimonies from the Bible and the Fathers of the first six centuries to prove the antiquity of the Catholic doctrine of the real presence of Christ in the Eucharist.

61. *Testimonies for the Real Presence of Christes body and blood in the blessed Sacrament of the aultar set foorth at large, & faithfully translated out of six auncient fathers which lyved far within the first six hundred yeres, together with certain notes, declaring the force of those testimonies, and detecting sometimes the Sacramentaries false dealing, as more plainly appeareth in the other syde of this leaf. By Robert Pointz student in Divinitie.* 1566   (STC 20082, AR 656, ERL 327)

62. *The Parliament of Chryste avouching and declaring the enacted and receaved trueth of the presence of his bodie and bloode in the blessed*

Sacrament, and of other articles concerning the same, impugned in a wicked sermon by M. Iuell, Collected and set furth by Thomas Heskyns Doctour of dyvinitie. Wherein the reader shall fynde all the scripturs commonlie alleaged oute of the newe Testament, touching the B. Sacrament, and some of the olde Testament, plainlie and truely expownded by a nombre of holie learned Fathers and Doctours. 1566 (STC 13250, 13842, AR 393, ERL 313)

Of these two books only the second was dealt with by Fulke in a composite work against Sanders and Rastell as well as Heskyns. He merely mentions 'Poyntes of the Sacrament' in his 'Catalogue of Popish Books' as among those remaining to be answered.

63. [= 23, 46] 'Heskins Parleament Repealed', in *D. Heskins, D. Sanders, and M. Rastel, accounted (among their faction) three pillers and Archpatriarches of the Popish Synagogue, (utter enemies to the truth of Christes Gospell, and all that syncerely professe the same) overthrowne, and detected of their severall blasphemous heresies. By D. Fulke, Maister of Pembroke Hall in Cambridge.* 1579   (STC 11433)

Another related controversy arose, not from any Protestant book or sermon, but from the Queen's decision to retain a cross in her private chapel — though the cross was being removed from altars in parish churches throughout the realm. This decision greatly heartened the Catholics; and one of Harding's young colleagues from New College, John Martial, was led to compose a *Treatyse of the Crosse* and to dedicate it to the Queen.

64. *A Treatyse of the Crosse gathred out of the Scriptures, Councelles, and auncient Fathers of the primitive church, by Iohn Martiall Bachiler of Lawe and Student in Divinitie.* 1564   (STC 17496, AR 524, ERL 174)

This book was strongly criticised by Alexander Nowell in a sermon preached before the Queen in March 1565, but he was publicly reproved by her for his excessive language. Martial's refutation was therefore undertaken, not by Nowell, but by James Calfhill, who used hardly less excessive language. Martial wrote in reply; but no further response was forthcoming from the Protestant side, till Fulke produced his composite work against both Martial and Stapleton in 1580.

65. *An Aunswere to the Treatise of the Crosse: wherin ye shal see by the plaine and undoubted word of God, the vanities of men disproved: by the true and Godly Fathers of the Church, the dreames and dotages of other controlled: and by the lawful Counsels, conspiracies overthrowen.* 1565   (STC 4368)

(The author's name is appended to the Preface.)

66. *A Replie to M. Calfhills blasphemous Answer made against the Treatise of the Crosse, by Iohn Martiall, Bachiler of Lawe, and studient in Divinitie.* 1566 (STC 17497, AR 523, ERL 203)

67. [= 36] 'A Reioynder to Iohn Martials reply against the answere of Maister Calfhill, to the blasphemous treatise of the Cross', in *T. Stapleton and Martiall (two Popish Heretikes) confuted, and of their particular heresies detected. By D. Fulke, Master of Pembrooke hall in Cambridge.* 1580 (STC 11456)

Another but unrelated controversy on the question of the royal supremacy was being conducted in Latin at the same time between a Portuguese bishop, Osorio da Fonseca, and the Master of the Court of Requests in England, Walter Haddon. Osorio began with a complimentary Epistle to the Queen in 1563 in the graceful Latin style for which he was famous in Europe; and he was answered in the same year by Haddon, who undertook to have his book published in Paris, like that of Osorio.

68. *Epistola ad Elizabetham Angliae Reginam de Religione.* 1563

69. *Gualtheri Haddoni pro Reformatione Anglicana Epistola Apologetica ad Hier. Osorium, Lusitanum.* 1563

Both these books were translated into English by the opposing sides in 1565 – that of Osorio by Richard Shacklock, and that of Haddon by Abraham Hartwell. Hartwell's translation was followed by another anonymous answer to Osorio in English, referring to his Epistle as 'a Pearle for a Prince' from the running title printed in Shacklock's translation.

70. *An Epistle of the Reverend Father in God Hieronymus Osorius Bishop of Arcoburge in Portugale, to the most excellent Princesse Elizabeth by the grace of God Quene of England, Fraunce, and Ireland, &c. Translated oute of Latten in to Englishe by Richard Shacklock M. of Arte and student of the Civill Lawes in Lovaine.* 1565 (STC 18887, AR 586, ERL 329)

71. *A sight of the Portugall Pearle, that is the Aunswere of D. Haddon Maister of the requests, against the epistle of Hieronimus Osorius, a Portugall, entitled a Pearle for a Prince. Translated out of lattyn into englishe by Abraham Hartwell, Student in the kynges colledge in Cambridge.* 1565 (STC 12598)

72. *An answere in action to a Portingale Pearle, called a Pearle for a Prince: Geven by a Laye man in a Legacie, which Legacie he desireth to se executed before his death.* 1570 (STC 7679, where the authorship is doubtfully attributed to the publisher, Dionis Emilie.)

In the next stage of this bilingual controversy Osorio replied to Haddon in a substantial work of three books in 1567; and his Latin was immediately translated into English by John Fen and published the following year.

73. *Amplissimi atque Doctissimi Viri D. Hieronymi Osorii, Episcopi Sylvensis, in Gualterum Haddonum Magistrum Libellorum Supplicum apud clarrisimam Principem Helisabetham Angliae, Franciae, & Hiberniae Reginam. libri tres.* 1567.

74. *A Learned and very Eloquent Treatie, writen in Latin by the famouse man Hieronymus Osorius Bishop of Sylva in Portugal, wherein he confuteth a certayne Aunswere made by M. Walter Haddon against the Epistle of the said Bishoppe unto the Queenes Maiestie.* 1568
(STC 18889, AR 587, ERL|318)

(The translator's name is appended to the Preface.)

Haddon again took up his pen in reply to Osorio, but he was unable to complete his work owing to his untimely death in 1572. His place was taken by the Protestant martyrologist, John Foxe, who eventually published the whole work in 1577. This was now translated into English by James Bell and published in 1581. In connection with this controversy, Foxe also engaged Osorio on the subject of inherent justice.

75. *Contra Hieron. Osorium, eiusque odiosas insectationes pro Evangelicae veritatis necessaria Defensione, Responsio Apologetica. Per clariss. virum, Gualt. Haddonum inchoata: Deinde suscepta & continuata per Ioann. Foxum.* 1577   (STC 12593)

76. *Against Ierome Osorius Bysshop of Silvane in Portingall and against his slaunderous Invectives. An Aunswere Apologeticall: for the necessary defence of the Evangelicall doctrine and veritie. First taken in hand by M. Walter Haddon, then undertaken and continued by M. Iohn Foxe, and now Englished by Iames Bell.* 1581   (STC 12594)

77. *De Christo gratis iustificante. Contra Osorianam iustititiam, caeterosque eiusdem inhaerentis iustitiae patronos, Stan. Hosium. Andrad. Canisium. Vegam. Toletanum. Lorichium, contra universam denique Turbam Tridentinam & Iesuiticam. Amica & modesta defensio. Ioan. Foxii.* 1583   (STC 11234)

Shacklock was also the translator of another Latin work by Cardinal Hosius, *De Origine haeresium nostri temporis*, which had been published in 1559. His translation, to which he gave the running title of 'The hatchet of heresies', was answered by the Puritan writer, John Barthlet, in a somewhat eccentric book entitled *The Pedegrewe of Heretiques.*

78. *A most excellent treatise of the begynnyng of heresyes in oure tyme, compyled by the Reverend Father in God Stanislaus Hosius Byshop of Wormes in Prussia. To the moste renomed Prynce Lorde Sigismund*

*myghtie Kyng of Poole, greate Duke of Luten and Russia, Lorde and
Heyre of all Prussia, Masovia, Samogitia &c. Translated out of Laten in
to Englyshe by Richard Shacklock M. of Arte, and student of the Civil
Lawes, and intituled by hym: The hatchet of heresies.* 1565
(STC 13888, AR 403, ERL 24)

79. *The Pedegrewe of Heretiques. Wherein is truely and plainely set out,
the first roote of Heretiques begon in the Church, since the time and
passage of the Gospell, together with an example of the ofspring of the
same.* 1566 (STC 1534)

Another translation of a work by a continental Catholic theologian was
published in the same year by Lewis Evans. This was Lindanus' *Tabulae
Grassantium passim Haereseon anasceusticae atque analyticae*, which had
appeared in 1562. Considering it would be of use for the Catholics in
England, Evans translated it into English with the running title, 'The betra-
yng of Heresye'. He also added his own pungent criticism of the newly made
ministers in England, published separately in the same year.

80. *Certaine Tables sett furth by the right Reverend father in God, William
Bushopp of Rurimunde, in Ghelderland: wherein is detected and made
manifeste the doting dangerous doctrine, the haynous heresyes, of the
rashe rablement of heretikes: translated into Englishe by Lewys Evans,
And by hym intitled, The betraing of the beastlines of heretykes.*
1565 (STC 15653, AR 461, ERL 52)

81. *A brieve Admonition unto the nowe made Ministers of Englande:
Wherein is shewed some of the fruicte of this theyr late framed fayth:
Made by Lewys Evans student in Lovain.* 1565 (STC 18589, AR 297,
ERL 67)

In spite of his invectives against the Anglican ministers, Evans soon afterwards returned to England and renounced his Catholic profession, following
this up with two books of no less pungent criticism against Roman prelates.
Of his Catholic books Fulke makes the brief entry in his 'Catalogue of
Popish Books': 'Maister Evans answered by himselfe'.

82. *The Castle of Christianitie, detecting the long erring estate, aswell of
the Romaine Church, as of the Byshop of Rome: together with the
defence of the Catholique Faith: Set forth, by Lewys Evans.* 1568
(STC 10590)

83. *The Hatefull Hypocrisie, and rebellion of the Romishe prelacie. By
Lewys Evans.* 1570 (STC 10591)

One more translation, contributing to the controversies of this decade,
aimed at exposing the recent tumults occasioned by the Protestants of the
Low Countries – of which there is a detailed description in Stapleton's

Counterblast (39). The original was a Latin *Oration* by Peter Frarin, a scholar of Antwerp, where the tumults had been particularly destructive of church property. Pronounced in the School of Arts at Louvain in December 1565, it was published early in 1566, and then translated into English and published by the zealous Catholic printer, John Fowler. But for many years it remained unanswered by the Protestants, though Fulke noted it as 'Frarins oration translated' among the Popish books awaiting refutation – till eventually in 1586 he published a small treatise 'against the Railing declamation of P. Frarine' (cf. 59, 203).

84. *An Oration Against the Unlawfull Insurrections of the Protestantes of our time, under pretence to Refourme Religion. Made and pronounced in Latin, in the Schole of Artes at Lovaine, the xiiii. of December. Anno 1565. By Peter Frarin of Andwerp, M. of Arte, and Bacheler of both lawes. And now translated into English, with the advise of the Author.* 1566   (STC 11333, AR 344, ERL 226)

(The translator's name is appended to the Preface.)

85. *An Apologie of the Professors of the Gospel in Fraunce against the Railing Declamation of Peter Frarine a Lovanian turned into English by Iohn Fowler. Written by William Fulke.* 1586   (STC 5009)

(The second of two treatises by Fulke – for the first, see 59 – added to the *Treatise against the Defense of the Censure*, attributed to W. Charke (203).)

There remain a few items contributed by the imprisoned Catholic leaders to be noticed. Eminent among them for his scholarship was Nicholas Harpsfield, formerly Archdeacon of Canterbury, but now confined to the Tower of London. Besides sending information to Stapleton for his *Counterblast* against Horne, he contrived to write and publish *Six Dialogues* in Latin against Jewel's *Apologie* and Foxe's *Book of Martyrs* under the assumed name of Alan Cope. Much of his time he also devoted to a Latin *History of the Church in England*, which was not published till 1622 and so lies well outside the present controversies.

86. *Dialogi Sex contra Summi Pontificatus, Monasticae vitae, Sanctorum, Sacrarum imaginum oppugnatores, et Pseudomartyres: In quibus praeterquam quod nonnulla, quae alii hactenus vel attigerunt leviter, vel penitus omiserunt, paullo uberius & plenius explicantur; Centurionum Magdeburgensium, auctorum Apologiae Anglicanae, Pseudomartyrologorum nostri temporis, maxime vero Ioannis Foxi, & aliorum, qui adulterino Evangelio nomina dederunt, variae fraudes, putidae calumniae, & insignia in historiis Ecclesiae contaminandis mendacia deteguntur. Nunc primum ad Dei Optimi Maximi gloriam, & Catholicae religionis confirmationem ab Alano Copo Anglo editi.* 1566

Another eminent prisoner was the former Abbot of Westminster, John Feckenham, whose scruples over the Oath of Supremacy had touched off the controversy between Horne and Stapleton. Subsequently, he made certain objections in writing to a sermon by a Protestant minister, John Gough, in the Tower of London, concerning justification by faith and the invocation of saints. To his objections both Gough himself and another Puritan, Laurence Tomson, published their answers in 1570.

87. *The Aunswer of Iohn Gough Preacher, To Maister Fecknams Obiect-ions, against his Sermon, lately preached in the Tower of London, 15 Ianuarie. 1570.* 1570   (STC 12131)

88. *An Answere to certein Assertions of M. Fecknam, somtime Abbot of Westminster, which he made of late against a godly Sermon of M. Iohn Goughes, preached in the Tower the xv. of Ianuarie. 1570.* 1570 (STC 24113)

Another of the leading Catholic theologians in Mary's reign, Dr. Richard Smith, had made his way to Louvain, where he became Professor of Theology. He was one of the first to respond to Jewel's challenge, but as his answer was in Latin, it remained largely unnoticed in the English controversy. His criticism was also directed against Melanchthon and Calvin; but he devoted a good third of his book to Jewel's attack on the Mass.

89. *Confutatio eorum, quae Philippus Melanchthon obijcit contra Missae sacrificium propitiatorium. Autore Ricardo Smythaeo Wigorniensi, Anglo, Sacrae Theologiae Professore, Lovanii. Cui accessit & repulsio calumniarum Ioannis Calvini, & Musculi, & Ioannis Iuelli, contra Missam, eius canonem, & Purgatorium, denuo excusa.* 1562

By way of postscript to the Jewel–Harding controversy, there appeared three more books on the Anglican side in Latin as it were continuing the memory and cause of Jewel after his death – tributes from the two Regius Professors of Divinity at Oxford and Cambridge, Laurence Humphrey and William Whitaker. The former contributed a *Life* of Jewel, and a defence of his doctrine against his Catholic adversaries; while the latter translated Jewel's *Replie* to Harding's *Answere*. Then there appeared a combination of the two tributes, with the addition of the *Apologie* in Latin.

90. *Ioannis Iuelli Angli, Episcopi Sarisburiensis vita & mors, eiusque verae doctrinae defensio, cum refutatione quorundam obiectorum, Thomae Hardingi, Nicol. Sanderi, Alani Copi, Hieronymi Osorii Lusitani, Pontaci Burdegalensis, Laurentio Humfredo S. Theologiae apud Oxoni-enses professore Regio, Autore.* 1573   (STC 13963)

91. *Ioannis Iuelli, Sarisburiensis in Anglia nuper Episcopi adversus Thomam Hardingum, volumen alterum, in quo viginti septem quaestiones & scripturis, & omnium Conciliorum ac patrum monimentis, quaecunque*

sexcentis a nato Christo annis antiquiora sunt, disceptantur atque explicantur: Ex Anglico conversum in Latinum, a Guilielmo Whitakero Collegii Sanctae Trinitatis apud Cantabrigienses socio. 1578 (STC 14608)

92. *Ioannis Iuelli Sarisburiensis in Anglia Episcopi, adversus Thomam Hardingum volumen. In quo XXVII quaestiones & Scripturis, & omnium Conciliorum ac Patrum monimentis, quaecumque sexcentis a nato Christo annis antiquiora sunt, disceptantur, atque explicantur. Ex Anglico conversum in Latinum, a Guilielmo Whitakero, Collegii Sanctae Trinitatis apud Cantabrigienses socio. Huic operi praefixa est auctoris vita & mors, eiusque verae doctrinae defensio, cum refutatione quorundam obiectorum, Thomae Hardingi, Nicolai Sanderi, Alani Copi, Hieronymi Osorii, Pontaci Burdegalensis. Laurentio Humfredo. S. Theologiae apud Oxonienses professore Regio, auctore. Eiusdem Iuelli Apologia Ecclesiae Anglicanae.* 1585

On the other side, Harding's works were also translated into Latin by William Reynolds, who had been one of Jewel's assistants in the great controversy, but had been won over by Harding's arguments — as he relates in his *Refutation of Sundry Reprehensions* (172). His translations, however, remained in manuscript and were never published. He was more successful with his translation of Stapleton's *Fortresse of the Faith* (33), which was published in the second volume of the latter's *Opera* in 1620 (93, 559), under the title of *Propugnaculum Fidei Primitivae Anglorum*. Other works of Stapleton translated (by other hands) in the same volume were: his *Counterblast* (39), or *Replica Stapletoni ad Horni Flatum*; his *Returne of Untruthes* (35), or *Nota Falsitatis in Iuellum Retorta*; and his *Discourse uppon the doctrine of the protestants* (30), or *De Protestantismo et primis eiusdem authoribus . . . disertatio.*

93. [= 559] *Thomae Stapletoni Angli, Sacrae Theologiae Doctoris, et Professoris Regii, Duaci primo, deinde Lovanii Opera quae extant omnia, nonnulla auctius et emendatius, quaedam iam antea Anglice scripta, nunc primum studio & diligentia Doctorum virorum Anglorum Latine reddita. In quatuor tomos distributa, quorum Elenchum Pagina decima-nona indicabit.* 1620

(The translations of Stapleton's English works are all ranged in the second volume, from fol. 709 to the end. They are entitled respectively as follows:

a) 'Propugnaculum Fidei Primitivae Anglorum, quo fides illa, quae Anglis, ante mille annos per S. Augustinum tradita fuit, & quae tunc temporis ac deinceps per universam Christi Ecclesiam semper viguit, quam nunc Protestantes Papisticam vocant, orthodoxam esse, vereque Christianam, asseritur & probatur.'

b) 'Replica Thomae Stapletoni, S. T. Doctoris et Professoris ad Responsum Horni, Pseudo-Episcopi Wintoniensis, quo is Feckenhami Ven. Abbatis Westmonasteriensis rationes recusandi iuramentum de Regio in causis Ecclesiasticis Primatu impugnat.'

c) 'Nota Falsitatis in Iuellum Retorta. Opus sic inscriptum, quia in eo falsa quae Iuellus Pseudo-Episcopus Sarisburiensis responso Hardingi Doctoris Catholici imposuit, quo is nonnulla Catholicae fidei dogmata defendit, de quibus Iuellus publice pro concione, Londini, ad D. Pauli crucem suggestum totius Angliae celeberrimum habita, omnes in toto Christiano orbe Catholicos, magna cum ostentatione provocaverat, ut illa, vel uno aliquo sacrae Scripturae, generalis Concilii, aut alicuius antiqui Patris, qui intra primos sexcentos a Christo annos vixit, testimonio probarent.'

d) 'De Protestantismo et primis eiusdem authoribus, Martino Luthero, Philippo Melanctone, et Ioanne Calvino Disertatio.')

Another postscript, of a more practical nature, consisted of three royal proclamations published in quick succession during the years 1569–70 – the last two having special reference to the Bull of Excommunication which had recently been issued against the Queen by Pope Pius V in 1570. The effect of this Bull was to transform the Catholic works of controversy into 'trayterous bookes and writinges', and the writers, distributors and possessors of them into traitors – in the eyes of the English authorities.

94. *By the Queene. Wheras divers bookes made or translated by certayne the Queenes Maiesties subiectes, for the more part remayning on the other syde of the sea, without lawfull licence* ... 1 March 1569 (STC 8014)

95. *By the Queene. A Proclamation made agaynst seditious and trayterous Bookes, Billes, and Writinges. The Queenes Maiestie being of late certenly infourmed of the trayterous boldnes of certen wicked and seditious persons* ... 1 July 1570   (STC 8032)

96. *By the Queene. A Proclamation against mayntayners of seditious persons, and of trayterous bookes and writinges.* 14 November 1570 (STC 8035)

CHAPTER 2

Puritan Admonition

a) *The Vestiarian controversy*

FROM the beginning of the Protestant Reformation in England under Edward VI there had appeared a fundamental cleavage between the moderates and the radicals — between those who were content with the reform of what they regarded as abuses in the Church and those who aimed at a complete break with the past in the light of what they regarded as the true Church of God. This cleavage was first expressed in the controversy over the practical issue of the wearing of vestments and the observing of certain ceremonies as prescribed in the Anglican *Book of Common Prayer*. After the accession of Queen Elizabeth in 1558, the more radical ministers felt themselves at liberty to disregard these prescriptions, and thus a considerable variety in the manner of conducting religious services prevailed during the early years of the new reign. The Queen herself complained about this situation to her new Archbishop of Canterbury, Matthew Parker; and he accordingly set about enforcing a more exact conformity among his clergy. But when he summoned the London ministers to a meeting at his palace at Lambeth on 26 March 1566, he found himself faced with a strong opposition. No less than one-third of their number refused to conform and subscribe to his requirements, even at the cost of being deprived of their livings. It was in connection with this meeting that he drew up certain *Advertisements* in the name of the bishops, though without the formal ratification of the Queen herself.

> 97. *Advertisments partly for due order in the publique administration of common prayers and usinge the holy Sacramentes, and partly for the apparrell of all persons ecclesiasticall, by vertue of the Queenes maiesties letters commaunding the same, the xxv. day of Ianuary, in the seventh yeare of the reigne of our Soveraigne Lady Elyzabeth, by the grace of God, of Englande, Fraunce, and Irelande Queene, defender of the faith &c.* 1566   (STC 10026)

This document, reinforced by 'protestations to be made, promised and subscribed by them that shall hereafter bee admitted to any office, roome or cure in any Churche, or other place Ecclesiasticall', as well as Parker's subsequent action in depriving the recalcitrant ministers of their livings, at once brought on a bitter controversy. The first book on the side of the ministers was an anonymous work, entitled *A briefe discourse*, which is usually attributed to one of their leaders, Robert Crowley.

98. *A briefe discourse against the outwarde apparrell and Ministring garmentes of the popishe church.* 1566 (STC 6078)

(The inner title is more specific:
'A declaration of the doings of those Ministers of Gods worde and Sacraments, in the citie of London, which have refused to weare the outwarde apparell, and Ministring garmentes of the Popes church.'
Two editions of the book came out in 1566, and a third in 1578.)

This was followed by a reply, also anonymous, on behalf of the bishops, which has often been ascribed to Parker himself, and which in turn led to *An answere for the tyme* from the ministers.

99. *A briefe examination for the tyme, of a certaine declaration, lately put in print in the name and defence of certaine Ministers in London, refusing to weare the apparell prescribed by the lawes and orders of the Realme. In the ende is reported, the judgement of two notable learned fathers, M. doctour Bucer, and M. doctour Martir, sometyme in eyther universities here of England the kynges readers and professours of divinitie, translated out of the originals, written by theyr owne handes, purposely debatyng this controversie.* 1566 (STC 10387)

100. *An answere for the tyme, to the examination put in print, with out the authours name, pretending to mayntayne the apparrell prescribed against the declaration of the mynisters of London.* 1566 (STC 10388)

The judgement of Martin Bucer and Peter Martyr appended to the *Briefe examination*, as an appeal to authorities recognized on either side, was a signal for further appeals to authority of this kind. The ministers accordingly published translations of passages from the *Decades* of Henry Bullinger and other writings of Martin Bucer, which seemed to favour their position.

101. *The iudgement of the Reverend Father Master Henry Bullinger/ Pastor of the church of Zurick, in certeyne matters of religion, beinge in controversy in many countreys, even wher as the Gopel is taught.* 1566 (STC 4065)

102. *The mynd and exposition of that excellente learned man Martyn Bucer/ uppon the wordes of S. Mathew: Woo be to the wordle bycause of offences. Math. xviii. Faythfully translated in to Englishe, by a*

faythfull brother, with certayne obiections & answeres to the same.
1566   (STC 3964)

On their side, the bishops were able to publish a letter written by Bullinger concerning this very controversy to three of their number: Horne of Winchester, Grindal of London, and Parkhurst of Norwich. They now presented it both in its original Latin and in English translation in two editions that year, as well as in conjunction with a larger work on the duty of observing civil laws in matters of indifference, such as the apparel to be worn at religious services.

103. *The Iudgement of the Godly and learned Father, M. Henry Bullinger,*
     chiefe Preacher and Pastor of the Church of Zurich in Swicerlande,
     declaring it to be lawfull for the Ministers of the Church of Englande,
     to weare the Apparell prescribed by the Lawes and orders of the same
     Realme. 1566   (STC 4063)

104. *Whether it be mortall sinne to transgresse civil lawes, which be the*
     commaundementes of civill Magistrates. The iudgement of Philip
     Melancton in his Epitome of morall Philosophie. The resolution of D.
     Hen. Bullinger, and D. Rod. Gualter, of D. Martin Bucer, and D. Peter
     Martyr, concernyng thapparrel of Ministers, and other indifferent
     thinges. 1566   (STC 22572)

   (The documents attached to the latter publication are as follows:
   a) 'A Discourse of Philip Melanchthon on Rom. xiii.'
   b) 'The resolution of D. Hen. Bullinger and D. Rod. Gualter, of D.
      Martin Bucer, and D. Peter Martyr, concernyng the apparrell of
      Ministers and other indifferent thinges.'
   c) 'A briefe and lamentable consyderation, of the apparell now used by
      the Cleargie of England: Set out by a faithfull servant of God, for
      the instruction of the weake.'
   d) A letter from Martin Bucer to John Hooper, in the reign of
      Edward VI.

   The last two documents are omitted from the title-page of the
   publication — which may indicate that they were intended to be
   published separately.)

This array of authorities, however, was not enough to silence the ministers. Instead, they responded with an anthology of texts from the 'Fathers' of the Reformation in support of their position. The initials I.B. attached to this document have been variously ascribed to John Barthlet, author of *The Pedegrewe of Heretiques* (79), and to John Browne, a Marian exile and chaplain to the Duchess of Suffolk.

105. *The Fortresse of Fathers, ernestlie defending the puritie of Religion,*
     and Ceremonies, by the trew exposition of certaine places of Scripture:

against such as wold bring in an Abuse of Idol stouff, and of thinges
indifferent, and do appoinct th'auctority of Princes and Prelates larger
then the trueth is. Translated out of Latine into English for there sakes
that understand no Latine by I.B. 1566   (STC 1040)

A number of short letters of exhortation were also published, as an
encouragement to those who had been deprived of their livings. The
authorship was anonymous; but the first has been attributed to Anthony
Gilby, who enjoyed a safe living at Ashby-de-la-Zouch under the patronage
of the Earl of Huntingdon, while the second and the third may have been
written by William Whittingham, now Dean of Durham, who had formerly
been among the most radical of the Marian exiles.

106. *To my lovynge brethren that is troublyd abowt the popishe aparrell,*
    two short and comfortable Epistels. Be ye constant: for the Lorde shall
    fyght for yow, yowrs in Christ. 1566   (STC 10390)

107. *To my faythfull Brethren now afflycted, & to all those that unfaynedly*
    love the Lorde Iesus, the Lorde guyde us with his holy spret, that we
    maye always serve hym bothe in body and mynde in all synceryte to
    oure lyves ende. 1566   (STC 10389)

108. *To the Reader. To my faythfull Brethren, we geve thanks to God for*
    your constancie. 1566   (STC 10391)

Yet another letter, from William Turner, Dean of Wells, took the form of
a Preface added to a new edition of his popular anti-popish pamphlet, *The*
huntyng of the Romyshe Wolfe, which he had originally published in 1554
against Bishop Gardiner.

109. 'To al my faithful Brethren in Christ Iesu, and to all other that labour
    to weede out the weedes of poperie', in *The Hunting of the Fox and*
    the Wolfe, because they make havocke of the sheepe of Christ Iesus.
    1566   (STC 24357)

There the matter rested for the time being. Many years later, in 1593,
other published materials from this controversy came to light with the
publication of the Puritan compilation entitled *A parte of a register*.

110. *A parte of a register, contayninge sundrie memorable matters, written*
    by divers godly and learned in our time, which stande for, and desire
    the reformation of our Church, in Discipline and Ceremonies,
    according to the pure worde of God, and the Lawe of our Lande.
    1593   (STC 10400)

    (This work contained the following documents dated around the year
    1570:
    a) 'A comfortable epistle written (as it is thought) by Maister D. W.
       [Doctor Perceval Wiburn] Doctour of Divinitie, in his owne defence,

and the brethren that suffer deprivation for the popish ceremonies urged by the Bishops, about the yere 1570.'

   b) 'A Godly and zealous letter written by Mai. A. G. [Anthony Gilby] 1570. To my Reverend Fathers and Brethren in Christ, Master Coverdale, Mai. Turner, M. Whittingham, M. Sampson, M. Doctor Humphry, M. Leaver, M. Crowley, and others that labour to roote out the weedes of Poperie: Grace and Peace.'

   c) 'Certaine Questions, Argumentes, and Obiections, conteyning a full answere to all the chiefe reasons that are used for defence of popish apparell, and other ceremonies urged: with foure causes why they should be remooved. Written about An. 1570.'

   d) 'A viewe of Antichrist, his lawes and ceremonies, in our English Church unreformed.' [by Anthony Gilby])

The two pamphlets by Anthony Gilby were also incorporated into his *Pleasaunt Dialogue*, which he wrote about 1574 but for various reasons (detailed in a prefatory note) did not publish till 1581 — as a last Puritan word on this particular controversy.

111.   *A Pleasaunt Dialogue, Betweene a Souldior of Barwicke, and an English Chaplaine. Wherein are largely handled & laide open, such reasons as are brought in for the maintenaunce of popishe Traditions in our Eng. Church. Also is collected, as in a short table, 120 particular corruptions yet remaining in our saide Church, with sundrie other matters, necessarie to be knowen of all persons. Togither with a letter of the same Author, placed before this booke, in way of a Preface.* 1581   (STC 6810)

b) The Admonition controversy

All these writings were, however, merely a foreshadowing of the great Puritan controversy that broke out towards the end of the Parliament of 1572. The Puritans had pinned their hopes on this Parliament for the realization of their proposals for reform. But they found themselves baffled, not so much by the members of the House of Commons, among whom they had many sympathisers, as by the personal intervention of the Queen, who refused to allow Parliament to discuss ecclesiastical affairs. So towards the end of the session two young Puritans, John Field and Thomas Wilcox, published an anonymous *Admonition*, in which they severely criticized the bishops for their popish tyranny and appealed once more to Parliament to institute measures for reform. Of this highly sensational document two editions are recorded for the year 1572, but there were probably more. It was reprinted much later in 1617. There was at once an official denunciation, and the two authors were soon identified and put in prison.

112. *An Admonition to the Parliament.* 1572 (STC 10847–9)
(This document was published not alone, but as the first of 'two treatises yee have heere ensuing'. The second is entitled: 'A View of Popish Abuses yet remayning in the Englishe Church, for the which godly Ministers have refused to subscribe.' It also carried two letters of continental reformers, favouring the Puritan position: one from Rudolph Gualter to Parkhurst, Bishop of Norwich; and the other from Theodore Beza to Grindal, then Bishop of London.)

During the following months other Puritan pamphlets were written and disseminated, culminating in *A Second Admonition*, whose authorship has often been attributed to Thomas Cartwright, now the unofficial leader of the Puritan party.

113. *A Second Admonition to the Parliament.* 1572 (STC 4713, 10849)

(Two other pamphlets were printed with this *Second Admonition*:
a) 'An Exhortation to the Bishops to deale brotherlie with their brethren.'
b) 'An Exhortation to the Bishops and their Clergie, to answer a little Booke that came foorth the last Parliament, and to other Brethren to iudge of it by Gods word, untill they see it answered, and not to be carried away with any respect of man.')

Finally, there appeared a justification of 'certaine articles' in the first *Admonition* to which the bishops had taken exception.

114. *Certaine Articles, collected and taken (as it is thought) by the Byshops out of a litle boke entituled an Admonition to the Parliament/ wyth an Answere to the same, Containing a confirmation of the sayde Booke in shorte Notes.* 1572 (STC 10850)

(The title of the bishops' compilation, which has not otherwise survived, is given in this work as:

'A view of the Churche/ that the Authors of the late publyshed Admonition would have planted wythin thys realme of Englande/ containing such Positions as they hold against the state of the sayd Churche/ as it is nowe.' The place of publication is enigmatically stated as 'Imprinted we know where/ and whan/ Judge you the place and you can. J.T.J.S.' It was probably Wandsworth, where the Puritans had recently set up their first presbyterian assembly.)

Apart from this compilation, the response of the bishops first took the form of a sermon delivered at Paul's Cross by Thomas Cooper, Bishop of Lincoln, on 27 June 1572, attacking the first *Admonition*. The Puritans circulated an answer in manuscript, 'An answer to certain pieces of a sermon made at Pauls Cross, &c. by Dr. Cooper, Bishop of Lincoln'; but it was never published by them. (It is given in full by John Strype, in his *Annals of the Reformation*, Vol. II, Pt. I, pp. 286–304.) The official reply in print was entrusted to John Whitgift, Master of Trinity College, Cambridge, who had already experienced Puritan troubles at his own university – particularly in connection with Cartwright. His *Answere* came out by the end of the year.

115. *An answere to a certen Libel intituled, An admonition to the Parliament, By Iohn Whitgifte, D. of Divinitie*. 1572 (STC 25427)

(In an appendix to his book, added after the main part had been sent to the press, Whitgift added two Epistles of Gualter and Bullinger supporting the bishops. He also appended 'A briefe answere to certain Pamphlets spred abroade of late', namely, the two exhortations to the bishops; together with 'A briefe viewe of the seconde Admonition'; and lastly, a review of the 'Articles collected out of the former Admonition', which the author claims are 'untruely sayd (of the fautors of that Admonition) to be falsified'.)

Whether Cartwright had indeed been the author of the *Second Admonition* or not, he came forward to defend both Admonitions against the bitter attack of Whitgift; and so the battle was joined between these two great adversaries, Anglican and Puritan.

116. *A Replye to an answere made of M. Doctor Whitgifte. Agaynst the Admonition to the Parliament. By T. C.* 1573 (STC 4711–2)

(The first edition of 'Cartwright's Book' (as it came to be known) was published in April 1573; and a second edition followed in June with a prefatory note by the printer, signed J. S. (John Stroud).)

That summer a royal proclamation was issued for the suppression of the *Admonition* and of Cartwright's *Replye*. By the end of the year Cartwright found it impossible for him to remain in England, and he crossed over to Germany where he might carry on the controversy with safety.

117. *By the Queene. The Queenes Maiestie consydering that notwithstanding that by great and mature deliberation of the wysest of this Realme, a godly and good order of publique prayer and administration of the Sacramentes hath ben set foorth . . . certayne books under the title of an admonition to the Parliament, and one other in defence of the sayde admonition . . .* 11 June 1573 (STC 8063)

In the following year there appeared two answers to his *Replye*, one by Whitgift himself, and the other anonymous but attributed (on the basis of a note written in a contemporary hand in the copy at Cambridge University Library) to Lord Henry Howard.

118. *The Defense of the Aunswere to the Admonition, against the Replie of T. C. By Iohn Whitgift Doctor of Divinitie*. 1574 (STC 24530)

119. *A Defense of the Ecclesiasticall Regiment in Englande, defaced by T. C. in his Replie agaynst D. Whitgifte.* 1574 (STC 10393)

To Whitgift's book Cartwright published his *Second replie* in two parts over a period of three years, as he was preoccupied with other activities on the continent and had difficulties with the printing of his books. He altogether ignored the anonymous *Defense*, which strangely produced no reaction from among the Puritans. Meanwhile, in 1575, independently of Cartwright's *Second replie*, there appeared another Puritan criticism of a portion of Whitgift's *Defense*, under the title of *An Examination*.

120. *An Examination of M. Doctor Whytgiftes Censures, contained in two Tables, sett before his booke, Entituled, The Defence of the Aunswer to the Admonition, &c.* 1575 (STC 24533)

121. *The second replie of Thomas Cartwright: agaynst Maister Doctor Whitgiftes second answer/ touching the Churche Discipline.* 1575 (STC 4714)

122. *The rest of the second replie of Thomas Cartwright: agaynst Master Doctor Whitgifts second answer, touching the Church discipline.* 1577 (STC 4715)

Cartwright now joined a former colleague of his from Cambridge, Walter Travers, in the important task of elaborating the platform of Church discipline for the Puritan party in England (as they now came to be known from the recent controversy). The Latin text of the work they produced is generally attributed to Travers, while to Cartwright belonged the composition of the Preface and the English translation, both of which were published in 1574.

123. *Ecclesiasticae Disciplinae, et Anglicanae Ecclesiae ab illa aberrationis, plena e verbo Dei, & dilucida explicatio.* 1574

124. *A full and plaine declaration of Ecclesiasticall Discipline owt off the word off God/ and off the declininge off the churche off England from the same.* 1574 (STC 24184)

Already, early in 1573 a younger Puritan at Cambridge, William Fulke, had written another explanation of the ideal of discipline; but his manuscript had been stayed, for prudential reasons, by the Puritan leaders, Laurence Tomson, Christopher Goodman and Anthony Gilby. It was only published later, against the author's wishes, in 1584, when it became a direct cause of the Marprelate controversy, to which it therefore belongs. It bore the confusingly similar title of *A Briefe and plaine declaration* (288). The further development of the Puritan platform also belongs to this later period, when the *Directory* was again elaborated by Cartwright and Travers, but not published owing to various disagreements among the Puritans themselves till the time of the Commonwealth, when it became the textbook of the Presbyterians (298). Meanwhile, in 1575 an anonymous Puritan author, probably William Whittingham, who had been intimately concerned with the events as the chief associate of John Knox, published a nostalgic account of the troubles among the Marian exiles at Frankfurt between the 'moderates' and the 'radicals'. These troubles he regarded as the root of the present evils in the English Church.

125. *A Brieff discours off the troubles begonne at Frankford in Germany Anno Domini 1554. Abowt the Booke off common prayer and Ceremonies/ and continued by the English men theyre/ to thende off Q. Maries Raigne/ in the which discours/ the gentle reader shall see the very originall and beginninge off all the contention that hathe byn/ and what was the cause off the same.* 1575 (STC 25442)

It was about this time that Matthew Parker died, and his place in the See of Canterbury was taken in 1576 by Edmund Grindal, who was more sympathetic to the Puritan cause. During his period of office fewer repressive measures were taken against the Puritans, and so the controversy stirred up by Parker's actions largely disappeared for the time being. He even incurred the Queen's displeasure for his spirited defence of the Puritan practice of 'prophesying', or gathering in private for the study of Scripture. On the other hand, while the Puritans ceased their attacks on the established Church and redirected their energies against the growing Popish threat, there now appeared two openly schismatical, and even heretical, movements to disturb the peace both of the Church and of the State.

c) *The Family of Love*

The first of these movements, the Family of Love, was a form of Anabaptism and had been introduced from the Low Countries into England early in Elizabeth's reign, where it mainly flourished among the lower classes. Its original founder had been David George of Basle; but its principal prophet in England was Henry Nicholas of Cologne, usually known from his initials as 'H. N.' In 1574 and 1575 many of his books were translated into English by his leading representative in England, Christopher Vitel, and probably published in Amsterdam. Three of them, in particular, met with vigorous criticism in England:

126. *The Prophetie of the Spirit of Love. Set-fourth by HN: And by Him Perused a-new/ and more distinctlie declared. Translated out of Base-almayne into English.* 1574 (STC 18560)

127. *Exhortatio I. The first Exhortation of H. N. to his Children/ and to the Famelye of Love by Him newlye perused/ and more distinctlye*

declared. Translated out of Base-almayne into English. [1574?]   (STC 18557)

128. *Evangelium Regni. A Joyfull Message of the Kingdom, published by the holie Spirit of the Love of Iesu Christ, and sent-fourth unto all Nations of People, which love the Trueth in Iesu Christ. Set-fourth by HN, and by him perused a-new and more distinctlie declared. Translated out of Base-almayne*. [1575?]   (STC 18556)

The first English publication against the movement took the form of a public recantation by one Robert Sharpe, in which he outlines the doctrine and specifies various books of 'H.N.' by name.

129. *The Confession and declaration of Robert sharpe Clerke, and other of that secte, tearmed the Familie of Love, at Paules Crosse in London the xii of Iune, An. 1575*. 1575   (STC 22378)
   (Sharpe particularly condemned 'those two wicked Bookes, Whereof the one hee nameth The Evangely or Gospell of the Kingdome . . . And the other Booke he calleth, The Declaration of the Masse'. The second book is not recorded in the STC.)

There followed a succession of books against the Family of Love in 1578 and 1579 by Puritan writers, who wished (no doubt) to shake off the imputation of Anabaptism which had been made by Whitgift in his *Answere* to the *Admonition*. The first of these writers was John Rogers, who complained in his Preface that 'many bookes are abroade, which I have not seene, and many I have seene, which I could not have the use of to reade. For except one will be pliant to their doctrine, and shewe good will thereto, he shall hardly get any of their bookes'. He also engaged in a controversy with Christopher Vitel, in *An Answere* to what he terms 'a wicked & infamous Libel' (which is not otherwise known).

130. *The Displaying of an horrible secte of grosse and wicked Heretiques, naming themselves the Familie of Love, with the lives of their Authors, and what doctrine they teach in corners. Newely set foorth by I. R. 1578. Whereunto is annexed a confession of certain Articles, which was made by two of the Familie of Love, being examined before a Iustice of peace, the 28. of May 1561. touching their errours taught amongest them at their assemblies*. 1578   (STC 21181)

131. *An Answere unto a wicked & infamous Libel made by Christopher Vitel, one of the chiefe English Elders of the pretended Family of Love: Maintaining their doctrine, & carpingly answeringe to certaine pointes of a boke called the displaing of the Fam. Aunswered by I. Rogers*. 1579   (STC 21180)

Two other confutations were penned by William Wilkinson and John

Knewstub, the latter of whom was to represent the Puritans at the Hampton Court Conference.

132. *A Confutation of Certaine Articles delivered unto the Familye of Love, with the exposition of Theophilus, a supposed Elder in the sayd Familye upon the same Articles. By William Wilkinson Maister of Artes and student of Divinitye. Hereunto are prefixed By the right reverend Father in God I. Y. [John Young] Byshop of Rochester, certaine notes collected out of their Gospell, and aunswered by the Fam. By the Author, a description of the tyme, places, Authors, and manner of spreading the same: of their lives, and wrestyng of Scriptures: with Notes in the end how to know an Heretique.* 1579   (STC 25665)

133. *A Confutation of monstrous and horrible heresies, taught by H. N. and embraced of a number, who call themselves the Familie of Love, by I. Knewstub.* 1579   (STC 15040)

The criticisms of Rogers and Knewstub, as well as an unidentified book by Stephen Bateman entitled *The golden Booke of the leaden Gods*, were jointly and generally answered by a Familist named Abia Nazarenus in *A Reproofe*, which was published in the same year.

134. *A Reproofe/ spoken and geeven-fourth by Abia Nazarenus/ against all false Christians seducing Ypocrites/ and Enemies of the Trueth and Love. Wher-withall their false Devices/ Punnishment/ and Condemnation. together with the Convertion from their Abhominations. and their Preservation in the Godlynes, is figured-fourth before their Eyes. Translated out of Nether-Saxon.* 1579   (STC 77)

A more effective measure against the Familists, however, was the royal proclamation published against them in October 1580; and for a time they were driven underground — to reappear in the following reign.

135. *By the Queene. A Proclamation against the Sectaries of the Family of Love.* 3 October 1580   (STC 8125)

(Special mention is made of the 'Dutch books of H. N. otherwise nameless, called Evangelium Regni, or a joyfull Message of the Kingdom. Documentall sentences. The Prophecie of the spirit of love. A publishing of the peace upon the earth, &c.')

d) *The first Brownists*

Hardly had the Family of Love disappeared from the scene than a separatist Puritan movement appeared in the district round Norwich about 1580. This movement was led by Robert Browne and Robert Harrison; but it was soon detected by the ecclesiastical authorities, and the two leaders were forced to emigrate to Middelburg in Zeeland in 1581. To this early period belong two writings in manuscript, which found their way into *The Seconde Parte of a Register* (edited by A. Peel, Cambridge, 1915): 'The Supplication of Norwich men to the Queenes Matie', signed among others by Browne and Harrison; and 'A treatise of the Church and the Kingdom of Christ', by Harrison. Their first publications, however, were written in exile and smuggled in sheets into England, where they were bound and disseminated by their disciples. Three books of Browne were sent over in this way in 1582, and bound together in one volume.

136. *A Treatise of reformation without tarying for anie, and of the wickednesse of those Preachers, which will not reforme themselves and their charge, because they will tarie till the Magistrate commaunde and compell them. By me, Robert Browne.* 1582   (STC 3910)

137. *A Treatise upon the 23. of Matthewe, both for an order of studying and handling the Scriptures, and also for avoyding the Popishe disorders, and ungodly communion of all false christians, and especiallie of wicked Preachers and hirelings.* 1582   (STC 3910)

138. *A Booke which sheweth the life and manners of all true Christians, and howe unlike they are unto Turkes and Papistes, and Heathen folke. Also the pointes and partes of all divinitie, that is of the revealed will and worde of God, and declared by their severall Definitions, and Divisions in order as followeth. Robert Browne.* 1582   (STC 3910)

(The bibliographical details of these three books in one may be unravelled as follows:

The title-page of the whole volume reads: *A Booke which sheweth the life and manners*, etc. The volume then begins (on sig. A2) with *A Treatise of reformation without tarying for anie*, whose running title is 'Of Reformation Without Tarying'. There follows (on sig. D1) 'A Preface of the use of this Booke which followeth, of the life of Christians', introducing (on sig. D2) *A Treatise upon the 23. of Matthewe*, whose running title is 'An Order for Studying the Scriptures'. Finally, with a new title-page and fresh pagination, comes *A Booke which sheweth the life and manner of all true Christians.*)

Two other books by Robert Harrison followed in 1583, of a less controversial nature.

139. *A Little Treatise upon the firste Verse of the 122. Psalm. Stirring up unto carefull desiring & dutifull labouring for true church Governement. R. H.* 1583   (STC 12861)

140. *Three Formes of Catechismes, conteyning the most principall pointes*

of Religion. R. H. 1583   (Not in STC. The only known copy is at the Lambeth Palace Library.)

These books of Browne and Harrison elicited no immediate refutation; but that was in any case rendered unnecessary by a royal proclamation against their movement in June 1583.

141. *By the Queene. A Proclamation against certaine seditious and scismaticall Bookes and Libelles &c . . . set foorth by Robert Browne and Richard Harrison.* 30 June 1583   (STC 8141)

In the same month of June two unfortunate disciples of Browne, Coppin and Thacker, were executed for dispersing these books. It was not long, however, before Browne and Harrison fell out with each other — establishing a pattern to be repeated by future separatists. Browne took ship for Scotland, and was back in England by 1584, where he made a temporary peace with the Church authorities. Harrison stayed on in Zeeland till his death there a few years later. On his return home, Browne published two more books: one giving an account of his breach with Harrison, and the other replying to a letter of Cartwright to Harrison, in which the Puritan leader expressed his disapproval of their schism.

142. *A True and Short Declaration, Both of the Gathering and Ioyning together of certaine Persons: and also of the Lamentable Breach and Division which fell amongst them.* 1584   (Not in STC; the only known copy of this book is at the Lambeth Palace Library.)

143. *An answere to Master Cartwright his Letter for Ioyning with the English Churches: whereunto the true copie of his sayde letter is annexed.* [1585?]   (STC 3909)

In the latter book Cartwright's letter is given in full (pp. 86–96), with the title: 'An Answere unto a Letter of Master Harrisons by Master Cartwright being at Middleborough'. It expresses the writer's constant policy, in that, however strongly he criticized the established Church, he no less strongly disapproved of any kind of schism. Meanwhile, another Brownist group emerged under the leadership of Edward Glover, who wrote a book, entitled *A Present Preservative*, expressing similar ideas to those of Browne. The book, which has not survived, was refuted by Stephen Bredwell in his *Detection*, to which he added an 'Admonition to the followers of Glover and Browne'. This Admonition evidently stimulated Browne to break his silence and defend himself in another book which has not survived. In answer to Browne, Bredwell published his *Rasing of the Foundations of Brownisme* in 1588, including 'A Defence of the Admonition to the followers of Browne: made in reply to a raging Libell of Brownes, sent abroad, in sundrie written copies, against the same'.

144. *Detection of Ed. Glovers hereticall confection, lately contrived and proffered to the Church of England, under the name of A Present Preservative. Wherein With the laying open of his impudent slander against our whole Ministrie, the Reader shal find a new built nest of old hatcht heresies discovered, (and by the grace of God) overthrowne: togither with an admonition to the followers of Glover and Browne. By Steph. Bredwell, Student in Phisicke.* 1586   (STC 3598)

145. *The Rasing of the Foundations of Brownisme. Wherein, against all the writings of the principall Masters of that sect, those chiefe conclusions in the next page, are, (amongst sundry other matters, worthie the Readers knowledge) purposely handled, and soundly prooved. Also their contrarie arguments and obiections deliberately examined, and clearly refelled by the word of God.* 1588   (STC 3599)

This latter book touches on the next stage of the Brownist movement, which is associated with the names of Henry Barrow and John Greenwood, and which belongs to the later Marprelate controversy. These books of Bredwell, however, remained unchallenged, except for a manuscript answer by Browne to the latter book, as recorded by Peter Fairlambe in his subsequent *Recantation of a Brownist* in 1606.

CHAPTER 3

Catholic Reasons

a) *Bristow's* Motives

THE Catholic response to Jewel's challenge had been vigorous enough while it lasted; but from the nature of the case, conducted as it was under unequal conditions, the controversy could not last very long. By the end of the '60s the religious outlook in England had fundamentally changed, owing to the failure of the Rising in the North and the decision of Pope Pius V to excommunicate Queen Elizabeth. From this time onwards, as William Allen realized, the chief need of the English Catholics was a supply of priests to take the increasingly vacant places of the older Marian clergy. Already with this idea in mind he had founded the English Seminary at Douai in 1568; and from the mid-'70s onwards priests who had been educated and ordained at the Seminary began to return to their native country, to undertake their dangerous pastoral task in England. For the purpose of strengthening the Catholics in their faith and of winning back the Protestants, they were supplied with a *Book of Motives*, which had been drawn up by one of the professors at Douai, Richard Bristow, at the suggestion of Allen himself. It was a small book, but it already had a somewhat complex history, which was to become even more complex with the passing of time. Its history is related by Bristow himself in his *Reply to Fulke* in 1580:

> Twelve or thirteene yeres agoe M. D. Allen, having amongst other learned Catholickes of our time and country of this side the sea, opened and defended in print most perspicuously and substantially, certayne speciall articles of the catholicke faith: and beeing driven not long after by sickness to seeke the ayre of his native soyle, did in the short space of his abode there, deale also the other waye with many Gentlemen, confirming some, and setting up agayne others, by most evident and undouted rules of truth, which were always common for the most part among Catholikes, but the weight of them deeply considered of very few, and the number of them as yet neither by him nor by any other bound up together. Only to one gentleman requesting so much he gave a copie of

them, such a one as of extemporall and private writing might be looked for.

It is now nine yeres since I heard the same of his own mouth, what time I came first into his blessed familie, and was present very often when amongst us he discoursed familiarly upon the said rules, to such liking of my part, that I left him not untill I had intreated him to take his penne one morning, and out of his memories to frame me also a copie. Which copie a friende having seene here with me, who afterward was sent home into our lords harvest, in a letter from thence desired instantly to be made partaker therof, affirming that he saw how medicinable it would be to many soules, I communicated the matter to the Author of it. He beeing wholly occupied him selfe in publike teaching of Divinitie, would have me who then had more leasure, though for skill not worthy to bear his booke, to devise somewhat upon those and the like rules, which might in print be published to the world.

There were thus several versions in existence of what soon came to be known as 'Allen's Articles' by the time Bristow came to publish his *Motives*; and the number of 'articles' changed with each version. To make the bibliographical situation even more complicated, when the first consignment of the *Motives* was shipped across to England, it was seized and destroyed by the authorities. Then, instead of simply bringing out a second edition, Bristow decided to recast his book in a new form, with the new title of *Demaundes* and 51 items in place of the previous 48 motives. In this book he made mention of an 'intended Latin booke of the same matter'; but this did not appear till long after his untimely death in 1581, when Allen's successor, Thomas Worthington, edited it in two volumes in 1608. By that time a second edition of the *Motives* had been published in 1599.

146. *A Briefe Treatise of diverse plaine and sure wayes to finde out the truthe in this doubtful and dangerous time of Heresie: conteyning sundry worthy Motives unto the Catholike faith, or Considerations to move a man to beleve the Catholikes, and not the Heretikes. Sette out by Richard Bristow Priest, Licentiat in Divinitie. 1574* (STC 3799, AR 146, ERL 209)

(The running title is simply 'Motives to the Catholike Faith'. A second edition was printed in 1599.)

147. *Demaundes to bee proponed of Catholickes to the Heretickes. By Richard Bristow. Priest and Doctor of Divinitie. Taken partely out of his late Englishe Booke of Motives to the Catholicke faith, partely out of his intended Latin booke of the same matter. 1576* (STC 3801, AR 148, ERL 53)

148. *Richardi Bristoi Vigorniensis, eximii suo tempore sacrae Theologiae*

Doctoris & Professoris Motiva, omnibus Catholicae Doctrinae Orthodoxis Cultoribus pernecessaria; ut quae singulas omnium aetatum ac praesentis maxime temporis haereses funditus extirpet; Romanae autem Ecclesiae auctoritatem fidemque firmissimis argumentis stabiliat. Tomus Primus. 1608 (*Motives 1–17*)

149. *Richardi Bristoi Vigorniensis, eximii suo tempore sacrae Theologiae Doctoris & Professoris, Antihaeretica Motiva, cunctis unius verae atque solius salutaris Christiano-Catholicae Ecclesiae Fidei & Religionis Orthodoxis cultoribus longe conducibilissima. Tomus Secundus.* 1608 (*Motives 18–25*)

Another version of Allen's Articles was also published in 1575, as an appendix to an English translation of *A notable Discourse* against the Calvinists by Jean Albin de Valsergues. This took the form of 22 'offers' made to the Protestants, followed by 6 'certaine and sure signes'.

150. *A notable Discourse, plainelye and truely discussing, who are the right Ministers of the Catholike Church: written against Calvine and his Disciples, By one Master Iohn de Albine, called De Seres, Archedeacon of Tolosa in Fraunce. With an Offer made by a Catholike to a learned Protestant, wherin shall appere the difference betwixte the open knowen Church of the Catholikes, from the hid and unknowen Congregation of the Protestantes.* 1575 (STC 274, 21058, AR 3, ERL 28)

In the Protestant answers to these Articles, or Reasons, or Motives, or Demands, or Questions, or Offers (as they were variously called), it is not the above-mentioned books which were originally aimed at. They seem rather to be dealing with manuscript material in various forms, and with a varying number of items. The first to write was William Fulke, who had answered what he terms 'a proude challenge of the Papist against the Protestant' as early as 1568–9, though he did not publish it till 1577, when he joined it with his refutation of Allen's 'defence of Purgatory'. This challenge contained 29 articles, and had originally been supposed by Fulke 'to have ben private, or in few mens handes'. What now made him publish his answer was partly the publication in 1575 of the *Notable Discourse* with its 'Offer made by a Catholike to a learned Protestant' (though the Offer contains, as has been noted, only 22 articles), and partly the subsequent publication of Bristow's *Demaundes* in 1576. It is for this reason that in his 'Catalogue of Popish Books', appended in 1580 to his *Retentive* and his *T. Stapleton and Martiall*, he claims to have answered the Offer 'under the name of Ristons articles', or (as he calls it in the second list) 'Ristons challeng'. At the same time, as Bristow pointed out in his *Reply to Fulke* (1580), 'where as D. Allens writing was called onely by the name of Articles, this man at every Article hath also printed the word Demaundes', as though to suggest he is also aiming at the work of Bristow. Fulke's attribution of these Articles to 'Riston', or Edward Rishton (the assistant of William Allen at Douai), is possibly due to a mistaken deduction from the insertion of Rishton's 'Table of the Church' as an appendix to Bristow's *Demaundes*; and in his subsequent *Reply* Bristow corrected him by identifying the manuscript as 'M. D. Allens scroll of Articles'. Fulke was followed in 1579 by Oliver Carter, who wrote *An Answere* to 18 demands or questions, which correspond neither to the 22 offers of 'a Catholike' nor to the 48 questions or 51 demands of Bristow, but presuppose yet another manuscript — though in his second Catalogue Fulke refers to Carter's book as answering the same 'Ristons challeng' as he himself had. Thirdly, in the same year another Puritan, John Knewstub, published an *Aunsweare* to 'certaine assertions', which were only 8 in number. It was not till 1580, when Fulke returned to the attack in *A Retentive*, that the Motives of Bristow were explicitly refuted in their precise number of 48; though in making mention of his work in his Catalogue, Fulke speaks as if he has dealt with both of Bristow's books together: 'Bristowes motives and demaunds, aunswered by W. Fulke'.

151. [= 58] *Two Treatises written against the Papistes, the one being an answere of the Christian Protestant to the proud challenge of a Popish Catholicke: the other a confutation of the Popish Churches doctrine touching Purgatory & prayers for the dead: by William Fulke Doctor in divinitie.* 1577   (STC 11458)

152. *An Answere made by Oliver Carter, Bacheler of Divinitie: Unto certaine Popish Questions and Demaundes.* 1579   (STC 4697)

153. *An Aunsweare unto certaine assertions, tending to maintaine the Church of Rome to bee the true and Catholique church. By I. Knewstub.* 1579   (STC 14038)

154. [= 47] *A Retentive, to stay good Christians, in true faith and religion, against the motives of Richard Bristow. Also A Discoverie of the Daungerous Rocke of the Popish Church, commended by Nicholas Sander D. of Divinitie. Done by William Fulke Doctor of divinitie, and Maister of Pembroke hall in Cambridge.* 1580   (STC 11449)

In reply, Bristow took up his pen in defence of Allen against Fulke's *Two Treatises*: and Fulke came back with his *Reioynder* in 1581. But there the controversy ended, as Bristow died in that year — unknown to Fulke, who complained in his 'Confutation of the Papistes quarels against the writings of W. Fulke', appended to his *Defence of the sincere and true Translations* in 1583, that 'he hath my reioynder unto his reply these two yeares in his hand to consider upon'.

155. *A Reply to Fulke, In defense of M. D. Allens scroll of Articles, and*

booke of Purgatorie. By Richard Bristo Doctor of Divinitie.
1580   (STC 3802, AR 151, ERL 34)

156. [= 43] *A Reioynder to Bristows Replie in defence of Allens scroll of*
Articles and Booke of Purgatorie. Also the cavils of Nicholas Sander D.
in Divinitie about the supper of our Lord, and the Apologie of the
Church of England, touching the doctrine thereof. 1581   (STC 11448)

Another Protestant theologian who set himself the task of refuting Bristow was John Reynolds, or Rainolds. In the Preface to his *Six Conclusions*, published in 1584, he relates how he had prepared himself for battle, when he came across Fulke's *Retentive*; so laying aside his former purpose, he 'thought on that demaund and promise of Bristow touching the scripture and the Church', and directed his attack chiefly against the writings of Stapleton and Gregory Martin, as will be seen (169). As for the 'Offer' appended to the *Notable Discourse*, it was not refuted – in spite of Fulke's profession of having done so – till 1587, when it came to the attention of Robert Crowley as having been a 'great cause of the Apostacie, of so many young men, as have in late yeeres fallen away from the pure profession of the gospell'; and this prompted him to publish his *Deliberat Answere*. Three years later the *Notable Discourse* was itself answered by Thomas Spark, another leading Puritan, who also appended 'A short answere to a new offer, not published at the first, when D. Fulke and Master Carter answered the 22 demands'.

157. [= 468] *A Deliberat Answere made to a rash offer, which a popish*
Antichristian Catholique, made to a learned protestant (as he saieth)
and caused to be publyshed in printe: Anno Do. 1575. Wherein the
Protestant hath plainly & substantially prooved, that the papists that
doo nowe call themselves Catholiques are in deed Antichristian
schismatiks: and that the religious protestants, are in deed the right
Catholiques: Written by Robert Crowley: in the yeere, 1587.
1588   (STC 6084)

158. *An Answere to Master Iohn de Albines, Notable Discourse against*
heresies (as his frendes call his booke) compiled by Thomas Spark
pastor of Blechley in the county of Buck. 1591   (STC 23019)

A response of a more eccentric kind came from the pen of an 'unlearned Christian', in three stages. First, he set forth what Bristow refers to in his *Demaundes* as 'a vaine libell against the Aucthoritie of the Church of God, comparing and opponing unto it the Authority of the word of God'; but this book has apparently not survived. Then, after waiting (as he complains) five years for an answer, and finding none in books of Bristow and Laurence Vaux printed in Antwerp in 1574, he brought out a strange compilation entitled *A New Yeares Gifte*, which he described as 'The third new years gift and the second Protest, and the first proclamation of outlawry for this year

1576'. The part of his book in which this sentence occurs was printed by John Allde in 1576, but the whole book was not published till 1579, under the imprint of Henry Bynneman. The compilation consisted of a Preface 'addressed to Cardinall Poole in 1537', as 'worthy a new imprinting', followed by a miscellany of anti-Papal material, and a challenge to 'all the learned Papists in England, Antwerp, or els where the Papists books are printed and sent in to England'. When he found still no answer forthcoming, he addressed yet a third pamphlet *To the Seminarye Priests*, which was not published till 1592, though said to have been printed more than ten years earlier by Edward Allde. This he presented as 'The sixt New-yeres gift, and the fourth Proclamacion of Outlawrye &c. against the silence of Richard Bristowe priest, and all other learned Papists, in England or else where' — though there is no record of the intervening new year's gifts or proclamations. It is strangely enough only in this obscure pamphlet that the Protestants made a direct answer to Bristow's 51 'demands', in response to which the author proposes 27 marks for recognizing the true Church of Christ.

159. *A New Yeares Gifte, dedicated to the . . . Holinesse, and all . . . -cted to the Sea of Rome.* 1579   (STC 18490)

(The title-page of the only existing copy, in the Bodleian Library, Oxford, is defective.)

160. *To the Seminarye Priests lately come over, some like Gentlemen, some like Marchants, some like serving-men, and some like maymed Soldiours: who in wordes speake like Angelles of light, but are Angelles of darkenes, and so proved in this small pamphlet, who are not to be beleeved against any unlearned Protestant, before they have aunswered and confuted the Author heerof. Which being printed more then x. yeeres past, and to this day not aunswered by Richard Bristowe Priest (notwithstanding he was spoken unto and required to answer) nor answered by any other: And the same proveth the wordes of Christ Iesus our only Saviour to be true, which are under written. Luke 21. 15. For I will give you a mouth, and wisedome, where against all your adversaries shall not be able to speake, nor resist.* 1592   (STC 22185)

(It is interesting to notice that the challenge contained in this pamphlet was later echoed by two books published in 1609: one by another 'unlearned Protestant', presenting *Six Demaunds* (STC 6574); and the other by 'a simple layman' with the initials 'R. M. Gent.', entitled *A Profitable Dialogue for a perverted Papist* (STC 17149).)

Bristow's *Motives* was further honoured by special mention in a royal proclamation of October 1584 'for the suppressing of seditious Bookes'; and it was frequently referred to in official interrogation of priests after their arrest.

161. *By the Queene. A Proclamation for the suppressing of seditious Bookes and Libelles.* 12 October 1584   (STC 8146)

> (It was in the same year that a consignment of 367 copies of the *Motives* had been seized by the English authorities.)

Out of this controversy with Allen and Bristow the Protestant apologists were increasingly led to retort by proving the marks of the true Church to be in their own favour. For this purpose they found useful material in two works of prominent French Huguenots, each entitled *Traité de l'Eglise* and published about the same time. The first was that of Philippe de Mornay, which appeared in French in 1578 and was translated into English the following year by the Puritan, John Field. (It was also translated into Latin in 1579 under the title of *Tractatus de Ecclesia*.) The second to appear in England was that of Bertrand de Loque, whose French (published before that of de Mornay in 1577) was translated into English in 1581 by Field's collaborator, Thomas Wilcox.

162. *A Treatise of the Church, in which are handled all the principall questions, that have beene mooved in our time concerning that matter. By Philip of Mornay, Lorde of Plessis Marlyn, Gentleman of Fraunce. Translated out of Frenche into Englishe by I. F.* 1579   (STC 18158)

163. *A Treatie of the Churche, conteining a true discourse, to knowe the true Church by, and to discerne it from the Romish Church, and all other false assemblies, or counterfet congregations. Written by M. Bertrande de Loque of Dolphinee, and dedicated unto my Lord the Vicount of Turenne. And faithfully translated out of French into English, by T. W.* 1581   (STC 16812)

> (Both these books went into several editions within a few years, under changing titles. That of de Mornay was re-named *A Notable Treatise of the Church* in subsequent editions of 1579 and 1580, but resumed its original title in the edition of 1581. That of de Loque bore the altered title of *An excellent and plaine discourse of the Church* in its second edition of 1582.)

Also in 1581 there appeared a translation and adaptation of Theodore Beza's speech on the Church at the recent Colloquy of Poissy. This was the work of another leading Puritan, Thomas Sampson. In the same year an original discourse on the four usual marks of the true Church was published by the Puritan minister, Robert Crowley.

164. *A Briefe collection of the Church, and of certayne Ceremonies thereof, gathered by Thomas Sampson.* 1581   (STC 21682)

165. [= 467] *A briefe discourse, concerning those foure usuall notes, whereby Christes Catholique Church is knowen: wherein it appeareth*

> *manifestly, that the Romish Church that nowe is, and that hath bene*
> *almost a thousand yeeres last past, is not, neither hath bene Catholique,*
> *but Schismaticall.* 1581   (STC 6081)

(This is the wording of the inner title, as the title-page is missing.)

b) *The Rheims Testament*

Another important need of the seminary priests working in England was a
Catholic translation of the Bible, with notes, to counteract the various
Protestant versions, especially the Geneva Bible with its notes attached. This
important task was entrusted to Gregory Martin, one of the professors at
Douai, with the assistance of Allen and Bristow (who contributed the notes).
The text of the New Testament was published first in 1582, and it became
known as the Rheims version, since the Seminary had been forced to move
from Douai to Rheims in 1575. The translation of the Old Testament was
also completed about this time, but its publication was postponed, as Martin
explains in his Preface, 'for lack of good meanes to publish the whole in such
sort as a work of so great charge and importance requireth'. It did not, in
fact, appear till it was published in two volumes in 1609 and 1610. To the
edition of the New Testament Martin added a long Preface, explaining the
reasons and method of his translation. in the same year he also published *A
Discoverie of the Manifold Corruptions* he had noticed in the Protestant
translations.

166. *The New Testament of Iesus Christ, translated faithfully into English,*
     out of the authentical Latin, according to the best corrected copies of
     the same, diligently conferred with the Greeke and other editions in
     divers languages: With Arguments of bookes and chapters, Annotations,
     and other necessarie helpes, for the better understanding of the text,
     and specially for the discoverie of the Corruptions of divers late
     translations, and for cleering the Controversies in religion, of these
     daies: In the English College of Rhemes. 1582   (STC 2884, AR 567,
     ERL 267)

167. *A Discoverie of the Manifold Corruptions of the Holy Scriptures by the*
     Heretikes of our daies, specially the English Sectaries, and of their foule
     dealing herein, by partial & false translations to the advantage of their
     heresies, in their English Bibles used and authorized since the time of
     Schisme. By Gregory Martin one of the readers of Divinitie in the
     English College of Rhemes. 1582   (STC 17503, AR 525, ERL 127)

These two publications, the Catholic translation with its notes and the
attack on the Protestant translations, were regarded in England as a serious
threat to the Protestant position. A detailed refutation of the translation and
notes was entrusted to the Puritan leader, Thomas Cartwright; while the task

of defending the Protestant translations fell to his friend, William Fulke, who brought out his *Defense* of them in 1585.

168. *A Defense of the sincere and true Translations of the holie Scriptures into the English tong, against the manifolde cavils, frivolous quarels, and impudent slaunders of Gregorie Martin, one of the readers of Popish divinitie in the trayterous Seminarie of Rhemes. By William Fulke D. in Divinitie, and M. of Pembroke haule in Cambridge. Whereunto is added a briefe confutation of all such quarrels & cavils, as have bene of late uttered by diverse Papistes in their English Pamphlets, against the writings of the saide William Fulke.* 1583   (STC 11430)

The Puritan theologian at Oxford, John Reynolds, also attacked Martin together with Stapleton (whose Latin writings on this subject will be dealt with in a later chapter) in his *Six Conclusions*, which he published in 1584 as an appendix to his *Summe of The Conference* (220) recently held between himself and the seminary priest, John Hart. This work had originally been published in Latin in 1580, without reference to Martin; but in the English translation Reynolds explained, in a note 'To the Christian Reader', that this 'may serve as a reply' to Martin as well as to Stapleton. This reference to Martin was included in the title both of the English translation and of the 1602 edition of the Latin original. Another eminent scholar from Cambridge who joined in the attack on Martin was William Whitaker. He likewise added to an already existing work in Latin, his criticism of Sanders' *De Visibili Monarchia* (otherwise known as his 'Book of Antichrist'), a preface 'Ad Christianum Lectorem', dealing at some length with Martin's *Discoverie*.

169. *Six Conclusions touching the Holy Scripture and the Church. Proposed, expounded, and defended, in publike disputations at Oxford. With a defense of such thinges as Thomas Stapleton and Gregorie Martin have carped at therein.* 1584   (STC 20626)

    (Bound with *The Summe of The Conference betwene Iohn Rainoldes and Iohn Hart*. The work of Stapleton chiefly aimed at in these *Conclusions* in his *Principiorum Fidei Doctrinalium Demonstratio Methodica* (543), which first came out in 1578.)

170. *Sex Theses de Sacra Scriptura et Ecclesia. Publicis in Academia Oxoniensi Disputationibus propositae, explicatae, et defensae, a Iohanne Rainoldo. 1. Sacra Scriptura docet ecclesiam, quicquid ad salutem est necessarium. 2. Ecclesia militans errare potest, & moribus, & doctrina. 3. Maior est authoritas sacrae Scripturae, quam ecclesiae. 4. Sancta catholica ecclesia, quam credimus, est coetus universus electorum Dei. 5. Romana ecclesia, nec est ecclesia catholica, nec sanum membrum catholicae. 6. Ecclesiae reformatae in Anglia, Scotia,*

> *Gallia, Germania, caeterisque regnis & rebuspub. seipsas a Romana iure*
> *segregarunt.* 1580 (STC 20624)

(The second revised edition of 1602 bears the altered title:

Iohannis Rainoldi Angli Sex theses de sacra Scriptura & Ecclesia: Ut
publicis in Academia Oxoniensi disputationibus explicatae, sic editae,
ante annos viginti; nunc autem recognitae, & apologia contra Pontificios
Elymos, Stapletonum, Martinum, Bellarminum, Baronium, Justum
Calvinum Veteracastrensem auctae. (STC 20625))

171. [= 54] *Ad Nicolai Sanderi Demonstrationes quadraginta, in octavo*
     libro visibilis Monarchiae positas, quibus Romanum Pontificem non esse
     Antichristum docere instituit, responsio Guilielmi Whitakeri,
     Theologiae in Academia Cantabrigiensi professoris Regii, Accessit
     eiusdem Thesis de Antichristo, defensa in Comitiis Cantabrigiensibus.
     1583 (STC 25357)

Whitaker's attack on Martin, though largely confined to the Preface of his
work, occasioned a spirited defence of the latter by his colleague at Rheims,
William Reynolds, the Catholic brother of John Reynolds. (Incidentally, the
religious opposition of these two brothers is the subject of an amusing
anecdote told by Thomas Fuller in his *Church-History of Britain* (x.3):

> This John Reynolds at the first was a zealous Papist, whilst William his
> Brother was as earnest a Protestant, and afterwards Providence so ordered
> it, that by their mutuall disputation John Reynolds turned an eminent
> Protestant, and William an inveterate Papist.

A somewhat different account is, however, given of his own conversion by
William in his *Refutation* of Whitaker.) Though Whitaker's criticism of
Martin had been in Latin, Reynolds had answered him in English; and so
Whitaker now published his response in English, while protesting that Latin
would have been more appropriate, as being more academic.

172. *A Refutation of Sundry Reprehensions, Cavils, and false sleightes, by*
     which M. Whitaker laboureth to deface the late English translation, and
     Catholike annotations of the new Testament, and the booke of
     Discovery of heretical corruptions. By William Rainolds, Student of
     Divinitie in the English Colledge at Rhemes. 1583 (STC 20632,
     AR 702, ERL 263)

173. *An Answere to a certeine booke, written by M. William Rainolds*
     Student of Divinitie in the English Colledge at Rhemes, and Entituled,
     A Refutation of sundrie reprehensions, Cavils, &c. By William Whitaker
     professor of Divinitie in the Universitie of Cambridge. 1585 (STC
     25364)

The main task allotted to Thomas Cartwright (at the entreaty of Sir

Francis Walsingham and the University of Cambridge) had in the meantime been held up by the hostility of the new Archbishop of Canterbury, John Whitgift. Instead, a preliminary attack on 'the Rhemish Testament' was undertaken by the Warden of Winchester, Thomas Bilson, in his *True Difference*, which he published in 1585, primarily against two books of William Allen (249, 257).

174. [= 259] (The fourth part of) *The True Difference betweene Christian Subiection and Unchristian Rebellion: Wherein the Princes lawful power to command for truth, and indeprivable right to beare the sword, are defended against the Popes censures and the Iesuites sophismes, uttered in their Apologie and Defence of English Catholikes: With a Demonstration that the things reformed in the Church of England by the lawes of this Realme are truly Catholike, notwithstanding the vaine shew made to the contrarie in their late Rhemish Testament: by Thomas Bilson Warden of Winchester.* 1585 (STC 3071)

Bilson was followed three years later by George Wither, who offered *A View of the Marginal Notes*; by Edward Bulkeley, who wrote *An Answere* to Martin's Preface, with a detailed criticism of his translation; and, above all, by William Fulke, who subjected the Preface, the text and the notes to a thorough examination. This was Fulke's final work of controversy against the Catholics, as he died in the very year of its publication. It was perhaps his most notable work, fulfilling what had been looked for from the pen of Cartwright. To give greater weight to his criticisms, he incorporated the full text of the Rheims version in parallel columns with that of the Bishops' Bible, as well as the Preface of Martin and the Notes of Bristow, to which he added his sharp comments.

175. *A View of the Marginal Notes of the Popish Testament, translated into English by the fugitive Papists resiant at Rhemes in France. By George Wither.* 1588 (STC 25889)

176. *An Answere to ten frivolous and foolish reasons, set downe by the Rhemish Iesuits and Papists in their Preface before the new Testament by them lately translated into English, which have mooved them to forsake the originall fountaine of the Greeke, wherein the Spirit of God did indite the Gospell, and the holie Apostles did write it, to follow the streame of the Latin translation, translated we know not when nor by whom. With a discoverie of many great Corruptions and faults in the said English Translation set out at Rhemes. By E. B.* 1588 (STC 4024)

177. *The Text of the New Testament of Iesus Christ, translated out of the vulgar Latine by the Papists of the traiterous Seminarie at Rhemes.*

With Arguments of Bookes, Chapters, and Annotations, pretending to discover the corruptions of divers translations, and to cleare the controversies of these dayes. Whereunto is added the Translation out of the Original Greeke, commonly used in the Church of England, with A Confutation of all such arguments, glosses, and annotations, as conteine manifest impietie, of heresie, treason, and slander, against the Catholike Church of God, and the true teachers thereof, or the Translations used in the Church of England: Both by the auctoritie of the holy Scriptures, and by the testimonie of the ancient fathers. By William Fulke, Doctor in Divinitie. 1589 (STC 2888)

As for Cartwright's work, only his *Answere to the Preface* of Martin came out before his death in 1603. His actual *Confutation* did not appear till many years later, in 1618. Incidentally, both he and Bulkeley speak of the Rhemists as Jesuits, whereas they were all members of the secular clergy; and this odd mistake has been carried over into modern times.

178. Σὺν Θεῷ ἐν Χριστῷ. *The Answere to the Preface of the Rhemish Testament. By T. Cartwright.* 1602 (STC 4716)

179. *A Confutation of the Rhemists Translations, Glosses and Annotations on the New Testament, so farre as they conteine manifest Impieties, Heresies, Idolatries, Superstitions, Prophanesse, Treasons, Slanders, Absurdities, Falsehoods, and other evills. By occasion whereof the true sence, scope, and Doctrine of the Scriptures, and humane Authors, by them abused, is now given. Written long since by order from the chiefe instruments of the late Queene and State, and at the speciall request and encouragement of many godly-learned Preachers of England, as the ensuing Epistles shew. By that Reverend, Learned, and Iudicious Divine, Thomas Cartwright, sometime Divinitie Reader of Cambridge.* 1618 (STC 4709)

c) *The question of schism*

A practical question facing the seminary priests on their arrival in England was that of attendance at the Anglican services, which had been made obligatory by statute. From the beginning they took a clear stand against such attendance, as savouring of heresy or at least of schism. Already in the early '70s John Feckenham, the imprisoned Abbot of Westminster, had stated his reasons for refusing attendance in a manuscript entitled: 'Certaine considerations and causes, movyng me not be bee presente at, nor to receive, neither use the service of the new booke, otherwise called the Common boke of praiers'. Seeing that this manuscript was widely copied and circulated among the Catholics, William Fulke undertook the task of confuting it, as his first controversial work against the Catholics. He speaks of the manuscript as 'a certain small pamphlette, conteinyng an Apollogie, or aunswere of a Papiste, to some frendes of his, that perswaded hym to conforme hymself, to the Religion now received in the realme, by publike aucthoritie'; and he now printed it together with his confutation.

180. *A confutation of a Popishe and sclaunderous libelle, in forme of an apologie: geven out into the courte, and spread abrode in diverse other places of the Realme. Written by William Fulke, Bacheler in Divinitie, and felowe of S. Ihons Colledge in Cambridge.* 1571 (STC 11426)

Gregory Martin later on wrote a fuller explanation of the Catholic position on this subject for the guidance of the seminary priests in England; but his book remained unanswered by the Protestants.

181. *A Treatise of Schisme. Shewing, that al Catholikes ought in any wise to abstaine altogether from heretical Conventicles, to witt, their prayers, sermons, &c. devided into foure Chapters whereof 1. Conteineth sundry reasons to that purpose, grounded for the most part uppon Scriptures and Fathers. 2. Examples out of holy Scripture. 3. Examples out of ecclesiastical histories. 4. Answers to the chiefe obiections. By Gregorie Martin Licentiate in Divinitie.* 1578 (STC 17508, AR 535, ERL 117)

When the first Jesuits, Robert Persons and Edmund Campion, reached England in 1580, they found themselves faced with this same question. About that time a book by a Catholic priest, identified as Dr. Alban Langdale, was being circulated in manuscript to the effect that in certain cases it might be permissible for Catholics to attend the Anglican services. The manuscript, which was never printed and was without title-page, begins: 'And for so muche as yt semethe that this question was never thus moved, nor the case in experience in any age before this tyme, therfor this is nowe made a question, argumentes are sett dowen for Iudgment, And these be the reasons to prove that in the case sett dowene ys nether P. nor mortale synn. a perswasion dd to Mr. Sheldon 1580'. This was the occasion for Persons' first book, which he wrote soon after his arrival in England as the result of a conference with the other priests in the London area. He added a Preface under the name of John Howlet, appealing directly to the Queen on behalf of the afflicted Catholics. It was the first of several books published at a secret printing-press by Stephen Brinkley.

182. [= 241] *A Brief Discours contayning certayne reasons why Catholiques refuse to goe to Church. Written by a learned and vertuous man, to a frend of his in England. And dedicated by I. H. to the Queenes most excellent Maiestie.* 1580 (STC 19394, AR 616, ERL 84)

The importance of this little book, often known from its running title as *Reasons of Refusall*, may be gauged by the number, the immediacy and the violence of the confutations it elicited in the following year — by William Fulke, John Field, and Perceval Wiburn, all prominent Puritans.

183. *A briefe Confutation, of a Popish Discourse: Lately set forth, and presumptuously dedicated to the Queenes most excellent Maiestie: by John Howlet, or some other Birde of the night, under that name. Contayning certaine Reasons, why Papistes refuse to come to Church, which Reasons are here inserted and set downe at large, with their severall answeres. By D. Fulke, Maister of Pembroke Hall, in Cambridge.* 1581   (STC 11421)

184. *A Caveat for Parsons Howlet, concerning his untimely flighte, and scriching in the cleare day lighte of the Gospell, necessarie for him and all the rest of that dark broode, and uncleane cage of papistes, who with their untimely bookes, seeke the discredite of the trueth, and the disquiet of this Church of England. Written by Iohn Fielde, student in Divinitie.* 1581   (STC 10844)

185. *A Checke or reproofe of M. Howlets untimely shreeching in her Maiesties eares, with an answeare to the reasons alleadged in a discourse therunto annexed, why Catholikes (as they are called) refuse to goe to church: Wherein (among other things) the Papists treaterous and treacherous doctrine and demeanour towardes our Soveraigne and the State, is somewhat at large upon occasion unfolded: their divelish pretended conscience also examined, and the foundation thereof undermined. And lastly shewed that it is the duety of all true Christians and subiectes to haunt publike church assemblies. P. W.* 1581   (STC 25586)

d) The Nichols affair

Persons replied to none of these pamphlets; but his controversial temper was aroused in the same year, 1581, by a public recantation made by John Nichols, who professed to have been 'the Popes Scholer' in the newly founded English College at Rome. Not content with his formal recantation in the Tower of London, Nichols went on to publish it in book form, as well as two other items critical of the Pope and the Roman Church.

186. *A declaration of the recantation of Iohn Nichols (for the space almost of two yeeres the Popes Scholer in the English Seminarie or Colledge at Rome) which desireth to be reconciled, and received as a member into the true Church of Christ in England.* 1581   (STC 18533)

187. *The Oration and Sermon made at Rome by commaundement of the foure Cardinalles, and the Dominican Inquisitour, upon paine of death. By Iohn Nichols, latelie the Popes Scholler. Which Sermon and Oration was presented before the Pope and his Cardinalles in his*

Consistorie, the xxvii day of Maie. 1578. and remaineth there registred. Now by him brought into the English tongue for the great comfort and commoditie of all faithfull Christians. Herein also is aunswered an infamous Libell, maliciouslie written and cast abroad, against the saide Iohn Nichols, with a sufficient discharge of himselfe from all the Papists lying reports, and his owne life both largelie and amplie discovered. 1581   (STC 18535)

188. *Iohn Niccols Pilgrimage, wherein is displaied the lives of the proude Popes, ambitious Cardinals, lecherous Bishops, fat bellied Monkes, and hypocriticall Iesuites.* 1581   (STC 18534)

The 'infamous Libell' mentioned in the *Oration* is not otherwise known. In his *Pilgrimage*, too, Nichols complains that 'there are certaine bookes scattered against mee, and against my workes'. One of these books may have been Persons' reply to the *Recantation* and the *Oration*: it appeared that year under the title of *A Discoverie*.

189. *A Discoverie of I. Nicols Minister, misreported a Iesuite, latelye recanted in the Tower of London. Wherin besides the declaration of the man, is contayned a ful answere to his recantation, with a confutation of his slaunders, and proofe of the contraries, in the Pope, Cardinals, Clergie, Studentes, and private men of Rome. There is also added a reproofe of an oration and sermon, falsely pretended by the sayd Nicols to be made in Rome, and presented to the Pope in his Consistorye. Wherto is annexed a late information from Rome touching the autentical copie of Nicols recantation.* 1581   (STC 19402, AR 627, ERL 57)

Towards the end of his reply Persons took occasion to criticise an attack on the Papists by Thomas Lupton, entitled *A Persuasion from Papistrie*, which had recently been published. Lupton responded to this criticism in the following year with *The Christian against the Iesuite*; but Persons paid no further attention to him.

190. *A Persuasion from Papistrie: Wrytten chiefely to the obstinate, determined, and dysobedient English Papists, who are herein named & proved English enimies and extreme Enimies to Englande.* 1581   (STC 16950)

191. *The Christian against the Iesuite. Wherein the secrete or namelesse writer of a pernitious booke, intituled A Discoverie of I. Nicols Minister &c. privily printed, covertly cast abrod, and secretely solde, is not only iustly reprooved: But also a booke, dedicated to the Queenes Maiestie, called A persuasion from papistrie, therein derided and falsified, is defended by Thomas Lupton the author thereof.* 1582   (STC 16946)

The following year a fuller answer to Persons' book came from the pen of a young Puritan, Dudley Fenner.

192. *An Answer unto the Confutation of Iohn Nichols his Recantation,*
in all pointes of any weight conteyned in the same: Especially in the
matters of Doctrine, of Purgatorie, Images, the Popes honor, and the
question of the Church. By Dudley Fenner, Minister of Gods word.
1583   (STC 10764)

About the same time, Nichols crossed over to France, where he was induced to withdraw his recantation. An anonymous account of the fact was published in 1583, under the title of *A true report*, probably by William Allen himself, who referred to the work in a letter of 30 May 1583 as 'the little book in English containing the various accounts of the apologies and repentance of the Catholics who have lapsed in this persecution'. It was also translated into Latin and published in the *Concertatio Ecclesiae Catholicae in Anglia* (251) in 1583.

193. *A true report of the late apprehension and imprisonment of Iohn Nicols*
Minister, at Roan, and his confession and answers made in the time of
his durance there. Whereunto is added the satisfaction of certaine, that
of feare or frailtie have lately fallen in England. 1583   (STC 18537,
AR 12, ERL 63)

e) *Campion's Challenge*

The major controversy of these years, however, raged round the writings not of Persons, but of his milder companion, Edmund Campion. To begin with, before leaving London on his apostolic journey through the provinces, he resolved to write a letter 'To the Right Honourable Lords of Her Maiesties Privy Council', stating the aims of his mission in case he was arrested.

This is the document known as Campion's Brag, or Challenge; and it was presented in the form of nine points or articles. He made two copies, one of which he left with a Catholic gentleman, Thomas Pounde, who had long been a prisoner in the Marshalsea in London; but Pounde could not forbear showing it to his fellow-prisoners. Thus it soon came to the attention of the authorities; and two ministers, William Charke and Meredith Hanmer, undertook the task of refuting it. In his reply Hanmer printed Campion's text in full, referring to it as 'the great bragge and challenge'. Charke went further and took this opportunity to vilify the whole Jesuit order. For the same purpose he also translated a recent book against the Jesuits by Christian Francken, *Colloquium Iesuiticum* (1580). He was soon able to bring out a second edition of his *Answere to a seditious pamphlet*, this time adding Campion's text, 'the rather, because the same is alreadie published in print in a booke entituled, The great bragge &c.'

194. *An answere to a seditious pamphlet lately cast abroade by a Iesuite, with a discoverie of that blasphemous sect. By William Charke.* 1580 (STC 5005)

   (The second edition, published in 1581, bore the altered title:

   An answere to a seditious Pamphlet lately cast abroade by a Iesuite, conteyning ix. Articles heere inserted and set downe at large, with a discoverie of that blasphemous sect. By William Charke. (STC 5006))

195. *A conference or Dialogue discovering the sect of Iesuites: most profitable for all Christendome rightly to knowe their religion. Written in Latine by Christian Francken, and translated by W. C.* 1580 (STC 11325)

196. *The great bragge and challenge of M. Champion a Iesuite, commonlye called Edmunde Campion, latelye arrived in Englande, contayninge nyne articles here severallye laide downe, directed by him to the Lordes of the Counsail, confuted & aunswered by Meredith Hanmer, M. of Art, and Student in Divinitie.* 1581 (STC 12745)

There followed yet another translation of an anti-Jesuit book, the *Assertio veteris ac veri Christianismi*, by the Huguenot Pierre Boquin, which had been published at Lyons in 1576. Thus began what was shortly to develop into an almost endless flood of anti-Jesuit propaganda in England.

197. *A Defence of the Olde, and True profession of Christianitie, against the new, and counterfaite secte of Iesuites, or fellowship of Iesus: Written in Latine by P. Boquine a Frenchman, borne in Borges, & Professor of Divinitie, in the Universitie of Heidelberge: Translated into Englishe by T. G. Whereby may bee perceived, how falslye the Iesuites usurpe the name of Iesus, and how farre off they are, from the thing signified thereby, and what their profession, and purpose is in truth: otherwise then they beare the worlde in hande.* 1581 (STC 3371)

Meanwhile Campion had been arrested and imprisoned in the Tower of London. So the task of defending his challenge was undertaken by Persons, who wrote *A Brief Censure* on both the books that had come out against him. This immediately elicited replies from both the authors, who added further vilification of the Jesuits in general.

198. *A Brief Censure uppon two bookes written in answere to M. Edmonde Campions offer of disputation.* 1581 (STC 4534, 19393, AR 615, ERL 1)

199. *A Replie to a Censure written against the two answers to a Iesuites seditious Pamphlet. By William Charke.* 1581 (STC 5007)

200. *The Iesuites Banner. Displaying their original and successe: their vow*

and othe: their hypocrisie and superstition: their doctrine and
positions: with A Confutation of a late Pamphlet secretly imprinted
and entituled: A briefe Censure upon two bookes written in answeare
to M. Campions offer of disputation &c. Compiled by Meredith Hanmer
M. of Arte, and Student in Divinity. 1581   (STC 12746)

Once again Persons undertook a combined refutation of the two ministers;
but this time he met with a strange silence. Only an anonymous writer came
forward with *An Answeare for the time* on behalf of Charke, who was
alleged to be working on a fuller response. But this response never appeared.
Instead, another *Treatise against the Defense of the Censure* came out on
Charke's behalf, bound with two treatises of Fulke against Allen and Peter
Frarin. It is not unlikely that the anonymous writer was Fulke himself.

201. *A Defence of the Censure, gyven upon two bookes of William Charke*
     and Meredith Hanmer mynysters, whiche they wrote against M.
     Edmond Campian preest, of the Societie of Iesus, and against his offer
     of disputation. Taken in hand since the deathe of the sayd M. Campian,
     and broken of agayne before it could be ended, upon the causes sett
     downe in an epistle to M. Charke in the begyninge. 1582   (STC 19401,
     AR 626, ERL 1)

202. *An Answeare for the time, unto that foule and wicked Defence of*
     the Censure, that was given upon M. Charkes Booke, and Meredith
     Hanmers. Contayning a maintenance of the credite and persons, of all
     those woorthie men: namely, of M. Luther, Calvin, Bucer, Beza, and
     the rest of those Godlie ministers of Gods worde, whom he, with a
     shamelesse penne most slanderously hath sought to deface: finished
     sometime sithence: And now published for the stay of the Christian
     Reader till Maister Charkes Booke come foorth. 1583   (STC 5008)

203. [cf. 59, 85] *A Treatise against the Defense of the Censure, given upon*
     the Bookes of W. Charke, and Meredith Hanmer, by an unknowne
     Popish Traytor, in maintenance of the seditious challenge of Edmond
     Campion, lately condemned & executed for high Treason. Hereunto are
     adioyned two treatises, written by D. Fulke: the one against Allens
     booke of the authoritie of Priesthode to remitte sinnes, of confession of
     sinnes to a Priest, and of the Popes Pardons: The other against the
     Railing declamation of P. Frarine. 1586   (STC 5009)

f) *Campion's* Reasons

Meanwhile, Pounde had developed *Six Reasons* of his own out of Campion's
challenge, and circulated them in manuscript under the title: 'Six Reasons
set downe to shew, that it is no orderly way in controversies of faith, to
appeale to be tryed only by Scriptures (as the absurde opinion of all

Sectaries is) but the sentence & definition of the Catholike Church, by whome, as by the spowse of Christ, always inspired by the holy ghost, the holy Scripture is to be iudged'. These 'Reasons' were taken up by Robert Crowley, who had visited Pounde in prison, and now printed them together with his refutation of them. In an appendix at the end of Crowley's *Aunswer* is also printed 'A breefe Aunswer to Maister Pownds six Reasons. Written by Maister Henrie Trippe', which only occupies four pages.

204. *An Aunswer to sixe Reasons, that Thomas Pownde, Gentleman, and*
    Prisoner in the Marshalsey, at the commaundement of her Maiesties
    Commissioners, for causes Ecclesiasticall: required to be aunswered.
    Because these Reasons doo move him to think, that controversies and
    doubts in Religion, may not be Judged by the Scriptures, but that the
    Scriptures must be Judged by the Catholique Church. 1. The first is, for
    that the Scriptures are mute and dum. 2. The second, for that they be
    full of harde and deepe mysteries. 3. The thirde, for that S. Peter sayth:
    No Scripture is to be taken after any private interpretation. 4. The
    fourth, for that to appeale to the Scriptures, dooth seeme to denie all
    unwritten verities. 5. The fyft is, for that it were a great absurditie, not
    to have a certaine Iudge of absolute Authoritie, in the interpreting of
    Scriptures, &c. 6. The sixt is, for that in refusing the Authoritie of the
    Churches absolute Iudgement herein: we seeme to denie the holie
    ghost, to be the spirite of truth. Written by Robert Crowley. 1581
    (STC 6075)

In addition to his brief challenge Campion composed a more elaborate work in Latin, entitled *Rationes Decem*, showing how he placed his reliance not on any private opinion, but on ten powerful reasons. This was secretly printed at Stonor Park in 1581, and distributed on the benches of St. Mary's Church in Oxford, causing even more of a sensation than the previous challenge. For its refutation the Regius Professors of Divinity at both universities, William Whitaker at Cambridge and Laurence Humphrey at Oxford, wrote their respective books in Latin at the request of John Aylmer, Bishop of London. Whitaker's reply was first in the field, and led to further controversy with a Scottish Jesuit, John Dury. In the next ten years no less than six Latin editions of Campion's book were published in Europe; and it was translated into Polish, Flemish, German and French before 1600. Strangely enough, however, it was not translated into English till 1606, when the Protestant Richard Stock undertook the translation of Whitaker's *Answere* – including Campion's text. A Catholic translation did not appear till many years later, in 1632, under the title *Campian Englished*.

205. [cf. 251, 264] *Rationes Decem, quibus fretus certamen Anglicanae*
    Ecclesiae ministris obtulit in causa fidei Edmundus Campianus. 1581
    (AR 192, ERL 1)

206. *Ad Rationes Decem Edmundi Campiani Iesuitae, quibus fretus certamen Anglicanae ecclesiae ministris obtulit in causa fidei Responsio Guilielmi Whitakeri Theologiae in Academia Cantabrigiensi professoris Regii.* 1581   (STC 25358)

207. *Confutatio Responsionis Gulielmi Whitakeri in Academia Cantabrigiensi Professoris Regii ad Rationes Decem, quibus fretus Edm. Campianus, Anglus, Societatis Iesu theologus, certamen Anglicanae Ecclesiae ministris obtulit in causa fidei. Authore Joanne Duraeo Scoto, Soc. Iesu presbytero.* 1582.

208. *Responsionis ad Decem illas Rationes, quibus fretus Edmundus Campianus certamen Ecclesiae Anglicanae ministris obtulit in causa fidei, Defensio contra Confutationem Ioannis Duraei Scoti, Presbyteri, Iesuitae: Authore Guilielmo Whitakero Theologiae in Academia Cantabrigiensi professore Regio. In hoc libro controversiae pleraeque omnes, quae inter nostras & pontificias Ecclesias intercederunt, breviter ac dilucide pertractantur.* 1583   (STC 23561)

209. *An Answere to the Ten Reasons of Edmund Campian the Iesuit, in confidence whereof he offered disputation to the Ministers of the Church of England, in the controversie of faith. Whereunto is added in briefe marginall notes, the summe of the defence of those reasons by Iohn Duraeus the Scot, being a Priest and a Iesuit, with a reply unto it. Written first in the Latine Tongue by the Reverend and faithfull servant of Christ and his Church, William Whitakers, Doctor in Divinitie, and the Kings Professor and publike Reader of Divinitie in the Universitie of Cambridge. And now faithfully translated for the benefit of the unlearned (at the appointment and desire of some in authoritie) into the English tongue: by Richard Stocke, Preacher in London.* 1606 (STC 25360)

210. *Campian Englished. or A Translation of the Ten Reasons, in which Edmund Campian (of the Societie of Iesus) Priest, insisted in his Challenge, to the Universities of Oxford and Cambridge. Made by a Priest of the Catholike and Roman Church.* 1632   (STC 4535, AR 193, ERL 71)

As for Laurence Humphrey, he brought out two substantial volumes against what he chose to call 'Jesuitism' or 'Puritanopapism', the first being of a more general nature, and the second dealing with the first five reasons of Campion in 667 pages. These books were shortly afterwards republished at La Rochelle, in the second and third tomes of a massive Protestant onslaught against the Jesuits, entitled *Doctrinae Iesuitarum Praecipua Capita*. The first tome, published in 1584, contained Boquin's *Assertio* (197) and Francken's *Colloquium Iesuiticum* (195). The second tome, published in 1585, contained – in addition to the first part of Humphrey's work – Whitaker's *Responsio* to Campion and his *Defensio* against Duraeus. The third tome, also published in 1585, contained – in addition to Humphrey's second part – John Foxe's disputation *De Christo gratis iustificante* against Osorius (77). The fifth tome, published in 1586, included the *Sex Theses* of John Reynolds (170).

211. *Iesuitismi pars prima: sive de Praxi Romanae Curiae contra respublicas et principes, et de nova legatione Iesuitarum in Angliam, προθεράπεια et praemonitio ad Anglos; cui adiuncta est concio eiusdem argumenti, cuius titulus est Pharisaismus vetus et novus, sive de fermento Pharisaeorum et Iesuitarum: authore Laurentio Humfredo.* 1582 (STC 13961)

212. *Iesuitismi Pars Secunda: Puritanopapismi, seu doctrinae Iesuiticae aliquot Rationibus ab Ed. Campiano comprehensae, & a Ioan. Duraeo defensae, Confutatio: Et ex iisdem Fundamentis Reformatae nostrae Religionis Assertio: Autore Laurentio Humfredo S. Theologiae in Acad. Oxoniensi Professore Regio.* 1584 (STC 13962)

213. *Doctrinae Iesuitarum Praecipua Capita, doctis quibusdam Theologis (quorum libri sequente pagina continentur) retexta, solidis rationibus testimoniisque sacrarum Scripturarum & Doctorum veteris Ecclesiae confutata.* 1584–88

g) *Conference in the Tower*

Already, before Campion was arrested in the summer of 1581, several of his companions – Sherwin, Hart, Bosgrave and Briant – had been apprehended and imprisoned in the Tower of London. There, in addition to various interrogations, they were subjected to denunciatory sermons, first by William Fulke in March, then by John Keltridge in May. These sermons were published shortly afterwards.

214. *A Sermon Preached upon Sunday, beeing the twelfth of March. Anno 1581, within the Tower of London: In the hearing of such obstinate Papistes as then were prisoners there: By William Fulke Doctor in Divinitie, and M. of Pembroke Hall in Cambridge.* 1581 (STC 11455)

215. *Two Godlie and learned Sermons, appointed, and Preached, before the Iesuites, Seminaries, and other adversaries to the Gospell of Christ in the Tower of London. In which, were confuted to their faces, the most principall and cheefe poincts of their Romish and Whoarish religion: And all such Articles as they defend, contrarie to the woord of God, were layed open and ripped up unto them. In Maye 7. and 21. Anno 1581. By Iohn Keltridge, Preacher of the worde of God, in London.* 1581 (STC 14921)

When it came to his own turn to be arrested and imprisoned in the same Tower, Campion was at length granted his desire of a disputation, but not altogether under the conditions he had desired. The attendance at the disputation was strictly limited; and he himself was considerably weakened by his prison life, including subjection to the torture of the rack. A number of conferences were held in August and September of 1581, first with Alexander Nowell, Dean of St. Paul's, and William Day, Dean of Windsor, then with William Fulke, Roger Goad, John Walker and William Charke. The reports of both series of conferences were put together by the Puritan, John Field, and published in one volume later on, in 1583.

216. *A true report of the Disputation or rather private Conference had in the Tower of London, with Ed. Campion Iesuite, the last of August, 1581. Set downe by the Reverend learned men them selves that dealt therein. Whereunto is ioyned also a true report of the other three dayes conferences had there with the same Iesuite. Which nowe are thought meete to be published in print by authoritie.* 1583   (STC 18744)

217. *The three last dayes conferences had in the Tower with Edmund Campion Iesuite, the 18: 23: and 27. of September, 1581. collected and faithfully set downe by M. Iohn Feilde student in Divinitie. Nowe perused by the learned men themselves, and thought meete to be published.* 1583   (STC 18744 – bound with 216)

This publication further inspired one H. D. to compose *A Godlie and fruitfull Treatise* in the same year, attacking the opinions put forward at the conference by Campion on the subject of faith and works.

218. *A Godlie and fruitfull Treatise of Faith and workes. Wherein is confuted a certaine opinion of merit by workes, which an adversary to the Gospell of Christ Iesu, held in the conference, had in the Tower of London.* 1583   (STC 6168) (The dedication is signed H. D.)

This practice of holding private conferences with Catholic priests in prison and of publishing them in support of the Protestant cause had already been followed by William Fulke the year before at Wisbech Castle, where many of the old Catholic leaders were still in custody. On that occasion he had failed to make much headway against John Feckenham's distrust of all such disputations. Subsequently, John Reynolds arranged a similar conference, with better success, with the seminary priest, John Hart (who was later received into the Society of Jesus). His report of it, published with Hart's approval, went into several editions, and was also translated into Latin – though it was not till 1610 that the translation was eventually published by order of Archbiship Bancroft.

219. *A True reporte of a Conference had betwixt Doctour Fulke, and the*

Papists, being at Wisbiche Castle: Doctour Fulke beeyng sent thither by
the Bishop of Ely the 4. of October. 1580. 1581   (STC 11457)

220. *The Summe of The Conference betwene Iohn Rainoldes and Iohn Hart:*
touching the Head and the Faith of the Church. Wherein by the way are
handled sundrie points, of the sufficiencie and right expounding of the
Scriptures, the ministerie of the Church, the function of Priesthood, the
sacrifice of the Masse, with other controversies of religion; but chiefly
and purposely the point of Church-government, opened in the branches
of Christes supreme soveraintie, of Peters pretended, the Popes usurped,
the Princes lawfull Supremacie. 1584   (STC 20626)

221. *Summa Colloquii Johannis Rainoldi cum Johanne Harto De Capite et*
Fide Ecclesiae. Ubi variae obiter tractantur quaestiones, de Sufficientia,
& orthodoxa expositione Scripturarum, Ministerio Ecclesiae, Functione
Sacerdotali, Sacrificio Missae, una cum aliis, quae in religione agitantur,
controversiis; praecipue vero, & ex instituto, quaestio de Ecclesiae
regimine, explicata in iis, quae de Christi suprema Monarchia, de Petri
praetensa, Papae usurpata, Principis legitima supremitate disputantur. A
Johanne Rainoldo conscripta, convenienter compendiis illis quae
uterque scripto mandarat: examinata demum, a Johanne Harto, atque
(post addita quaedam, quaedam mutata ut ipsi commodum videbatur)
pro fideli narratione eorum, quae inter ipsos in Colloquio disserebantur,
habita & comprobata. Ante quatuor et viginti annos ex Anglico
sermone in Latinum versa, nunc autem primum jussu, curaque
Reverendissimi atque vigilantissimi Praesulis, Richardi Bancrofti,
Cantuariensis Archiepiscopi (qui non domesticarum modo, quibus
praeest, sed etiam exterarum Ecclesiarum bono impense studet) e situ &
pulvere evocata, & in lucem emissa. Henrico Parraeo, Gloucestrensi
Episcopo, interprete. 1610   (STC 20630)

h) *The arrest and execution of Campion*

The smallest details of Campion's arrest, imprisonment in the Tower,
tortures, trial and execution, were controverted in innumerable pamphlets
on either side. These began with a strange altercation between Anthony
Munday, another 'Popes scholar' turned informer and future dramatist, and
George Eliot, who had actually betrayed Campion to the authorities,
concerning the circumstances of his arrest.

222. *A Breefe discourse of the taking of Edmund Campion, the seditious*
Iesuit and divers other Papistes, in Barkeshire: who were brought to the
Towre of London, the 22. day of Iuly. 1581. Gathered by A. M. 1581
(STC 18264)

223. *A very true Report of the apprehension and taking of that arch-papist Edmund Campion, the Pope his right hand, with three other lewd Iesuit priests, and diverse other lay people, most seditious persons of like sort. Containing also a controulment of a most untrue former book set out by A. M. concerning the same, as is to be proved and justified by Geo. Ellyot, one of the ordinary yeomen of her Maiesties chamber, author of this booke, and chiefest cause of the finding of the said lewd and seditious people.* 1581   (STC 7629)

Concerning the trial of Campion and his companions in Westminster Hall various reports were circulated among the Catholics. They soon elicited an anonymous rebuttal under the title of *An advertisement*. An unsympathetic account of Campion's subsequent execution in December, 1581, *A Triumph for true subjects*, came from the scurrilous pen of William Elderton. Early in the following year Munday added his account of the arraignment and execution in *A Discoverie of Edmund Campion*.

224. *An advertisement and defence for Trueth against her Backbiters, and specially against the whispring Favourers, and Colourers of Campions, and the rest of his confederats treasons.* 1581   (STC 18259)

225. *A Triumph for true subjects and a terror unto all traitors. By the example of the late death of Edmund Campion, Ralph Sherwin and Alexander Briant, Jesuits and Seminary Priests: who suffered at Tyburn the first day of December, Anno Domini, 1581.* 1581   (STC 7564)

226. *A Discoverie of Edmund Campion, and his Confederates, their most horrible and traiterous practises, against her Maiesties most royall person, and the Realme. Wherein may be seene, how thorowe the whole course of their Araignment: they were notably convicted of every cause. Whereto is added, the Execution of Edmund Campion, Raphe Sherwin, and Alexander Brian, executed at Tiborne the 1. of December. Published by A. M. sometime the Popes Scholler, allowed in the Seminarie at Roome amongst them: a Discourse needefull to be read of every man, to beware how they deale with such secret seducers.* 1582 (STC 18270)

On the other hand, a Catholic view was presented in an anonymous eye-witness *Reporte of the death & martyrdom of M. Campion*, now accepted as the work of a seminary priest, Thomas Alfield, which became a main source for the Catholic versions of the event that were soon circulating everywhere in Europe. The author enumerates his adversaries as 'Charke, Hanmer, Whitakers, Fyld, Keltrigh, Eliot, kogging Munday, riming Elderton, and Iohn Nichols the disciple of bawdy Bale', and appends 'A Caveat to the reader touching A. M. his discovery'. His pamphlet was shortly translated into both French and Latin.

227. *A true reporte of the death & martyrdom of M. Campion Iesuite and preiste, & M. Sherwin, & M. Bryan preistes, at Tiborne the first of December 1581. Observid and written by a Catholike preist, which was present therat. Wherunto is annexid certayne verses made by sundrie persons.* 1582 (STC 4537, AR 4, ERL 56)

228. *L' Histoire de la Mort que le R. P. Edmonde Campion, prestre de la Compagnie du nom de Jesus, et autres ont souffert en Angleterre pour la foy Catholique et Romaine, le premier jour de Decembre 1581. Traduit d' Anglois en Francois.* 1582.

229. *Martyrium R. P. Edmundi Campiani Presbyteri e societate nominis Iesu, qui cum duobus aliis Presbyteris, Radulpho Sherwino & Alexandro Briano in Anglia propter constantem Romanae Catholicae fidei confessionem, mortis supplicio affectus est ipsis calendis Decembris, anno a Christo nato MDLXXXI. Per G. Estium e Gallico Latine redditum. Adiuncta sunt et alia quaedam similis argumenti.* 1582

Munday promptly responded both to the English original and to the French version with *A breefe Aunswer*, adding a particular 'aunswer to his Caveat' and a parody on the 'Verses in the Libell'.

230. *A breefe Aunswer made unto two seditious Pamphlets, the one printed in French, and the other in English. Contayning a defence of Edmund Campion and his complices, their moste horrible and unnaturall Treasons, against her Maiestie and the Realme. by A. M.* 1582 (STC 18262)

About the same time there appeared an official justification of Campion's execution and a reproof of books in which he was glorified as a martyr.

231. *A particular declaration or testimony, of the undutifull and traiterous affection borne against her Maiestie by Edmond Campion Iesuite, and other condemned Priestes, witnessed by their owne confessions: in reproofe of those slaunderous bookes & libels delivered out to the contrary by such as are malitiously affected towards her Maiestie and the state. Published by authoritie.* 1582 (STC 4536)

Other priests involved with Campion in the trial and executions that followed were made the subjects of conflicting reports during 1582. The dying confession of Ralph Sherwin, 'I acknowledge that in me, and of me, there is nothing but sinne and abhomination, and I trust onelie to be saved by the death and blood shedding of Iesus Christ', was pounced upon by Peter White as an apparent rejection of the Catholic teaching on the merit of good works; and after sounding out the beliefs of other priests in the Tower concerning this matter, he published the result in a book, entitled *A Discoverie of the Iesuitical Opinion of Iustification.*

232. *A Discoverie of the Iesuitical Opinion of Iustification, guilefullie uttered by Sherwine at the time of his execution. Gathered and set foorth by Peter White, verie necessarie and profitable for this daungerous time.* 1582   (STC 25401)

The execution of a second batch of priests in May 1582 was reported by Munday in yet another of his pamphlets, entitled *A breefe and true reporte.* On the other side, the various reports concerning both groups of victims were sifted by William Allen and published that same year in *A Briefe Historie of the Glorious Martyrdom.* A Latin translation of the *Historie* appeared later in the *Concertatio Ecclesiae Catholicae in Anglia* (251).

233. *A breefe and true reporte, of the Execution of certaine Traytours at Tiborne, the xxviii. and xxx. dayes of Maye. 1582. Gathered by A. M. who was there present. The names of them executed on Monday, the xxviii. of Maye. Thomas Foord. Iohn Shert. Robert Iohnson. The names of them executed on Wednesday, the xxx. of Maye. William Filbie. Luke Kirbie. Lawrance Richardson. Thomas Cottom.* 1582. (STC 18261)

234. *A Briefe Historie of the Glorious Martyrdom of XII. Reverend Priests, executed within these twelve monethes for confession and defence of the Catholike Faith. But under the false pretence of Treason. With a note of sundrie things that befel them in their life and imprisonment: and a preface declaring their innocencie. Set furth by such as were much conversant with them in their life, and present at their arraignement and death.* 1582   (STC 13526, AR 7, ERL 55)

Finally, Munday carried out a promise he had made in his *Discoverie*, and followed the example of John Nichols by giving a full account of the lives of English seminarians at Rome as a former 'Popes scholar'. His book was, however, ignored by the Catholics.

235. *The English Romayne Lyfe. Discovering: The lives of the Englishmen at Roome: the orders of the English Seminarie: The dissention betweene the Englishmen and the Welshmen: the banishing of the Englishmen out of Roome: the Popes sending for them againe: a reporte of many of the paltrie Reliques in Roome: their Vautes under the grounde: their holy Pilgrimages: and a number other matters, worthy to be read and regarded of every one. There unto is added, the cruell tiranny, used on an English man at Roome, his Christian suffering and notable Martirdome, for the Gospell of Iesus Christe, in Anno. 1581. Written by A. M. sometime the Popes Scholler in the Seminarie among them.* 1582 (STC 18272)

i) *The English persecution*

It was chiefly out of these controversies, and the actions and sufferings that lay behind them, that there now grew among English Catholics an increasing sense of persecution — in which they compared their plight to that of the Christians under the Roman Empire. It was Robert Persons who first gave utterance to this sense with his *Epistle of the Persecution*. This was first written in Latin and published in several editions, before being translated into French by Matthieu de Launoy, and then into English by G. T. (who added an epistle of his own to the Lords of the Council).

236. *De Persecutione Anglicana, Epistola. Qua explicantur afflictiones, aerumnae, & calamitates gravissimae, cruciatus etiam & tormenta, & acerbissima martyria, quae Catholici nunc Angli, ob fidem patiuntur.* 1581

(This first edition was published at Rouen. Two other editions followed in 1582 from Rome and Ingolstadt, with the following changes in the title:

Rome: *De Persecutione Anglicana Libellus, Quo explicantur Afflictiones, calamitates, cruciatus, & acerbissima martyria, quae Angli Catholici nunc ob fidem patiuntur. Quae omnia in hac postrema editione aeneis typis ad vivum expressa sunt.*
Ingolstadt: *De Persecutione Anglicana Commentariolus, A Collegio Anglicano Romano, hoc Anno Domini MDXXCII in Urbe editus, & iam denuo Ingolstadii excusus: Additis Literis S.D.N.D. Gregorii Papae XIII hortatoriis ad subveniendum Anglis, &c.*)

237. *Epistre de la Persecution meue en Angleterre contre l'Eglise Chrestienne Catholique & Apostolique, & fideles membres d'icelle, ou sont declares les tres grandes afflictions, miseres, et calamites, les tourmens tres cruelz et martyres admirables que les fideles Chrestiens Anglois souffrent pour leur foy et religion.* 1582

238. *An Epistle of the Persecution of Catholickes in Englande. Translated owt of frenche into English and conferred with the Latyne copie, by G. T. To whiche there is added an epistle by the translator to the right honorable Lordes of her maiesties preevie councell towchynge the same matter.* 1582   (STC 19406, 4834, 3724, AR 629, ERL 125)

This epistle of the English translator prompted a reply from the pen of the Puritan, Walter Travers.

239. *An Answere to a Supplicatorie Epistle, of G. T. for the pretended Catholiques: written to the right Honorable Lords of her Maiesties*

privy Councell. By Water Travers, Minister of the worde of God. 1583
(STC 24181)

At the same time, there appeared a 'literature of consolation' written by various priests for the comfort of their afflicted flock in England. It was accompanied by a smaller 'literature of complaint' written to those in authority in England. Thomas Hide led the way with *A Consolatorie Epistle* in 1579. He was followed in 1580 by Robert Persons, who (under the pseudonym of John Howlet) painted a lamentable picture of the sufferings of English Catholics in the Dedicatory Epistle to the Queen prefaced to his *Brief Discours*.

240. *A Consolatorie Epistle to the afflicted Catholikes: set foorth by Thomas Hide Priest.* 1579   (STC 13376, AR 394, ERL 105)

241. [= 182] *A Brief Discours contayning certayne reasons why Catholiques refuse to goe to Church. Written by a learned and vertuous man, to a frend of his in England. And dedicated by I. H. to the Queenes most excellent Maiestie.* 1580   (STC 19394, AR 616, ERL 84)

In 1581 came William Allen's 'Admonition and comfort to the afflicted Catholikes', appended to his *Apologie* on behalf of the two English Colleges; and this was also translated into Latin as part of a larger work entitled *Concertatio Ecclesiae Catholicae in Anglia* (251).

242. 'An admonition and comfort to the afflicted Catholikes', published as Ch. VII of *An Apologie and True Declaration* (249) 1581   (STC 369, AR 6, ERL 67)

243. 'D. Guilielmi Alani piissima admonitio & consolatio vere Christiana ad afflictos Catholicos Angliae', published as an appendix to Allen's *Duo Edicta Elizabethae*, the Latin translation of his *Apologie* (250), itself appended to the *Concertatio Ecclesiae Catholicae in Anglia*, 1583 (251, 264)

Subsequently, Robert Southwell published his *Epistle of Comfort* in 1588; and about the same time there appeared *A Consolatory Letter* by one 'H. B.' Finally, Southwell's deeply moving *Humble Supplication*, though written in the early '90s, was not published till 1600 (with the false imprint of 1595, the year of his death). Apart from Persons' Dedicatory Epistle to his *Brief Discours*, it is interesting that this literature elicited no response from the Protestant side.

244. *An Epistle of Comfort, To the reverend Priestes & To the Honorable, Worshipful, & other of the Laye sort restrayned in Durance for the Catholicke Fayth.* 1588   (STC 22946, AR 781, ERL 211)

(The Preface bears the signature R. S.)

245. *A Consolatory Letter to all the afflicted Catholikes in England.* 1588
(STC 1032, AR 59, ERL 10)

(The initials H. B. occur in the opening salutation.)

246. *An Humble Supplication to Her Maiestie.* 1600 (STC 7586, AR 784,
ERL 123)

(The title-page bears the false imprint of 1595.)

Further point was given to this sense of persecution by the publishing of
two royal proclamations against the Jesuits and the seminary priests on 15
July 1580 and 10 January 1581. As they were specifically directed against
the English Colleges at Rheims and Rome, Allen felt it incumbent on him to
write in defence of his two foundations. The result was his *Apologie* both for
his own priests and pupils and for the fathers of the Society of Jesus. This
was soon translated into Latin and published as an appendix to the
Concertatio Ecclesiae Catholicae in Anglia, a compilation of documents in
Latin relating to the whole situation arising out of Campion's challenge, and
edited by the Marian priest, John Fen, and the Jesuit, John Gibbons, in
1583.

247. *By the Queene. The Queens Maiestie findeth the continuance, or rather
increase, of the traiterous and malicious purposes and solicitations of
such rebels and traitors as do live in foreign parts* . . . 15 July 1580
(STC 8124)

248. *By the Queene. A Proclamation for revocation of Students from
beyond the seas, and against the reteining of Iesuites.* 10 January 1581.
(STC 8127)

249. *An Apologie and True Declaration of the institution and endevours of
the two English Colleges, the one in Rome, the other now resident in
Rhemes: against certaine sinister informations given up against the
same.* 1581 (STC 369, AR 6, ERL 67)

250. *Duo Edicta Elizabethae Reginae Angliae contra sacerdotes Societatis
Iesu, & alumnos seminariorum, quae a Gregorio XIII Pont. Max. Romae
& Remis pro Anglis sunt instituta; quibus non solum illi ut perduelles
proscribuntur, sed Angli omnes, qui in iisdem Collegiis vivunt
revocantur: Una cum Apologia doctissimi viri D. Gulielmi Alani pro
iisdem sacerdotibus societatis Iesu, & aliis seminariorum Alumnis; in
qua explicantur causae institutionis praedictorum seminariorum, & cur
sacerdotes Catholici in Angliam mittantur. Additur eiusdem Gulielmi
Alani piissima admonitio & consolatio vere Christiana ad afflictos
Catholicos Angliae.* 1583

251. [cf. 264] *Concertatio Ecclesiae Catholicae in Anglia, adversus*

Calvino papistas & Puritanos, a paucis annis singulari studio quorundam hominum doctrina & sanctitate illustrium renovata. 1583

(This important work was originally published in two separate parts, with *Duo Edicta* added as a second part bearing a new title-page later in the same year. The individual contents of the first part are as follows:

a) 'Epistolae duae Edmundi Campiani Sacerdotis Societatis Iesu; altera, ad Reginae Angliae Consiliarios, qua profectionis suae in Angliam institutum declarat, ex Anglico sermone latine reddita: altera ad R. P. Everardum Mercurianum Praepositum Generalem Societatis Iesu, qua, postquam in Anglia aliquot menses egisset, statum ecclesiae Anglicanae, suorumque laborum fructum exponit, ab ipso auctore latine conscripta.'

b) 'Rationes Decem: quibus fretus certamen adversariis obtulit in causa fidei idem Edmundus Campianus allegatae ad clarissimos viros, Anglos Academicos ab ipso auctore latine editae.' [= 205]

c) 'De Persecutione Anglicana, Epistola. Qua explicantur afflictiones, aerumnae, & calamitates gravissimae, cruciatus etiam & tormenta, & acerbissima martyria, quae Catholici nunc Angli, ob fidem patiuntur.' [= 236]

d) 'Vita et Martyrium Edmundi Campiani, diligenter collecta ex variis scriptis tam Anglicis quam Latinis; una cum martyriis Radulphi Scheruini, Alexandri Brianti, & aliorum duodecim, qui ob fidei Catholici professionem in Anglia occisi sunt, annis 1581 & 1582. His adiunctae sunt insignes quaedam Epistolae ab iisdem martyribus ex carceribus sub mortem scriptae, redolentes pietatem & fervorem antiquorum martyrum primitivae ecclesiae.' [cf. 234]

e) 'Martyrium aliorum septem sacerdotum, qui ob Catholicae fidei confessionem, passi sunt 28 & 30 Maii, anno incarnationis dominicae 1582. Una cum quaestionibus ipsis propositis, & responsionibus ad easdem.'

f) 'Apologia Martyrum; qua ipsorum innocentia variis rationibus demonstratur; eosque solius religionis Catholicae causa, quam susceperant propagandam & propugnandam, crudelissime enecatos fuisse.'

g) 'Literae et confessio publica Ioannis Nicolai, quibus fatetur se falso accusasse supra nuncupatos martyres, causamque praebuisse non postremam, eorumdem crudelissimae necis.' [cf. 193]

These and other accusations of the use of torture and other forms of cruelty on the Catholic priests by the English authorities now prompted Lord Burghley to publish an official reply, of which he was generally recognized as author. First, in a brief document of six pages he made a *Declaration* about the allegations of torture, which was published in English in 1583, then also in Latin in 1584. Also in 1583 he brought out an ampler justification of official procedure under the title *The Execution of Justice in England*. To this latter document great importance was attached. It was printed twice in its original English in 1583, and translated into a variety of languages, not only Latin and French, but also Dutch and Italian.

252. *A Declaration of the favourable dealing of her Maiesties Commissioners appointed for the Examination of certaine Traitours, and of tortures uniustly reported to be done upon them for matters of religion.* 1583 (STC 4901)

253. *De Summa Eorum Clementia, qui habendis quaestionibus praefuerant, contra proditores quosdam, deque tormentis quae in eosdem, ob Proditionem, expromkpta sunt.* 1584   (STC 4904)

(This was bound in one volume with 255, though with its own title-page.)

254. *The Execution of Iustice in England for maintenaunce of publique and Christian peace, against certeine stirrers of sedition , and adherents to the traytours and enemies of the Realme, without any persecution of them for questions of Religion, as is falsely reported and published by the fautors and fosterers of their treasons.* 1583   (STC 4902–3)

255. *Iustitia Britannica. Per quam liquet perspicue, aliquot in Anglia perditos cives, propter turpes Proditiones mulctatos esse: propter Religionem vero aut ceremonias Romanas neminem.* 1584   (STC 4904)

256. *L'execution de iustice faicte en Angleterre, pour maintenir la Paix publique & Chrestienne, contre les autheurs de sedition, adherens aux traistres & ennemis du Royaume: sans aucune persecution contre eux esmeuë, pour matiere de religion comme il a esté faucement advancé et publié, par les fauteurs & nouricciers de leurs traisons. Descrite premierement en Anglois, puis traduite en langue Françoise, en faveur des autres nations & personnes, qui ont l'usage d'icelle.* 1584 (STC 4906)

These two works of Burghley prompted an immediate reply from William Allen, as being the acknowledged leader of the English Catholics and president of the English Colleges at Rheims and Rome. In what was perhaps the principal controversial work from the Catholic side during the whole period, his *Defence of English Catholiques*, he sought to demonstrate that the priests and laymen who had been executed in England in the past few years were not traitors to their country, but martyrs for the Catholic faith. His book was also translated into Latin by William Reynolds, under the title *Ad Persecutores Anglos*.

257. *A True, Sincere and Modest Defence of English Catholiques that suffer*

> for their Faith both at home and abrode: against a false, seditious and
> slaunderous Libel intituled; The Execution of Iustice in England.
> Wherin is declared, how uniustlie the Protestants doe charge
> Catholiques with treason; how untrulie they deny their persecution for
> Religion; and how deceitfullie they seeke to abuse strangers about the
> cause, greatnes, and maner of their sufferinges, with divers other
> matters perteining to this purpose. 1584   (STC 373, AR 13, ERL 68)

258. *Ad Persecutores Anglos pro Catholicis domi forisque persecutionem
   sufferentibus; contra falsum, seditiosum, & contumeliosum Libellum,
   inscriptum; Iustitia Britannica. Vera, sincera, & modesta Responsio:
   qua ostenditur, quam iniuste Protestantes Angli Catholicis
   perduellionem obijciant; quam falso negent se quemquam religionis
   cause persequi; & quam callide laborent hominibus externis imponere,
   ne earum quae inferuntur afflictionum causam, modum, &
   magnitudinem vere intelligant; cum aliis permultis ad hoc argumentum
   pertinentibus. Scripta primum idiomate Anglico, & deinde translata in
   Latinum.* 1584

The official Anglican reply to Allen was entrusted to Thomas Bilson,
Warden (later Bishop) of Winchester, who dealt with Allen's *Apologie* and
Defence together in dialogue form in his *True Difference betweene Christian
Subiection and Unchristian Rebellion*. Another reply, commissioned by Cecil
himself, was undertaken by the Puritan, John Stubbs, and entitled
Vindication of the English Justice; but it was never published. (cf. J. Strype,
Annals of the Reformation, Vol. I, Pt. II, pp. 305–6)

259. [= 174] *The True Difference betweene Christian Subiection and
   Unchristian Rebellion: Wherein the Princes lawful power to command
   for truth, and indeprivable right to beare the sword, are defended
   against the Popes censures and the Iesuites sophismes, uttered in their
   Apologie and Defence of English Catholikes: With a demonstration that
   the things reformed in the Church of England by the lawes of this
   Realme are truly Catholike, notwithstanding the vaine shew made to
   the contrarie in their late Rhemish Testament: by Thomas Bilson
   Warden of Winchester.* 1585   (STC 3071)

From the Catholic side two further books in Latin now appeared from the
pen of Nicholas Sanders, though he had died in 1581. The first, whose title
seems to imply a refutation of Burghley's *Iustitia Britannica*, and has led
unwary bibliographers to confuse it with Allen's reply in Latin translation,
was merely an excerpt of relevant passages from Book VII of Sanders' *De
Visibili Monarchia*, in which he had dealt with the Roman Pontiff and the
contrast between the city of God and that of the devil. The second was a
historical survey, *De Origine ac Progressu Schismatis Anglicani*, which had
been left unfinished by Sanders at his death and was now edited and

published, first in one book by Edward Rishton, then in three books by Robert Persons. It rapidly became the most popular book on England in sixteenth-century Europe, going into fifteen editions – including translations into French, Spanish, Italian and German – within ten years of its first appearance. Oddly enough, it was not translated into English till the nineteenth century (Dublin, 1827, and London, 1877).

260. *De Iustitia Britannica, sive Anglica, quae contra Christi martyres continenter exercetur.* 1584

(The inner title explains the nature of the book more precisely:

'Series et Catalogus eorum, quae in Anglis superioribus annis contra Christi Ecclesiam acciderunt, ex doctissimi Theologi Nicolai Sanderi libris de Monarchia Ecclesiae.'

For the continuation of these events it refers in the end to the *Concertatio*:

'Qui subsequentium annorum persecutiones & martyria cognoscere voluerit, librum earumdem persecutionum cum vita & martyrio Edmundi Campiani & aliorum, qui liber ubique habetur, & in omnes pene linguas conversus est, perlegere poterit.')

261. *Doctissimi Viri Nicolai Sanderi, De Origine ac Progressu Schismatis Anglicani, Liber. Continens historiam maxime Ecclesiasticam, annorum circiter sexaginta, lectu dignissimam: nimirum ab anno 21. regni Henrici 8, quo primum cogitare coepit de repudianda legitima uxore serenissima Catherina, usque ad hunc vigesimum septimum Elizabethae, quae ultima est eiusdem Henrici soboles. Editus & auctus per Edouardum Rishtonum.* 1585

(The enlarged second edition of 1586 is still attributed to Rishton, though the hand of Persons was generally admitted. It bears the altered title:

Nicolai Sanderi De Origine ac Progressu Schismatis Anglicani Libri Tres. Quibus Historia continetur maxime Ecclesiastica, annorum circiter sexaginta, lectu dignissima; nimirum, ab anno 21. regni Henrici octavi, quo primum cogitare coepit de repudianda legitima uxore serenissima Catharina, usque ad hunc vigesimum octavum Elizabethae, quae ultima est eiusdem Henrici soboles. Aucti per Edouardum Rishtonum, & impressi primum in Germania, nunc iterum locupletius & castigatius editi.)

262. *Les trois livres de Nicolas Sander, touchant l'origine et progres du Schisme d'Angleterre. Esquelz est contenue l'Histoire principalement Ecclesiastique de 60. ans ou environ, tresdigne d'estre levé, assavoir, depuis l'an 21. du regne de Henry 8. auquel il se mit à penser de*

repudier sa femme legitime, la Serenissime Catherine, iusques au 28. an d'Elizabeth, laquelle est le dernier enfant du sus-dit Henry. Augmenté par Edoüard Rishton, & imprimez premierement en Allemagne: & depuis l'annee passee à Rome, augmentez davantage, & mieux disposez, Avec privilege & licence. Traduits en François, selon la copie Latine de Rome, par I.T.A.C. Et maintenant imprimé par le commandement de Monseigneur Illust. & Reverend. Cardinal de Vaudemont, à la requeste de certains Gentilzhommes Anglois refugiez pour la foy Catholique. 1587

(Another French translation, also dated 1587, is entitled:

Les trois livres du docteur Nicolas Sanders, contenants l'origine & progrez du Scisme d'Angleterre. Esquels est descripte une narration ou histoire Ecclesiastique, depuis le temps de soixante ans, pitoyable certes & calamiteuse, sçavoir est depuis l'an vingt & unziesme de Henry huictiesme qu'il delibera de repudier la serenissime Royne Catherine, iusques au vingthuictiesme an, du regne d'Elisabeth, auiourd'huy vivante, & derniere de la race d'iceluy Henry. Augmentez par Edouart Rishton, premierement Imprimez en Latin, en Allemaigne, & depuis plus correctement à Rome.)

This book naturally caused grave concern to the English authorities, and it was frequently brought up in interrogations of Catholic priests, together with Sanders' *De Visibili Monarchia* (50) and Bristow's *Motives* (146), as charged with seditious matter. The task of its refutation was entrusted by Archbishop Whitgift to John Reynolds; but the latter was unable to complete the task, as he confesses in the Dedication to the 1602 edition of his *Sex Theses* (170). It was not till 1593 that a refutation appeared in Latin, under the title of *Anti Sanderus*, in the form of a letter supposedly written by a Catholic in Venice to a friend of his at Rheims, and now published by A. L. at Cambridge.

263. *Anti Sanderus. Duos continens Dialogos non ita pridem inter viros quosdam doctos Venetiis habitos: In quibus variae Nicholai Sanderi, aliorumque Romanensium calumniae in haec Anglorum ab excusso Pontifice tempora vaferrime confictae, licet obiter & fortuito, vere tamen candideque refelluntur.* 1593

(This book is mentioned in the STC under the letter A, but not numbered — as the reader is referred to Sanders, N., but in vain.)

At the end of both books by Sanders there appeared a list of those priests and laymen who had suffered for the faith in England. This was now brought up to date in a new, augmented edition of the *Concertatio* by John Bridgewater (to whom the compilation was subsequently attributed) in 1589, and again in 1594.

264. (anr. ed. of 251). *Concertatio Ecclesiae Catholicae in Anglia adversus Calvino-papistas et Puritanos sub Elizabetha Regina, quorundam hominum doctrina & sanctitate illustrium renovata & recognita. Quae nunc de novo centum et eo amplius martyrum, sexcentorumque insignium virorum rebus gestis variisque certaminibus, lapsorum Palinodiis, novis persecutorum edictis, ac doctissimis Catholicorum de Anglicano seu muliebri Pontificatu, ac Romani Pontificis in Principes Christianos auctoritate; disputationibus & defensionibus aucta, & in tres partes divisa.* 1589

   (The third part, containing the *Apologia Martyrum* with William Reynolds' Latin translations of Allen's *Apologie* and *Defence*, has a separate title-page, dated 1588.)

At the same time books of engravings by J. B. de Cavaleriis and Richard Verstegan, depicting the cruelty of the Protestant persecutors, became popular and occasioned much wonder in Europe. The latter's *Theatrum Crudelitatum*, in particular, went into four Latin editions between 1587 and 1602, as well as two French editions.

265. *Ecclesiae Anglicanae Trophaea Sive Sanctorum Martyrum, qui pro Christo Catholicaeque fidei Veritate asserenda, antiquo recentiorique Persecutionum tempore, mortem in Anglia subierunt, Passiones Romae in Collegio Anglico per Nicolaum Circinianum depictae; nuper autem Per Io. Bap. de Cavalleriis aeneis typis repraesentatae. Cum Privilegio Gregorii XIII P. M.* 1584

266. *Ecclesiae Militantis Triumphi Sive Deo amabilium Martyrum gloriosa pro Christi fide Certamina: prout opera RR. Patrum Societatis Iesu Collegii Germanici et Hungarici Moderator, impensa S.D.N. Gregorii PP. XIII in Ecclesia S. Stephani Rotundi, Romae Nicolai Circiniani pictoris manu visuntur depicta. Ad excitandam piorum devotionem a Joanne Bapta. de Cavalleriis, aeneis typis accurate expressa.* 1585

267. *Theatrum Crudelitatum Haereticorum Nostri Temporis.* 1587

268. *Theatre des cruautez des hereticques de nostre temps, traduit du latin.* 1588

j) *Persons'* Christian Directory

By way of postscript, it may be of interest to add the history of a book by Robert Persons, which, though of its nature devotional and unconnected with controversy, was drawn by various circumstances into the controversies of the age. This was his *Book of the Christian Exercise* (as it was originally entitled) – generally known as the *Book of Resolution*, or more simply the *Resolution* – which became the most popular book of devotion among both

Catholics and Protestants in Elizabethan and Jacobean England. It was developed out of the work of an Italian Jesuit, Gaspar Loarte, entitled *The Exercise of a Christian Life*, which had been translated into English by James Sancer in 1579. Persons expanded this work in his own vigorous style, and published his book at Rouen in 1582 soon after his escape from England. An unauthorized reprint came out two years later also at Rouen. That year, 1584, a revised version was published in London under the same title, but perused by a Protestant minister, Edmund Bunny, who made various deletions and alterations, besides adding a *Treatise tending to Pacification*. In this form it became, in the words of its London publisher, 'one of the most vendible books ever issued in this country'; and a pirated edition was brought out by Joseph Barnes at Oxford. By the end of Elizabeth's reign Bunny's revision had gone into no less than 13 editions (two of them at Oxford).

269. *The Exercise of a Christian Life. Written in Italian by the Reverend Father Gaspar Loarte D. of Divinitie, of the Societie of Iesus. And newly translated into Englishe. by I. S.* 1579   (STC 16642, AR 462, ERL 44)

270. *The First Booke of the Christian Exercise, appertayning to resolution. Wherein are layed downe the causes & reasons that should move a man to resolve hym selfe to the service of God: And all the impedimentes removed, which may lett the same.* 1582   (STC 19353, AR 619)

271. (anr. ed.) *A Booke of Christian exercise, appertaining to Resolution, that is shewing how that we should resolv our selvs to becom Christians indeed: by R. P. Perused, and accompanied now with a Treatise tending to Pacification: by Edmund Bunny.* 1584   (STC 19355)

Persons himself was far from pleased with this piracy and the Protestant alterations introduced into his text by Bunny. So in 1585 he brought out a new edition of his book at Rouen, altering its title to *A Christian Directorie*, and adding a stern reproof in his Preface of Bunny's falsified edition. To this reproof Bunny merely responded with *A Briefe Answer*, justifying his action, in 1589. Then in 1590 he proceeded to republish the *Christian Directorie* in its expanded form as *The Second Part of the Book of Christian Exercise*, which also became immensely popular, going into six editions during the last decade of Elizabeth's reign. To this further piracy of Bunny Persons paid no attention when he brought out the second edition of his *Christian Directorie* at Louvain in 1598. Nor again did he do so in the third edition, which he brought out at St. Omers in 1607. Here he made several radical alterations in its contents, 'by displacing certaine Chapters which seemed to some not to be so necessary to the end heere proposed' — though they were the chapters most praised by many of his English contemporaries. For it was his aim to reduce the bulk of the book, so as to allow for the addition of a second and third book promised in the title (but never completed). Of Persons' silence regarding his *Briefe Answer* Bunny subsequently complained in 1610, in a Note appended to his book *Of Divorce for Adulterie*, since in each new edition Persons merely reprinted his original reproof of Bunny without alteration.

272. *A Christian Directorie Guiding Men to their Salvation. Devided into*
three Bookes. The first wherof apperteining to Resolution, is only
conteined in this volume, devided into two partes, and set forth now
againe with many corrections, and additions by th' Authour himself,
with reprofe of the corrupt and falsified edition of the same booke
lately published by M. Edm. Buny. There is added also a methode for
the use of al; with two tables, and a preface to the Reader, which is
necessary to be reade. 1585   (STC 19362, AR 621)

(The third edition of 1607 bears the altered title:

The Christian Directory Guiding men to eternall salvation, Devided into
three Bookes. The First wherof teacheth how to make a good
Resolution. The Second, how to begin well. The Third, how to persevere
and end happily.   (STC 19371, AR 623, ERL 41))

273. *A Briefe Answer, unto those idle and frivolous quarrels of R. P. against*
the late edition of the Resolution: By Edmund Bunny. Wherunto are
praefixed the booke of Resolution, and the Treatise of Pacification,
perused and noted in the margent, on all such places as are misliked of
R. P. shewing in what section of this Answer following, those places are
handled. 1589   (STC 4088)

274. *The Second part of the Booke of Christian exercise, appertayning to*
Resolution. Or A Christian Directory, guiding all men unto theyr
salvation. Written by the former Authour. R. P. 1590   (STC 19380)

275. *Of Divorce for Adulterie, and Marrying againe: that there is no*
sufficient warrant so to do. With a note in the end, that R. P. many
yeeres since was answered. By Edm. Bunny Bachelour of Divinitie.
1610   (STC 4091)

Meanwhile, Bunny's treatise of *Pacification* was eventually answered by John Radford in his *Directorie* of 1605. To this Bunny added a brief reply in the above-mentioned Note, reserving a fuller refutation to 'a larger Discourse of mine', of which there is no further record.

276. *A Directorie Teaching the Way to the Truth in a briefe and plaine*
discourse against the heresies of this time. Whereunto is added, A Short
Treatise against Adiaphorists, Neuters, and such as say they may be
saved in any Sect or Religion, and would make of many divers sects one
Church. 1605   (STC 20602, AR 701, ERL 19)

To the first and second editions of his *Christian Directorie* Persons had added a couple of chapters outlining the proofs for the existence of God and the truth of the Christian religion. These chapters proved particularly influential in countering the growing irreligion of the age; and it is to them that both Robert Greene and Thomas Nash refer in their well-known commendations of the *Book of Resolution* — the former in his *Repentance of Robert Greene* (1592), and the latter in his *Christs Teares over Ierusalem* (1593). The proofs were also utilised, without acknowledgment, by two Protestant ministers of the time: Henry Smith, in his *Gods Arrow against Atheists,* and John Dove, in his *Confutation of Atheisme*. The general influence of Persons' book is also evident in Gabriel Powell's popular book, *The resolved Christian.*

277. *Gods Arrow against Atheists. By Henry Smith.* 1593 (STC 22666)

278. *A Confutation of Atheisme. By Iohn Dove Doctor of Divinitie.* 1605 (STC 7078)

279. *The resolved Christian, exhorting to Resolution, Written, To recall the Worldling, to comfort the Faint-harted, to strengthen the Faithfull, and to perswade all Men, so to runne, that they may obtaine. By Gabriel Powel.* 1600 (STC 20150)

CHAPTER 4

Presbyterian Discipline

a) *Subscription v. Discipline*

UNDER the mild rule of Edmund Grindal as Archbishop of Canterbury from 1576 till his death in 1583 — though he spent much of this period under the Queen's displeasure for having reprimanded her — the Puritan movement in England made considerable progress. The *Advertisments* of Archbishop Parker largely became a dead letter, and the prescriptions of the *Book of Common Prayer* were widely ignored by ministers in the Church of England. When John Whitgift, therefore, succeeded Grindal to the See of Canterbury in 1583, his first concern was to reinstate uniformity of liturgical observance in the Church. For this purpose he drew up a number of Articles, variously given as 12 (by Strype) and 16 (by a contributor to *The Seconde Parte of a Register*), which he presented to the Queen for her approval. The last, and most controversial, of these Articles was the following:

> That none be permitted to preach, read or catechise, to minister the Sacraments, or exercise any ecclesiastical function, unless he first subscribe to the following articles — in the meantime all licences to preach being suspended:
>
> 1. That the Queen has supreme authority — ecclesiastical and temporal;
>
> 2. That the Book of Common Prayer and of Ordering contains nothing contrary to the word of God; that it may be lawfully used; and that he will use it in public prayer, and none other;
>
> 3. That he allows the Articles agreed on in the Convocation of 1562, and believes them to be agreeable to the word of God.

These Articles were formally drawn up and approved at a Convocation of the Province of Canterbury held in London in November 1584, and were published in the same year.

280. *Articuli per Archiepiscopum, Episcopos & reliquum Clerum*
      Cantuariensis Provinciae in Synodo inchoata Londini, vicesimo quarto
      die Mensis Novembris, Anno Domini 1584. Regnique serenissimae in

> *Christo Principis Dominae Elizabethae, Dei gratia Angliae, Franciae &*
> *Hyberniae Reginae, fidei Defensoris &c. vicesimo septimo stabiliti, &*
> *Regia auctoritate approbati & confirmati.* 1584   (STC 4583)

On the basis of these Articles all ministers were once again required to subscribe or suffer deprivation of their livings and benefices; and once again the Puritan ministers rose up in protest. Only now their protest was more prolonged, as they were now better organized, thanks to the administrative skill of John Field. The first Puritan publication in this new movement of protest was a document reminding the ecclesiastical authorities of various legal and statutory provisions to which the Puritans attached great importance, but which they found disregarded by these authorities. The anonymous compiler of the document drew attention to the 'lamentable contention . . . in our English Church, about reformation of Ecclesiasticall discipline and popish ceremonies'; and he laid significant emphasis on the need of 'a learned Ministerie' as 'commanded by the Lawe'.

281. *An Abstract, of Certain Acts of parliament: of certaine her Maiesties*
    Iniunctions: of certaine Canons, Constitutions, and Synodalles
    provinciall: established and in force, for the peaceable government of
    the Church, within her Maiesties Dominions and Countries, for the
    most part heretofore unknowen and unpractized. 1584   (STC 10394)

The answer on behalf of the Church authorities was undertaken by the Dean of Arches, Richard Cosin, who suggested that the aim of this document was 'covertlie to bring the governours and governement ecclesiasticall of this church of England, into contempt, hatred and obloquie'. His *Answer* was refuted by the Puritan, Dudley Fenner, in *A Counter-Poyson*. Soon afterwards, speaking on behalf of the church, Dr. John Copquot criticised Fenner's book in a sermon at Paul's Cross in 1584. He was in turn taken to task by an anonymous Puritan author, writing on behalf of Fenner, in *A Defence of the reasons of the Counter-Poyson*, which did not appear till 1586. In his preface 'to the Christian Reader' he explains that Fenner himself had not replied to Copquot's sermon because he 'never could get the answeres in writing as now I have got them'. He adds that he has now 'falne upon the whole Sermon in writing', but he prints only that part of it which concerns the issue of Discipline. Both the *Counter-Poyson* and the *Defence*, including a small extract of Copquot's sermon, were again published in 1593.

282. *An Answer To the two first and principall Treatises of a certeine*
    factious libell, put foorth latelie, without name of Author or Printer,
    and without approbation by authoritie, under the title of An Abstract
    of certeine Acts of Parlement: of certeine hir Maiesties Iniunctions: of
    certeine Canons, &c. Published by authoritie. 1584   (STC 5815)

283. *A Counter-Poyson, Modestlie written for the time, to make answere to*
    the obiections and reproches, wherewith the answerer to the Abstract,

would disgrace the holy Discipline of Christ. 1584 (STC 10770, 10400 (*A parte of a register*))

284. *A Defence of the reasons of the Counter-Poyson, for maintenance of the Eldershippe, against an answere made to them by Doctor Copequot, in a publike Sermon at Paules Crosse, upon Psalm 84. 1584. Wherein also according to his demaund is prooved Syllogistically for the learned, and plainelie for all men, the perpetuitie of the Elders office in the Church. 1586* (STC 10772, 10400)

The year 1584 was an important one for Puritan publications. In addition to the *Counter-Poyson*, many other works which later came to be regarded as fundamental to the movement were published by the zealous printer, Robert Waldegrave. *A Dialogue, concerning the strife of our Churche*, attributed to John Udall, a minister at Kingston, was the first of a series of such Puritan dialogues. There was an anonymous protest entitled *The unlawfull Practises Of Prelates*, and an anonymous *Sermon* on Romans 12, attributed to Laurence Chaderton, a Puritan scholar at Cambridge. This sermon was subsequently accused of being 'the foundation of Brownisme' by Peter Fairlambe in his *Recantation of a Brownist* (1606).

Above all, the manuscript of William Fulke's *Briefe and plaine declaration*, which had been ready for the press in 1573, was now published without the author's permission by John Field, who gave it the running title of 'The Learned Discourse of Eccl. Government'.

285. *A Dialogue, concerning the strife of our Churche: Wherein are aunswered divers of those uniust accusations, wherewith the godly preachers and professors of the Gospell, are falsly charged: with a briefe declaration of some such monstrous abuses, as our Byshops have not bene ashamed to foster. 1584* (STC 6801, 10396)

286. *The unlawfull Practises Of Prelates Against Godly Ministers, The Maintainers Of The Discipline of God.* [1584?] (STC 20201, 10400)

287. *A Fruitful Sermon, upon the 3.4.5.6.7. and 8. verses of the 12. Chapter of the Epistle of S. Paule to the Romaines. Very necessary for these times to bee read of all men, for their further instruction and edification, in all things concerning their Faith and obedience to Salvation. 1584* (STC 4926)

288. *A Briefe and plaine declaration, concerning the desires of all those faithfull Ministers, that have and do seeke for the Discipline and reformation of the Church of Englande: Which may serve for a iust Apologie, against the false accusations and slaunders of their adversaries. 1584* (STC 10395)

On behalf of the established Church Thomas Rogers published a general defence of *The English Creede* in two parts, in 1585 and 1587, dealing successively with the thirty-nine Articles (from I to XIX, and from XX to XXXIX). In 1590 he went on to publish a Sermon on Romans 12, attacking the Puritan *Sermon* on the same text. In it he lists the principal writings of the Puritans as: 'The Ecclesiastical Discipline. A Learned Discourse of Eccles. goverment. The Counterpoyson. A Sermon upon the 12. to the Romans. And M. Cartwrightes last Replie'. He also refers to the year 1584 as 'that fertile yeare of contentious wrightings'.

289. *The English Creede, consenting with the true, auncient, catholique, and apostolique Church in al the points, and articles of Religion which every Christian is to knowe, and beleeve that would be saved. The first parte, in moste loyal maner to the glorie of God, credit of our Church, and displaieng of al haeresies, and errors, bothe olde and new, contrarie to the faith, subscribed unto by Thomas Rogers. Allowed by auctoritie.* 1585; part 2, 1587 (STC 21226–7)

290. *A Sermon upon the 6.7 and 8. Verses of the 12. Chapter of S. Pauls Epistle unto the Romanes; Made to the Confutation of so much of another Sermon, entituled, A Fruitful Sermon &c. as concerneth both the deprivation of the praesent goverment, and the perpetual, and uniforme regiment of our Church By certaine their described Officers to be in everie particular Parish through-out al her Maiesties Dominions; More fullie penned, then could by mouth be expressed, the tyme limitted to the speaker being verie short. Published at the request of certaine frendes by Thomas Rogers, Allowed by Auctoritie.* 1590 (STC 21240)

Of greater importance in the subsequent controversy was the lengthy refutation of the *Briefe and plaine declaration* by the Dean of Salisbury, John Bridges, in a tome of 1401 pages, in which he developed a sermon he had preached against the book some two years earlier. On that occasion, as he says in his Preface, he had promised 'the publishing both of the whole Sermon, and the aunswering at large of all the Learned Discourse'; but in fact he only kept the second part of this promise.

291. *A Defence of the Government Established in the Church of Englande for ecclesiasticall matters, Contayning an aunswere unto a Treatise called, The Learned Discourse of Eccl. Government, otherwise intituled, A Briefe and plaine declaration concerning the desires of all the faithfull Ministers that have, and do seeke for the discipline and reformation of the Church of Englande. Comprehending likewise an aunswere to the arguments in a Treatise named The judgement of a most Reverend and Learned man from beyond the Seas, &c. Aunswering also to the argumentes of Calvine, Beza, and Danaeus, with other our Reverend learned Brethren, besides Caenalis and Bondinus, both for the regiment of women, and in defence of her Maiestie, and of*

all other Christian Princes supreme Government in Ecclesiasticall causes, Against the Tetrarchie that our Brethren would erect in every particular congregation, of Doctors, Pastors, Governors and Deacons, with their severall and ioynt authoritie in Elections, Excommunications, Synodall Constitutions and other Ecclesiasticall matters. Aunswered by Iohn Bridges Deane of Sarum. 1587 (STC 3734)

The *Treatise* mentioned by Bridges in his title is an English translation of a work by Theodore Beza, entitled:

292. *The judgement of a most reverend and learned man from beyond the seas, concerning a threefold order of bishops, with a declaration of certaine other waightie points, concerning the discipline and governement of the church.* 1580 (STC 2021)

The first Puritan to answer this long-winded attack by Bridges was Dudley Fenner, who published his *Defence of the godlie Ministers* in the same year. His book was reprinted in *A parte of a register* in 1593, with an abbreviated title containing the information that it had been 'written a moneth before his death'. Only the previous year he had also written a Latin statement of the theological position of the Puritans, entitled *Sacra Theologia*; and this was later translated into English and published with the title of *The sacred doctrine of divinitie* in 1599.

293. *A Defence of the godlie Ministers, against the slaunders of D. Bridges, contayned in his answere to the Preface before the Discourse of Ecclesiasticall governement, with a Declaration of the Bishops proceeding against them. wherein chieflie, 1. The lawfull authoritie of her Maiestie is defended by the Scriptures, her lawes, and authorised interpretation of them, to be the same which we have affirmed, against his cavilles and slaunders to the contrarie. 2. The Lawfull refusinge also of the Ministers to subscribe, is maintayned by evident groundes of Gods worde, and her Maiesties lawes, against his evident wresting of both. 3. Lastlie, the forme of Church-governement, which we propounde, is according to his demaunde Sillogisticallie proved to be ordinarie, perpetuall, and the best.* 1587 (STC 10771)

(The title of this book is altered in the 1593 reprint in *A parte of a register* (STC 10400) as follows:

Master Dudley Fenners defence of the godlie Ministers against D. Bridges slaunders: with a true report of the ill dealings of the Bishops against them, written a moneth before his death. Anno 1587.)

294. *Sacra Theologia, sive Veritas quae est secundum Pietatem, ad Unicae & verae methodi leges descripta, & in decem libros per Dudleium Fennerum digesta.* 1586

295. *The sacred doctrine of divinitie.* 1599 (STC 10774)

Fenner was followed soon after by Walter Travers, who published his *Defence of the Ecclesiasticall Discipline* in 1588. It was, in fact, during these critical years that the platform of Church discipline, which had been outlined by Travers and Cartwright during their exile in the '70s, was seriously discussed and elaborated by the Puritans in England. In its Latin form the revised document, entitled *Disciplina Ecclesiae sacra*, was approved at a General Conference in 1586, but not published. The English translation was evidently again entrusted to Cartwright, for the manuscript was found in his study after his death in 1603; but it was not published till the time of the Civil War in 1644, under the title of *A Directory of Church-government*.

296. *A Defence of the Ecclesiasticall Discipline ordayned of God to be used in his Church. Against a Replie of Maister Bridges, to a briefe and plain Declaration of it, which was printed An. 1584. Which replie he termeth, A Defence of the governement established in the Church of Englande, for Ecclesiasticall matters.* 1588   (STC 24183)

297. *Disciplina Ecclesiae sacra Dei verbo descripta* (Part I). *Disciplina Synodica ex ecclesiarum quae eam ex verbo Dei instaurarunt usu Synodis atque libris de eadem re scriptis collecta, et ad certa quaedam capita redacta* (Part II). (1586, in MS)

298. *A Directory of Church-government. Anciently contended for, and as farre as the Times would suffer, practised by the first Non-conformists in the daies of Queen Elizabeth. Found in the study of the most accomplished Divine, Mr. Thomas Cartwright, after his decease; and reserved to be published for such a time as this. Published by Authority.* 1644   (Wing T 2066)

From the side of the establishment it was the Dean of Exeter, Matthew Sutcliffe, who now appeared as the leading opponent of the Puritans. His first anti-Puritan work was *A Treatise of Ecclesiasticall Discipline*, published in 1590, in which he criticised the platform of Travers and Cartwright. This he followed up with a Latin book, *De Presbyterio*, 1591.

299. *A Treatise of Ecclesiasticall Discipline: Wherein that confused forme of government, which certeine under false pretence, and title of reformation, and true discipline, do strive to bring into the Church of England, is examined and confuted: By Matth. Sutcliffe.* 1590   (STC 23471)

300. *De Presbyterio, eiusque nova in Ecclesia Christiana Politeia, adversus cuiusdam I.B.A.C. de politeia civili & Ecclesiastica libros duos, eiusdemque & reliquorum Presbyterii Patronorum gravissimos in Politeiae Iudaicae, & Christianae descriptione errores, Mathaei Sutlivii disputatio: in qua Presbyterium quod illi tuentur, oppugnatur;*

Christiani Magistratus potestas, quam illi oppugnant defenditur;
Episcoporum Evangelium amplectentium supra alios Ecclesiae ministros
dignitas, quam variis sermonibus nonnulli traducunt, confirmatur;
Ecclesiae denique Anglicanae pristinus ordo, quam omni ratione
Ecclesiasticae pacis hostes evertere conantur, ab eorum calumniis
vindicatur. 1591   (STC 23458)

Meanwhile, a greater work of refutation was quietly being undertaken by Richard Hooker, which will be considered in due place (398). He was assisted in his task by a full account and criticism of the Puritan movement, which was prepared at this time by a pupil of his, George Cranmer — though not published till 1642.

301. *Concerning the New Church Discipline, An Excellent Letter. Written by*
     Mr. George Cranmer to Mr. R. H. 1642   (Wing C 6826)

b) *Petitions to Parliament*

On their side, the Puritans were taking active measures to obtain a favourable hearing for their cause in Parliament, in Convocation, in the Privy Council and from the Queen herself. To them all they now submitted a series of complaints and petitions, which were published separately at the time and later collected with other documents in *A parte of a register* in 1593. The most substantial of these representations, *An Humble Motion*, addressed to the Lords of the Council, was not published till 1590 and was not included in *A parte of a register*; but in presenting it to the public, its publisher ranged it with such classical Puritan writings as Cartwright's replies to Whitgift (116, 121–2), the *Ecclesiasticae Disciplinae* (123), the 'Learned Discourse' (288), the *Sermon* on Romans 12 (287) and the *Demonstration* (314).

302. *A Lamentable Complaint of the Commonalty, By Way of Supplication*
     to the High Court of Parliament, For a Learned Ministry. 1585   (STC
     7739, 10400)

303. *A petition made to the Convocation house, 1586. by the godly*
     ministers tending to reconciliation, and translated into English. 1588
     (STC 10397, 10400)

304. *An humble petition of the Communaltie to their most renowned and*
     gracious Soveraigne, the Lady Elizabeth, by the grace of God, Queene
     of England, France and Ireland, defender of the faith, &c. [1588?]
     (STC 7584, 10400)

305. *An Humble Motion with Submission unto the Right Honourable LL. of*
     hir Maiesties Privie Counsell. Wherein is laid open to be considered, how
     necessarie it were for the good of this Lande, and the Queenes Maiesties

safety, that Ecclesiasticall discipline were reformed after the worde of God: And how easily there might be provision for a learned Ministery. 1590   (STC 7754)

One of the most zealous of these petitioners was a young Welshman, John Penry, who particularly urged his request for the provision of a learned ministry in his native land. He was supported in his plea by the Member of Parliament for Carmarthen, Edward Dunn Lee, during the session of 1587. To his petition he also added a *Supplication* printed in the form of *A Treatise*; the next year he followed it up with an *Exhortation* to the governors and people of Wales.

306. *A Treatise containing the Aequity of an Humble Supplication which is to be exhibited unto hir gracious Maiesty and this high Court of Parliament in the behalfe of the Countrey of Wales, that some order may be taken for the preaching of the Gospell among those people. Wherein also is set downe as much of the estate of our people as without offence it could be made known, to the end that our case (if it please God) may be pitied by them who are not of this assembly, and so they also may bee drived to labour on our behalfe.* 1587   (STC 19611)

307. *An exhortation unto the Governours and people of her Maiesties countrie of Wales, to labour earnestly to have the preaching of the Gospell planted among them.* 1588   (STC 19605)

The latter book now led to a strange controversy (not least from a bibliographical point of view) between Penry and his Anglican adversary, Dr. Robert Some, of Cambridge. It was to refute certain theological errors – particularly, the denial or doubt 'whether unpreaching ministers doe deliver a Sacrament' – expressed by Penry in his *Exhortation*, that Some brought out his first *Godly Treatise*. His initial response to this criticism Penry stated in a brief addendum appended to the second and third editions of his book, which also appeared in the course of 1588. He further promised to expose 'the weaknes of his reasons' in a separate book against Dr. Some; and this promise he fulfilled in *A defence of that which hath bin written*, also published in 1588. It elicited what amounted to another book by Dr. Some, though presented as a second edition of his *Godly Treatise* – seeing that, whereas the first edition contained only 37 pages, the second ran to 200. Penry now prepared 'an answere unto master D. Some'; but his study was raided by the authorities on 29 January 1589, and his manuscript was seized.

308. *A Godly Treatise containing and deciding certaine questions, moved of late in London and other places, touching the Ministerie, Sacraments, and Church: Written by Robert Some Doctor of Divinitie.* 1588   (first ed.) (STC 22908)

309. *A defence of that which hath bin written in the questions of the ignorant ministerie, and the communicating with them. By Iohn Penri.* 1588   (STC 19604)

310. (anr. ed. of 308) *A Godly Treatise containing and deciding certaine questions, mooved of late in London and other places, touching the Ministerie, Sacraments, and Church. Whereunto one Proposition more is added. After the ende of this Booke you shall finde a defence of such points as M. Penry hath dealt against: and a confutation of many grosse errours broched in M. Penries last Treatise. Written by Robert Some Doctor of Divinitie.* 1588   (STC 22909)

(The additional Proposition has a new title-page:

A Defence of such points in R. Somes last Treatise, as M. Penry hath dealt against. And a refutation of many Anabaptistical, blasphemous and Popish absurdities, touching Magistracie, Ministerie, Church, Scripture and Baptisme, &c. conteined in M. Penryes treatise, &c. By R. Some Doctour of Divinitie.)

The place of Penry was now taken by Job Throkmorton, who as Member of Parliament for Warwick had encouraged him in his petition of 1587 – that is to say, if Throkmorton is indeed (as is very probable) the anonymous author of *M. Some laid open in his coulers*, a masterpiece of anti-episcopal satire which was published in the late summer of 1589. To the same author may also be attributed the stylistically similar *Dialogue Wherin is plainly laide open, the tyrannical dealing of L. Bishopps*, which appeared about the same time. Between them, these two pamphlets provide a clear stylistic clue to the much disputed identity of Martin Marprelate, who had already announced himself in the autumn of 1588.

311. *M. Some laid open in his coulers: Wherin the Indifferent Reader may easily see, howe wretchedly and loosely he hath handeled the cause against M. Penri. Done by an Oxford man, to his friend in Cambridge.* 1589   (STC 12342)

(The book is signed I. G. – which led the STC to assign it to John Greenwood.)

312. *A Dialogue. Wherein is plainly laide open, the tyrannical dealing of L. Bishopps against Gods children: with certaine points of doctrine, wherein they approove themselves (according to D. Bridges his judgement) to be truely the Bishops of the Divell.* 1589   (STC 6805)

Another dialogue on the same subject, which had been published in the previous year by John Udall, a confederate of Penry and Throkmorton, was entitled *The state of the Church of England laid open*, but more commonly known as *Diotrephes* from the name of one of its characters. The author followed it up with a more abstract treatise on Church discipline entitled *A demonstration*, for which he was subsequently charged with sedition and sentenced to death. This book was answered from the Anglican side by an anonymous *Remonstrance*, which has been doubtfully attributed to Matthew Sutcliffe.

313. *The state of the Church of England laid open in a Conference between Diotrephes a Bishop, Tertullus a Papist, Demetrius an Usurer, Pandochus an Inne-keeper, and Paule a Preacher of the worde of God.* 1588   (STC 24505, 10400)

314. *A demonstration of the trueth of that Discipline which Christ hath prescribed in his worde for the government of his Church, in all times and places, untill the end of the world.* 1588   (STC 24499, 10400)

315. *A Remonstrance: or Plaine Detection of some of the faults and hideous sores of such sillie syllogismes and impertinent allegations, as out of sundrie factious Pamphlets and Rhapsodies, are cobled up together in a Booke, Entituled, A Demonstration of Discipline: Wherein also, The true state of the Controversie of most of the points in variance, is (by the way) declared.* 1590   (STC 20881)

Two more petitions to the 'high Court of Parliament' were published by Penry in 1589: another on behalf of Wales, in continuation of his *Exhortation*; and one on his own behalf, protesting against the unjust dealing of the Archbishop of Canterbury and the Court of High Commission.

316. *A viewe of some part of such publike wants & disorders as are in the service of God, within her Maiesties countrie of Wales, togither with an humble Petition, unto this high Court of Parliament for their speedy redresse. Wherein is shewed, not only the necessitie of reforming the state of religion among that people, but also the onely way, in regard of substaunce, to bring that reformation to passe.* 1589   (STC 19613)

   (Running title: 'A Supplication unto the High Court of Parliament'.)

317. *Th' Appellation of Iohn Penri, unto the Highe court of Parliament, from the bad and injurious dealing of th' Archb. of Canterb. & other his colleagues of the high commission: Wherin the complaint, humbly submitting himselfe and his cause unto the determination of this honorable assembly: craveth nothing els, but either release from trouble and persecution, or just tryall.* 1589   (STC 19602)

c) *The Marprelate controversy*

Events were now reaching a climax, as the Puritans found all their attempts at reform frustrated by the ecclesiastical Court of High Commission, and all their petitions to Parliament without effect. With the connivance of Penry, Udall and Throckmorton, the Puritan printer, Robert Waldegrave, set up a secret printing-press at East Molesey by the river Thames; and from there he published the first of the notorious Marprelate Tracts, known as the *Epistle*, in October, 1588. The sensation this tract aroused on account of its open and ribald attack on the bishops, by way of reply to Bridges, made it necessary for the printer to move to Fawsley in Northamptonshire; and from there he published the next tract, known as the *Epitome*, in November. In it the author admitted he had antagonised several of the Puritan preachers by going beyond the bounds of moderation; but this did not prevent him from issuing a third, though shorter tract, or broadside, known as the *Mineralls*, in January, 1589 — from yet another place, Coventry.

318. *Oh read over D. John Bridges/ for it is a worthy worke: Or an epitome of the fyrste Booke/ of that right worshipfull volume/ written against the Puritanes/ in the defence of the noble cleargie/ by as worshipfull a prieste/ John Bridges/ Presbyter/ Priest or elder/ doctor of Divillitie/ and Dean of Sarum. Wherein the arguments of the puritans are wisely prevented/ that when they come to answere M. Doctor/ they must needes say something that hath bene spoken. Compiled for the behoofe and overthrow of the Parsons/ Fyckers/ and Currats/ that have lernt their Catechismes/ and are past grace: By the reverend and worthie Martin Marprelate gentleman/ and dedicated to the Confocationhouse. The Epitome is not yet published/ but it shall be when the Bishops are at convenient leysure to view the same. In the meane time/ let them be content with this learned Epistle. Printed oversea/ in Europe/ within two furlongs of a Bounsing Priest/ at the cost and charges of M. Marprelate/ gentleman. 1588*   (STC 17454, GS 11)

319. *Oh read over D. John Bridges, for it is a worthy worke: Or an epitome of the fyrste Booke, of that right worshipfull volume, written against the Puritanes, in the defence of the noble cleargie, by as worshipfull a prieste, John Bridges, Presbyter, Priest or elder, doctor of Divillitie, and Deane of Sarum. Wherein the arguments of the puritans are wisely prevented, that when they come to answere M. Doctor, they must needes say something that hath bene spoken. Compiled for the behoofe and overthrow of the unpreaching Parsons, Fyckers, and Currats, that have lernt their Catechismes, and are past grace: By the reverend and worthie Martin Marprelat gentleman, and dedicated by a second Epistle to the Terrible Priests. In this Epitome, the foresaid Fickers, &c. are very insufficiently furnished, with notable inabilitie of most vincible reasons, to answere the cavill of the puritanes. And lest M. Doctor should thinke that no man can write without sence but his selfe, the senceles titles of the several pages, and the handling of the matter throughout the Epitome, shewe plainely, that beetle-headed ignoraunce*

must not live and die with him alone. Printed on the other hand of some of the Priests. 1588 (STC 17453, GS 11)

320. *Certaine Minerall and Metaphisicall Schoolpoints to be defended by the reverende Bishops and the rest of my cleargie masters of the Convocation house against both the universities and al the reformed Churches in Christendome. Wherin is layd open the very quintessence of all Catercorner divinitie. And with all to the preventing of the Cavils of these wrangling Puritans the persons by whom and the places where these miseries are so worthely maintayned are for the most part plainly set downe to the view of all men and that to the ternall prayse of the most reverend Fathers.* 1589 (STC 17455, GS 11)

The counter-attack of the bishops was led by Thomas Cooper, Bishop of Winchester, who wrote a dignified reply in the form of *An Admonition to the People of England*. This however, only elicited two more scurrilous pamphlets from Martin, addressing himself to Cooper by name, with punning reference to a common street-cry. The first of them was published at Coventry in March 1589, under the title of *Hay any worke for Cooper*. The second, entitled *More Worke for Cooper*, was seized at Manchester on 14 August and presumably destroyed.

321. *An Admonition to the People of England: Wherein are answered, not onely the slaunderous untruethes, reprochfully uttered by Martin the Libeller, but also many other Crimes by some of his broode, obiected generally against all Bishops, and the chiefe of the Cleargie, purposely to deface and discredite the present state of the Church.* 1589 (STC 5682)

(The Preface is signed T. C.)

322. *Hay any worke for Cooper: Or a briefe Pistle directed by waye of an hublication to the reverende Byshopps/ counselling them/ if they will needs be barrelled up/ for feare of smelling in the nostrels of her Maiestie & the State/ that they would use the advise of reverend Martin/ for the providing of their Cooper. Because the reverend T.C. (by which mistical letters/ is understood/ eyther the bounsing Parson of East-meane, or Tom Coakes his Chaplaine) to bee an unskilfull and a deceytfull tubtrimmer. Wherein worthy Martin quits himselfe like a man I warrant you/ in the modest defence of his selfe and his learned Pistles/ and makes the Coopers hoopes to flye off/ and the Bishops Tubs to leake out of all crye. Penned and compiled by Martin the Metropolitane. Printed in Europe/ not farre from some of the Bounsing Priestes.* 1589 (STC 17456, GS 11)

Another Anglican reply came from Richard Bancroft, who now emerged as the principal hammer of the Puritans by forceful as well as by literary methods. His first attack took the form of a sermon he preached at Paul's Cross on 9 February 1589; and this was shortly followed on 13 February by a royal proclamation enforcing his criticism. The *Sermon* was published the following month, and elicited two Puritan responses from Scotland. One of these, *A Brief Discovery*, has been ascribed to John Penry, who had meanwhile sought refuge north of the border. The other, taking Bancroft to task for his 'rashnes in rayling', particularly against the Scottish presbyterians, was by John Davidson.

323. *By the Queene. A Proclamation against certaine seditious and schismatical Bookes and Libels, &c.* 13 February 1589 (STC 8182)

324. *A Sermon preached at Paules Crosse the 9 of Februarie, being the first Sunday in the Parleament, Anno 1588. by Richard Bancroft D. of Divinitie, and Chaplaine to the right Honorable Sir Christopher Hatton Knight L. Chancelor of England.* 1589 (STC 1346)

325. *A Brief Discovery of the Untruthes and Slanders (against the true Governement of the Church of Christ) contained in a Sermon, preached the 8. of Februarie 1588. by D. Bancroft, and since that time, set forth in Print, with additions by the said Authour. This short answer may serve for the clearing of the truth, untill a larger confutation of the Sermon be published.* 1590 (STC 19603)

326. *D. Bancrofts Rashnes in Rayling against the Church of Scotland, noted in an answere to a letter of a worthy person of England, and some reasons rendred, why the answere thereunto hath not hitherto come fourth. By I. D. a brother of the sayd Church of Scotland.* 1590 (STC 6322)

There followed three more tracts in the Marprelate series before publication finally ceased in September 1589. The identity of Martin was now apparently multiplied. One tract, entitled *Theses Martinianae*, purported to have been written by a younger son of Martin (and so called *Martin Junior*), and another, entitled *The iust censure*, was supposedly written by his angry elder brother (and therefore known as *Martin Senior*). These two tracts were both printed at Wolston in Warwickshire in July 1589. Finally, *The Protestatyon of Martin Marprelat* — his last challenge — was also printed at Wolston, in September of that year.

327. *Theses Martinianae: That is, certaine demonstrative Conclusions, sette downe and collected (as it should seeme) by that famous and renowned Clarke, the reverend Martin Marprelate the great: serving as a manifest and sufficient confutation of al that ever the Colledge of Catercaps with their whole band of Clergie-priests, have, or can bring for defence of their ambitious and Antichristian Prelacie, Published and Set foorth as an after-birth of the noble Gentleman himselfe, by a pretty stripling of*

his, Martin Iunior, and dedicated by him to his good neame and
nuncka, Maister Iohn Kankerbury: How the yongman came by them,
the Reader shall understande sufficiently in the Epilogue. In the meane
time, whosoever can bring mee acquainted with my father, Ile bee
bounde hee shall not loose his labour. Printed by the assignes of Martin
Iunior, without any priviledge of the Catercaps. 1589   (STC 17457,
GS 11)

328. *The iust censure and reproofe of Martin Iunior. Wherein the rash and*
undiscreet headines of the foolish youth, is sharply mette with, and the
boy hath his lesson taught him, I warrant you, by his reverend and elder
brother, Martin Senior, sonne and heire unto the renowmed Martin
Mar-prelate the Great. Where also, least the springall should be utterly
discouraged in his good meaning, you shall finde, that hee is not
bereaved of his due commendations. 1589   (STC 17458, GS 11)

329. *The Protestatyon of Martin Marprelat. Wherin notwithstanding the*
surprizing of the printer, he maketh it known unto the world that he
feareth, neither proud priest, Antichristian pope, tiranous prellate, nor
godlesse catercap: but defieth all the race of them by these presents and
offereth conditionally, as is farthere expressed hearin by open
disputation to apear in the defence of his cause against them and theirs.
Which chaleng if they dare not maintaine against him: then doth he
alsoe publishe that he never meaneth by the assistaunce of god to leave
the assayling of them and theire generation untill they be uterly
extinguished out of our church. Published by the worthie gentleman D
martin marprelate D. in all the faculties primat and metropolitan.
1589   (STC 17459)

In addition to the more serious criticism of Cooper and Bancroft, Martin
was by this time being assailed by attacks of a more scurrilous kind – in
imitation of his own vein. At the instance (it is said) of Bancroft himself,
various anonymous rhymesters and satirists now entered the lists against
Martin, particularly three of the 'university wits', John Lyly, Thomas Nash
and Robert Greene. To begin with, already by May and June of 1589 rhymes
of various kinds were being circulated in London – *Mar-Martine*, *Rhythmes*
against Martin Marr-Prelate and *A Whip for an Ape*. Another rhyme, entitled
Marre Mar-Martin, criticised the critics of Martin.

330. *Mar-Martine. I know not why a trueth in rime set out/ Maie not as wel*
mar Martine and his mates/ As shamelesse lies in prose-books cast
about/ Mar priests, & prelates, and subvert whole states./ For where
truth builds, and lying overthroes,/ One truth in rime, is worth ten
lies in prose. 1589   (STC 17461)

331. *Rhythmes against Martin Marr-Prelate.* 1589   (STC 17465)

332. *A Whip for an Ape, or Martin displayed.* 1589 (STC 17464)

> (This is really another edition of 331 under a new title.)

333. *Marre Mar-Martin: Or Marre-Martins medling, in a manner misliked.* 1589 (STC 17462)

(Mention may here be made of a rhyme by Sir John Davies, entitled *Sir Martin Mar-people*, and published in 1590 (STC 6363), which merely reflected the contemporary sensation in its title, without dealing with the controversy in its contents. Similarly, the anonymous author of *Martine Mar-Sixtus*, writing in 1591 under the initials R. W. (STC 24913), merely applied the methods of Martin to what he called a better cause – against Pope Sixtus V for his rumoured approval of the recent murder of Henry III in France.)

In addition to the rhymes, various anti-Martinist plays were staged, apparently in the old Morality tradition, but none of them have survived; and all we know about them is from contemporary references. It was not long before they were prohibited for their excessive scurrility and withdrawn from public performance.

Among the satirists in prose the most prominent was one using the pseudonym of Pasquil, who has been identified with some probability as Thomas Nash. In August he came out with *A Countercuffe given to Martin Iunior*, and in October with *The Returne of the renowned Cavaliero Pasquill*. Another writer, styling himself Marphoreus, who may have been Robert Greene, also brought out in August his witty *Martins Months minde*, to celebrate the decease of old Martin implied by the two pamphlets of his sons. In November yet another writer, whom Gabriel Harvey identified in his *Pierces Supererogation* (354) as John Lyly, brought out the scurrilous *Pappe with an hatchet*. The last pamphlet in this series, *An Almond for a Parrat*, appeared in the following year, 1590, with general commendations of 'Pasquin and Marphoreus', as well as 'the pleasant author of Pap with a hatchet': it has been attributed to Nash.

334. *A Countercuffe given to Martin Iunior: by the venturous, hardie, and renowned Pasquill of England, Cavaliero. Not of olde Martins making, which newlie knighted the Saints in Heaven, with rise up Sir Peter and Sir Paule; But lately dubd for his service at home in the defence of his Countrey, and for the cleane breaking of his staffe uppon Martins face. Printed Betweene the skye and the grounde, within a myle of an Oake, and not many fieldes of, from the unpriviledged Presse of the Ass-ignes of Martin Iunior.* 1589 (STC 19456)

335. *The Returne of the renowned Cavaliero Pasquill of England, from the other side of the Seas, and his meeting with Marforius at London upon the Royall Exchange. Where they encounter with a little houshold talke of Martin and Martinisme, discovering the scabbe that is bredde in*

England: and conferring together about the speedie dispersing of the
golden Legende of the lives of the Saints. If my breath be so hote that
I burne my mouth, suppose I was Printed by Pepper Allie. 1589   (STC
17457)

336. *Martins Months minde, that is, A certaine report, and true description
of the Death, and Funeralls, of olde Martin Marreprelate, the great
makebate of England and father of the Factious. Contayning the cause
of his death, the manner of his buriall, and the right copies both of his
Will, and of such Epitaphs, as by sundrie his dearest friends, and other
of his well willers, were framed for him. Martin the Ape, the dronke,
and the madde,/ The three Martins are, whose workes we have had,/ If
Martin the fourth come, after Martins so evill,/ Nor man, nor beast
comes, but Martin the devill.* 1589   (STC 17452)

337. *Pappe with an hatchet. Alias, A figge for my God sonne. Or Cracke me
this nut. Or A Countrie cuffe, that is, a sound boxe of the eare, for the
idiot Martin to hold his peace, seeing the patch will take no warning.
Written by one that dares call a dog, a dog, and made to prevent
Martins dog daies. Imprinted by Iohn Anoke, and Iohn Astile, for the
Baylive of Withernam, cum privilegio perennitatis, and are to bee sold
at the signe of the crab tree cudgell in thwack-coate lane. A sentence.
Martin hangs fit for my mowing.* 1589   (STC 17463)

338. *An Almond for a Parrat, or Cuthbert Curry-knaves Almes. Fit for the
knave Martin, and the rest of those impudent Beggers, that cannot be
content to stay their stomakes with a Benèfice, but they will needes
breake their fastes with our Bishops. Rimarum sum plenus. Therefore
beware (gentle Reader) you catch not the hicket with laughing.
Imprinted at a Place, not farre from a Place, by the Assignes of Signior
Some-body, and are to be sold at his shoppe in Trouble-knave Street, at
the signe of the Standish.* 1590   (STC 28900)

One more pamphlet in the Pasquil series, entitled *The First parte of
Pasquils Apologie*, was written in response, not to Martin, but to John Penry
(identified with Martin by the author of *An Almond for a Parrat*), who had
recently published a *Treatise* with the running title, 'Reformation no enemy
to hir Maiestie and the State', from the press of Robert Waldegrave, then in
Edinburgh.

339. *A Treatise wherein is manifestlie proved, that Reformation and those
that sincerely favor the same, are uniustly charged to be enemies, unto
hir Maiestie, and the state. Written both for the clearing of those that
stande in that cause: and the stopping of the sclaunderous mouthes of
all the enemies thereof.* 1590   (STC 19612)

340. *The First parte of Pasquils Apologie. Wherein he renders a reason to his*

friendes of his long silence: and gallops the fielde with the Treatise of Reformation lately written by a fugitive, Iohn Penrie. Printed where I was, and where I will be readie by the helpe of God and my Muse, to send you the May-game of Martinisme for an intermedium, betweene the first and seconde part of the Apologie. 1590   (STC 19450)

Other pamphlets against Martin were of a more serious kind, and make very dull reading by comparison with those of the 'wits'. First came a Latin admonition to Martin, entitled *Anti-Martinus*, and signed 'A. L.' There followed three tedious pamphlets by the minister, Leonard Wright: *A Summons for Sleepers, The Hunting of Antichrist* and *A Friendly Admonition to Martine Marprelate*. In them he dealt more generally with 'the intollerable Sectes of Seditious Schismatikes', leaving the precise reference to Martin to be inferred by his readers. The same was true of *A Myrror for Martinists* by 'T. T.', whose only explicit mention of the culprits is in the title.

341. *Anti-Martinus, sive monitio cuiusdam Londiniensis, ad Adolescentes utriusque Academiae contra personatum quendam rabulam qui se Anglice, Martin Marprelat, hoc est, Martinum Μαστιγάρχον ἢ μισάρχον vocat.* 1589   (STC 681)

342. *A Summons for Sleepers. Wherein most grievous and notorious offenders are cited to bring forth true frutes of repentance, before the day of repentance, before the day of the Lord now at hand. Hereunto is annexed, A Patterne for Pastors, deciphering briefly the dueties pertaining to that function, by Leonard Wright.* 1589   (STC 26034)

343. *The Hunting of Antichrist. With a caveat to the contentious. By Leonard Wright.* 1589   (STC 26031)

344. *A Friendly Admonition to Martine Marprelate, and his Mates. By Leonard Wright.* 1590   (STC 26030)

345. *A Myrror for Martinists, And all other Schismatiques, which in these dangerous daies doe breake the godlie unitie, and disturbe the Christian peace of the Church. Published by T. T.* 1590   (STC 23628)

d) *The Harvey—Nash controversy*

In the year 1590 there appeared various attempts to bring about a reconciliation between the opposing parties. First, there was a work in Latin by 'some pious learned foreigner' (possibly Hadrian Saravia), entitled *Fraternum et amicum . . . consilium* (which is mentioned by John Strype in his *Annals of the Reformation*, Bk. III, Pt. I, p. 345). This was followed by a similar work in English, perhaps a translation of the former, by a gentleman named Anthony Marten, entitled *A Reconciliation*.

346. *Fraternum et amicum de resartienda inter ecclesiae Anglicanae doctores et ministros pace, concilium.* 1590

347. *A Reconciliation of all the Pastors and Cleargy of this Church of England. By Anthony Marten, Sewer of her Maiesties most honorable Chamber.* 1590   (STC 17490)

Other writers who proposed a similar aim to themselves only succeeded in prolonging the dispute in other directions. Eminent among them were the Harvey brothers, Richard the minister and Gabriel the scholar. The former was probably the author of the anonymous *Plaine Percevall*, which came out in 1590 with a proposal of reconciliation, but with abuse against either side. He soon returned to his theme in *A Theologicall Discourse of the Lamb of God*, in which he took the occasion of this printing of some old sermons to attack both Martinism and its critics. He thus drew upon himself the derision of Robert Greene in *A Quip for an upstart Courtier* in 1592.

348. *Plaine Percevall the Peace-Maker of England. Sweetly indevoring with his blunt persuasions to botch up a Reconciliation between Mar-ton and Mar-tother. Complied by lawfull art, that is to say, without witch craft, or sorcery: and referred specially to the Meridian and pole Artichocke of Nomans Land: but may serve generally without any great error, for more Countries then Ile speake of. Printed in Broad-streete at the signe of the Pack-staffe.* 1590   (STC 12914)

349. *A Theologicall Discourse of the Lamb of God and his Enemies: Containing a briefe Commentarie of Christian faith and felicitie, together with a detection of old and new barbarisme, now commonly called Martinisme. Newly published, both to declare the unfayned resolution of the wryter in these present controversies, and to exercise the faithfull subiect in godly reverence and duetiful obedience.* 1590 (STC 12915)

350. *A Quip for an upstart Courtier: Or, A quaint dispute between Velvet breeches and Clothbreeches. Wherein is plainely set downe the disorders in all Estates and Trades.* 1592   (STC 12300, GS 246)

(The name of Robert Greene comes in the Dedication.)

As Greene had attacked not only Richard, but also Gabriel Harvey in his pamphlet, the latter now joined in the dispute with his *Foure Letters*. Not content with criticising Greene (who had just died), Gabriel Harvey also attacked his friend, Nash, who had recently published his *Pierce Penilesse*. Thus it was that Nash came to grips with Harvey in a famous dispute, which continued through many pamphlets and many years, till the original occasion was completely lost to view. In his first pamphlet, *Strange Newes*, Nash referred to many of the books and authors involved in the recent Marprelate controversy. In his reply, *Pierces Supererogation*, Harvey included a long passage of criticism against Marprelate and his opponents, entitled 'An Advertisement for Pap-hatchet, and Martin Mar-prelate', where the author remarked of the former: 'Would God, Lilly had alwaies bene Euphues, and never Pap-hatchet'. In his next pamphlet, a religious work entitled *Christs Teares over Ierusalem* (1593), Nash made an offer of peace; but he was only ridiculed by Harvey, in *A New Letter of Notable Contents*. So in his next edition of *Christs Teares* in 1594, Nash indignantly withdrew his offer, and went on in *Have with you to Saffron-walden* (Harvey's home-town) to give a full answer to *Pierces Supererogation*, including Harvey's comments on Martinism. The last word in this strange controversy was claimed on behalf of Harvey, by his Cambridge barber, Richard Lichfield, in *The Trimming of Thomas Nashe*; and there the matter came to an end. Between the two combatants there appeared a peace-maker in William Covell, whose *Polimanteia* includes an appeal for unity not only between Harvey and Nash, but also among all Englishmen 'of what religion soever they are'.

351. *Foure Letters, and certaine Sonnets: Especially touching Robert Greene, and other parties, by him abused: But incidently of divers excellent persons, and some matters of note. To all courteous mindes, that will voutchsafe the reading.* 1592   (STC 12900, GS 47)

352. *Pierce Penilesse His Supplication to the Divell. Barbaria grandis habere nihil. Written by Tho. Nash, Gent.* 1592   (STC 18371, GS 114)

353. *Strange Newes, Of the intercepting certaine Letters, and a Convoy of Verses, as they were going Privilie to victuall the Low Countries. Unda impellitur unda. By Tho. Nashe Gentleman,* 1592   (STC 18377, GS 127)

(This book was re-titled in 1593: *The Apologie of Pierce Pennilesse.*)

354. *Pierces Supererogation or A New Prayse of the Old Asse. A Preparative to certaine larger Discourses, intituled Nashes S. Fame. Gabriell Harvey.* 1593   (STC 12903, GS 149)

355. *Christes Teares over Ierusalem. Wherunto is annexed, a comparative admonition to London. A Iove Musa. By Tho. Nashe.* 1593, 1594 (STC 18366—67, GS 186)

356. *A New Letter of Notable Contents. With a straunge Sonet, intituled Gorgon, Or the wonderfull yeare.* 1593   (STC 12902, GS 192)

357. *Have with you to Saffron-walden. or Gabriell Harveys Hunt is up. Containing a full Answere to the eldest sonne of the Halter-maker. Or, Nashe his Confutation of the sinfull Doctor. The Mott or Posie, in stead of Omne tulit punctum: Pacis fiducia nunquam. As much to say, as I sayd I would speake with him.* 1596   (STC 18369, GS 252)

358. *The Trimming of Thomas Nashe Gentleman, by the high-tituled patron*

> *Don Richardo de Medico campo, Barber Chirurgion to Trinitie Colledge in Cambridge. Faber quas fecit compedes ipse gestat.* 1597   (STC 12906, GS 302)

359. *Polimanteia, or, The meanes lawfull and unlawfull, to judge of the fall of a Common-wealth, against the frivolous and foolish coniectures of this age. Whereunto is added, a letter from England to her three daughters, Cambridge, Oxford, Innes of Court, and to all the rest of her inhabitants: perswading them to a constant unitie of what religion soever they are, for the defence of our dread soveraigne, and native country: most requisite for this time wherein wee now live.* 1595 (STC 5883)

e) *The Barrowists*

Such literary frivolity, a logical development of Martin's vein, stands in strange contrast to the tragic outcome of the controversy. The victims of the official wrath aroused by Martin's invectives were (directly) his two associates, John Penry and John Udall, and (indirectly) the two separatists, Henry Barrow and John Greenwood — who all suffered the extreme penalty of death. Udall, indeed, was reprieved after having been sentenced to death, but he died in prison a year or two later. Neither of the separatists had, it seems, any direct connection with the Marprelate tracts — though Barrow has been credited (by H. M. Dexter) with the authorship of the tracts on rather slender evidence, while Greenwood has been identified (by the STC) as the I. G. of *M. Some laid open in his coulers*. Barrow and Greenwood had both been influenced by the writings of Robert Browne, as well as by those of Cartwright; and these had persuaded them to adopt an extreme Puritan position and to separate themselves from the Church of England.

For their schism they were thrown into the Fleet prison; but from their prison they managed to carry on a brief but intense literary activity, until they were finally arraigned and hanged in 1593. It was here that Barrow composed the manifesto of their new Brownist movement, entitled *A True Description . . . of the Visible Church*, in 1589. This was apparently the outcome of his reaction to Dr. Some's first *Godly Treatise* against John Penry (308) — particularly its ninth point, that 'The Church of England is the Visible Church of Christ'. A copy of this *Treatise* is preserved in the Lambeth Palace Library, with interleaved pages on which Barrow made copious annotations in his clear hand, and which he evidently developed in his *True Description*. It was republished several times during the following years among the separatist groups in the Low Countries. In reply, Dr. Some published his third *Godly Treatise* in the same year.

360. *A True Description out of the Worde of God, of the Visible Church.* 1589   (STC 1526)

361. *A Godly Treatise, wherein are examined and confuted many execrable*
     fancies, given out and holden, partly by Henry Barrow and Iohn
     Greenewood: partly, by other of the Anabaptisticall order. Written by
     Robert Some Doctour of Divinitie. 1589   (STC 22912)

The two prisoners took careful notes of the various interrogations to
which they were subjected at various times by the ecclesiastical authorities,
and succeeded in smuggling out their manuscripts to the Low Countries,
where they were published in 1590 in the form of *Collections* of *Certaine*
Sclaunderous Articles and of *Certain Letters and Conferences*. To both these
Collections, and to the *True Description*, answer was made by Richard
Alison, an Anglican minister.

362. *A Collection of Certaine Sclaunderous Articles gyven out by the*
     Bisshops against such faithfull Christians as they now uniustly deteyne
     in their Prisons togeather with the answeare of the saide Prisoners
     therunto. Also the Some of Certaine Conferences had in the Fleete
     according to the Bisshops bloudie Mandate with two Prisoners there.
     1590   (STC 1518)

363. *A Collection Of Certain Letters and Conferences Lately Passed Betwixt*
     Certaine Preachers & Two Prisoners In The Fleet. 1590   (STC 5555)

364. *A Plaine Confutation of a Treatise of Brownisme, Published by some of*
     that Faction, Entituled: A description of the visible Church. In the
     confutation whereof, is shewed,that the Author hath neither described
     a true government of the Church, nor yet proved, that outward
     discipline is the life of the Church. Whereunto is annexed an answere
     unto two other Pamphlets, by the said Factioners latelie dispersed, of
     certaine conferences had with some of them in prison. Wherein is made
     knowen the inconstancie of this Sect, what the Articles are which they
     still maintaine: as also a short confutation of them. There is also added
     a short answere unto such argumentes as they have used to prove the
     Church of England not to be the Church of God. 1590   (STC 355)

At the same time Barrow also wrote *A Briefe Discoverie of the False*
Church and smuggled out his manuscript sheet by sheet for printing at Dort;
but the entire edition was confiscated and was used by his judges as
incriminating evidence against him at his trial in 1593. The *Examinations*
that took place on this occasion, not only of Barrow himself, but also of
Greenwood and Penry, were published in the same year as 'penned by the
Prisoners Themselves'. Many years later, in 1611, Barrow's *Platform* was
published in the setting of a dialogue. It had originally been composed in
September 1590 and submitted to Lord Burghley, who had rejected it; so it
had remained unfinished and unpublished.

365. *A Briefe Discoverie of the False Church. (As the Mother such the daughter is.)* 1590 (STC 1517)

366. *The Examinations of Henry Barrow, John Grenewood, and John Penrie before the High Commissioners and Lordes of the Counsel. Penned by the Prisoners Themselves before Their Deathes.* [1593?] (STC 1519)

367. *Mr. Henry Barrowes Platform, Which may serve, as a Preparative to purge away Prelatisme: with some other parts of Poperie. Made ready to be sent from Miles Mickle-bound to Much-beloved-England. Togither with some other memorable things. And, A familiar Dialogue, in and with the which, all the severall matters conteyned in this booke, are set forth and interlaced. After the untimely death of the penman of the foresaid Platforme, & his fellow prisoner; who being constant witnesses in points apperteyning to the true worship of God, and right government of his Church, sealed up their testimony with their bloud: And paciently suffred the stopping of their breath, for their love to the Lord. Anno 1593. Printed for the yeare of better hope.* 1611 (STC 1525)

Meanwhile, another controversy had been joined between a minister named George Gifford and John Greenwood — with support in the form of added contributions from Henry Barrow. Gifford attacked them in *A Short Treatise against the Donatists of England*, which he published in May 1590. Greenwood undertook to answer him, particularly on the point of 'read prayer' (of which the separatists had expressed their disapproval); but his first writing was (as he complained) 'by the Prelates taken from him' and suppressed. Still, he succeeded in publishing *An Answere* the same year; and Gifford immediately replied in the autumn with *A Plaine Declaration*. Barrow now made his contribution to the controversy with *A Plaine Refutation* in the following year. To this Greenwood appended his own refutation, with 'a fewe observations of M. Giff. his cavils about read prayer and devised Leitourgies', which were also added to the second edition of his *Answere* in 1603. Gifford again responded with *A short Reply* prompting Barrow's 'A Few observations to the Reader of M. Gifford His Last Replie'; but they remained unpublished till 1605(?), when Francis Johnson brought out the second edition of his *Plaine Refutation*.

368. *A Short Treatise against the Donatists of England, whome we call Brownists. Wherein, by the Answeres unto certayne Writings of theyrs, divers of their heresies are noted, with sundry fantasticall opinions, By George Giffard, Minister of Gods holy word in Maldon.* 1590 (STC 11869)

369. *An Answere to George Giffords Pretended Defence of Read Praiers and Devised Litourgies with his ungodly cavils and wicked sclanders comprised in the first parte of his last unchristian and reprochfull*

booke entituled *A Short Treatise Against the Donatists of England. By Iohn Greenwood Christs Poore Afflicted Prisoner in the Fleet for the truth of the Gospel.* 1590   (STC 12339)

370. *A Plaine Declaration that our Brownists be full Donatists, by comparing them together from point to point out of the writings of Augustine. Also a replie to Master Greenwood touching read prayer, wherein his grosse ignorance is detected, which labouring to purge himselfe from former absurdities, doth plunge himselfe deeper in the mire. by George Gyffard, Minister of Gods word in Maldon.* 1590   (STC 11862)

371. *A Plaine Refutation of M. G. Giffardes reprochful booke, intituled a short treatise against the Donatists of England. Wherein is discovered the forgery of the whole Ministrie, the confusion, false worship, and antichristian disorder of these Parish assemblies, called the Church of England. Here also is prefixed a summe of the causes of our seperation, and of our purposes in practise, which M. Giffard hath twise sought to confute, and hath now twise received answere, by Henrie Barrowe. Here is furder annexed a briefe refutation of M. Giff. supposed consimilituda betwixt the Donatists and us. Wherein is shewed how his Arguments have bene & may be by the Papists more iustly retorted against himself & the present estate of their Church, by I. Gren. Here are also inserted a fewe observations of M. Giff. his cavils about read prayer and devised Leitourgies.* 1591   (STC 1523)

372. *A short Reply unto the last printed books of Henry Barrow and Iohn Greenwood, the chief ringleaders of our Donatists in England: Wherein is layd open their grosse ignorance, and foule errors: upon which their whole building is founded. By George Gyfford, Minister of Gods holy worde, in Maldon.* 1591   (STC 11868)

373. 'A Few Observations to the Reader of M. Gifford His Last Replie', appended to the second edition of *A Plaine Refutation.* [1605?]   (STC 1524)

f) *Some Anglican champions*

Yet another of the Puritan petitions for reformation gave rise to a significant controversy of its own as an appendix to the Marprelate controversy. This was *A petition directed to her most excellent Maiestie*, which has been variously attributed to Barrow and Penry, though in his *Answere* to it Sutcliffe identified the author as 'one W. St.' — possibly William Stoughton. On account of a passing critical mention of Sutcliffe's *Treatise of Ecclesiasticall Discipline* (299), the latter was prompted in 1592 to publish his *Answere* to what he contemptuously described in his title as a 'Certaine Libel Supplicatorie'. In this *Answere* Sutcliffe ranged widely among the

Puritan controversies of the time, drawing particularly on his intimate knowledge of the Marprelate affair. Vague accusations he made against Job Throkmorton in this connection elicited a *Defence* from the latter in 1594, in the only published work of his that bears his name. To this *Defence* Sutcliffe responded the following year with *An Answere unto a certaine calumnious letter*, in which he added further valuable information about the Marprelate affair and openly identified Throkmorton as 'the author of Martins Satyres'. He also accused Cartwright of abetting Throkmorton and his associates; and thus Cartwright was in turn drawn to make a *Brief Apologie* in 1596. Sutcliffe, however, had the last word in this fascinating exchange, with an *Examination* of Cartwright's work in the same year.

374. *A petition directed to her most excellent Maiestie, wherein is delivered 1. A meane howe to compound the civill dissention in the church of England. 2. A proofe that they who write for the Reformation, do not offend against the stat. of 23. Eliz. c.2. and therefore till matters be compounded, deserve more favour. Hereunto is annexed: Some opinions of such as sue for Reformation: by which it maie appeare howe uniustlie they are slaundered by the Bishops, &c. pag. 53. Togither with the Authours Epistle to the Reader. pag. 58. Also: Certayne Articles wherein is discovered the negligence of the Bishoppes, their Officialls, Favourers and Followers, in performance of sundrie Ecclesiasticall Statutes Lawes and Ordinances Royall and Episcopall, published for the governement of the Church of England. pag. 60. Lastlie: Certayne Questions or Interrogatories drawen by a favourer of Reformation, wherein he desireth to be resolved by the Prelates, pag. 74.* [1592?]   (STC 1521)

375. *An Answere to a Certaine Libel Supplicatorie, or rather Diffamatory, and also to certaine Calumnious Articles, and Interrogatories, both printed and scattered in secret corners, to the slaunder of the Ecclesiasticall state, and put forth under the name and title of a Petition directed to her Maiestie: Wherein not onely the frivolous discourse of the Petitioner is refuted, but also the accusation against the Disciplinarians his clyents iustified, and the slaunderous cavils at the present governement disciphred by Mathew Sutcliffe.* 1592   (STC 23450)

376. *The Defence of Iob Throkmorton, against the slaunders of Maister Sutcliffe, taken out of a Copye of his own hande as it was written to an honourable Personage.* 1594   (STC 24055)

377. *An Answere unto a certaine calumnious letter published by M. Iob Throkmorton, and entituled, A defence of I. Throkmorton against the slaunders of M. Sutcliffe. Wherein the vanitie both of the defence of himselfe, and the accusation of others is manifestly declared, by Matthew Sutcliffe.* 1595   (STC 23451)

378. *A brief Apologie of Thomas Cartwright against all such slaunderous accusations as it pleaseth Mr. Sutcliffe in severall pamphlettes most iniuriously to loade him with.* 1596   (STC 4706)

379. *The Examination of M. Thomas Cartwrights late apologie, Wherein his vaine and uniust challenge concerninge certaine supposed slanders pretended to have bene published in print against him, is answered and refuted, by Matthew Sutcliffe.* 1596   (STC 23463)

Supporting Whitgift and Bancroft on the Court of High Commission with his considerable legal skill was Richard Cosin. He also came forward in the aftermath of the Marprelate controversy, both to defend the proceedings of that Court (particularly their requirement of the oath *ex officio*, whereby the examinee had to swear to answer faithfully whatever he was asked), and to attack those who still adhered to the presbyterian discipline. The oath *ex officio* had been widely criticised, even by Lord Burghley, as savouring too much of the methods of the Inquisition; and a leading Puritan lawyer, James Morice, now undertook to prove in his *Brief treatise of Oathes* that it was also unlawful. In answer to this *Treatise* Cosin published his *Apologie* for the proceedings of the Court in 1591, and it went two more editions in 1593.

380. *A briefe treatise of Oathes exacted by Ordinaries and Ecclesiastical Iudges, to answere generallie to all such Articles or Interrogatories, as pleaseth them to propound. And of their forced and constrained Oathes ex officio, wherein is proved that the same are unlawfull.* [1591?] (STC 18106)

381. *An Apologie: of, and for Sundrie proceedings by Iurisdiction Ecclesiasticall, of late times by some challenged, and also diversly by them impugned. Lex, Iustitiae: Iustitia Reipub. basis.* 1591   (STC 5820)

Cosin further undertook to give the official account of a *Conspiracie, for Pretended Reformation*, involving three fanatical Puritans, William Hacket, Edmund Coppinger and Henry Arthington, who had attempted to convince Londoners that the Messiah had come again in the person of Hacket. This fact, as well as Cosin's account, served to throw discredit on the whole Puritan movement, with which it seemed to be associated. The book derived further support from the confession of Arthington, which was published in 1592. In a subsequent book of his, on a devotional theme, Arthington looked back contritely to his 'late monstrous offence committed in Cheape'.

382. *Conspiracie, for Pretended Reformation: viz. Presbyteriall Discipline. A Treatise discovering the late designments and courses held for advancement thereof, by William Hacket Yeoman, Edmund Coppinger, and Henry Arthington Gent. out of others depositions and their owne letters, writings & confessions upon examination: Together With some*

> part of the life and conditions, and the two Inditements, Arraignment,
> and Execution of the sayd Hacket: Also An answere to the calum-
> niations of such as affirme they were mad men: and a resemblance of
> this action unto the like, happened heretofore in Germanie. 1591
> (STC 5823)

383. *The Seduction of Arthington by Hacket especiallie, with some tokens
of his unfained repentance and Submission. Written by the said Henrie
Arthington, the third person, in that wofull Tragedie.* 1592   (STC
799)

384. *The Exhortation of Salomon. By H. A.* 1594   (STC 796)

To Bancroft himself is justly attributed the principal authorship (though
he may well have been assisted by Sutcliffe) of two remarkable books, both
published in 1593, which expose the whole Puritan movement in its origins
and its development in Elizabethan England. From the first Bancroft had
been called upon by the Bishop of Ely to deal with the incipient schismatical
movement of Browne and Harrison at Norwich; and to him is ascribed the
authorship of a document, preserved at St. John's College, Cambridge,
outlining the heresies of Browne in particular and 'the opinions and dealinges
of the Precisians' in general. Now, as the fruit of his prosecution of the
Marprelate affair, he was able to publish his detailed *Survay of the Pretended
Holy Discipline* and his criticism of their *Dangerous Positions and Proceedings*. These works together stand for the temporary triumph of the
Anglican cause over that of the presbyterian discipline. They were widely
quoted, not only by Anglican but also by Catholic writers in the years to
come: they were never formally refuted by the Puritans, though the proposal
was made more than once.

385. *A Survay of the Pretended Holy Discipline. Contayning the
beginninges, successe, parts, proceedings, authority, and doctrine of it:
with some of the manifold, and materiall repugnances, varieties and
uncertainties, in that behalfe.* 1593   (STC 1352)

386. *Dangerous Positions and Proceedings, published and practised within
this Iland of Brytaine, under pretence of Reformation, and for the
Presbiteriall Discipline.* 1593   (STC 1344)

In the same year, Thomas Bilson, Warden of Winchester, brought out a
heavy, uninspired volume on *The Perpetual Governement of Christes
Church*. It was subsequently translated into Latin in 1611.

387. *The Perpetual Governement of Christes Church. Wherein are handled:
The fatherly superiority which God first established in the Patriarkes
for the guiding of his Church, and after continued in the Tribe of Levi
and the Prophetes; and lastlie confirmed in the New Testament to the
Apostles and their successours: As also the points in question at this*

day; Touching the Iewish Synedrion: the true Kingdome of Christ: the Apostles commission: the Laie Presbyterie: the Distinction of Bishops from Presbyters, and their succession from the Apostles time and hands: the calling and moderating of Provinciall Synodes by Primates and Metropolitanes: the allotting of Dioeceses, and the Popular electing of such as must feed and watch the flocke: And divers other points concerning the Pastorall regiment of the house of God; By Tho. Bilson Warden of Winchester Colledge. 1593   (STC 3065)

388. *De Perpetua Ecclesiae Christi Gubernatione. In qua tractantur Patria potestas quam Deus primum in Patriarchis pro regenda Ecclesia sua instituit; Deinde in Tribu Levi & Prophetis continuavit; Postremo in novo Testamento Apostolis eorumque successoribus confirmavit. Ut etiam quae hodie in quaestione versantur de Iudaeorum Synedrio; vero Christi regno; authoritate & legatione Apostolica: laico Presbyterio: Episcoporum a Presbyteris distinctione: eorumque ab Apostolorum temporibus Potestate ac Successione: Dioecesium assignatione; populari Pastorum electione: Synodorum in Ecclesia Dei antiquitate & necessitate; atque earundem in quavis Provincia convocatione & moderatione per Metropolis Episcopum. Cum multis aliis quae ad Pastoralem domus Dei procurationem pertinent. Liber ad utilitatem Patriae primum Anglice scriptus, nunc demum ab Authore Thom. Bilsono Episcopo Wintoniensi recognitus, auctus, & in publicum Ecclesiae bonum Latine redditus.* 1611   (STC 3067)

It was, interestingly enough, out of this controversy with the upholders of presbyterian discipline that the Anglicans came to fall back on the traditional Catholic doctrine of the apostolic succession and divine institution of the episcopacy. This had first been hinted at by Bancroft in his *Sermon* of 1589 (324) against Martin Marprelate, where he had maintained that Martin was heretical in opposing the institution of bishops, which (he said) had been in the Church of God 'ever since the apostles times'. On this point he was subsequently, though privately, taken to task by the Puritan theologian, John Reynolds. Now it was openly declared by Thomas Bilson, both in his *Perpetual Government of Christes Church* and in *A Compendious Discourse* on the subject which was published in 1595.

389. *A Compendious Discourse proving Episcopacy to be of Divine Institution.* 1595   (STC 3063)

(The only recorded copy of this book in the STC is unfortunately missing.)

The apostolic origin of bishops had a little earlier been defended by a foreign theologian who had settled in England, Hadrian Saravia, in a Latin treatise, *De Diversis Ministrorum Evangelii Gradibus*, which had been published in 1590 and translated into English in 1591. This occasioned a small controversy between him and Beza at Geneva — which was conducted in Latin and never apparently translated into English.

390. *De Diversis Ministrorum Evangelii Gradibus, sicut a Domino fuerunt instituti, & traditi ab Apostolis, ac perpetuo omnium Ecclesiarum usu confirmati, liber unus: Cui Duo alii additi, alter de Honore qui debetur Ecclesiae Pastoribus, alter de Sacrilegiis & Sacrilegorum poenis. Authore Hadriano Saravia Belga.* 1590   (STC 21746)

391. *D. Saravia. 1. Of the diverse degrees of the Ministers of the Gospell. 2. Of the honor which is due unto the Priestes and Prelates of the Church. 3. Of Sacrilege, and the punishment thereof.* 1591   (STC 21749)

392. *Ad Tractationem De Ministrorum Evangelii Gradibus, ab Hadriano Saravia Belga editam. Theodori Bezae responsio.* 1592

393. *Defensio tractationis de diversis ministrorum evangelii gradibus, ab Hadriano Saravia editae contra responsionem clarissimi viri D. Theodori Bezae, eodem Hadriano Saravia authore.* 1594   (STC 21748)

(Another edition was brought out in Germany in 1601 by Adam Herzog, a disciple of Saravia, with a longer title:

Defensio Tractationis de Diversis Ministrorum Evangelii Gradibus: Ab Hadriano Saravia editus, Contra Responsionem claris. viri D. Theodori Bezae. Eodem Hadriano Saravia autore. Nunc primum edita in Germania, opera et studio Adami Herzogaei: qui propter moderatissimam suam a D. Bezae opinione, dissensionem, invidiam atque iniuriam passus, hanc praestantissimi Theologi D. Hadriani de Saravia Apologiam, magna accessione rerum recognitam & Elencho utillissimo insignitam Ecclesiae & vere Germanis viris, ex verbo Dei ac continuo universae antiquitatis atque Ecclesiasticarum historiarum consensu diiudicandam committit. Liber varia rerum scitu dignissimarum cognitione refertus, ac lectu cum Ecclesiasticis tum politicis utilis atque necessarius.)

g) *The* Laws *of Hooker*

The final and most effectual answer to the Puritans came, however, from the pen of a retiring scholar, Richard Hooker, who had for a short time been Master of the Temple in London, but had decided to withdraw to the peace of the countryside in order to work on a refutation of the Puritans and a justification of the Anglican polity. This work eventually appeared in 1593, in four books out of a promised eight, under the title, *Of the Lawes of Ecclesiasticall Politie*. Its history goes back to the time when Hooker was appointed Master of the Temple by Archbishop Whitgift, over the head of the Puritan Walter Travers, who as Reader had expected to receive the appointment to the Mastership when this fell vacant. In his sermons there

Hooker dealt with the questions of justification by faith and the certainty of faith among the elect. He also proposed the idea, abhorrent to the Puritans, that the Church of Rome might be a true, if defective, part of the whole Church of Christ, and that consequently members of this Church might find salvation through their faith. His proposals were challenged by Travers from the same pulpit on the very afternoon of the day they were delivered. The outcome of this sensational dispute was that Travers was removed from his position as Reader. He appealed to the Privy Council for justice; but Hooker was invited to present his side of the case, with the result that Travers' appeal was not upheld. The sermons of Hooker, the appeal of Travers and Hooker's answer were eventually published by Joseph Barnes of Oxford in 1612.

394. *A Learned and Comfortable Sermon of the certaintie and perpetuitie of faith in the Elect; especially of the Prophet Habbakuks faith. By Richard Hooker, sometimes fellow of Corpus Christi College in Oxford.* 1612   (STC 13707)

395. *A Learned Discourse of Iustification, Workes, and how the foundation of faith is overthrowne. By Richard Hooker, sometimes Fellow of Corpus Christi College in Oxford.* 1612   (STC 13708)

396. *A Supplication made to the Privy Counsel. By Mr. Walter Travers.* 1612 (STC 24187)

397. *The Answere of Mr. Richard Hooker to a Supplication preferred by Mr. Walter Travers to the HH. Lords of the Privie Counsell.* 1612   (STC 13706)

Not long after this controversy Hooker himself retired from his position to devote his energy to his great project, first to Boscombe in Wiltshire, then Bishopsbourne in Kent. After the first four books came out in 1593, the fifth (as long as the other four together) followed in 1597. When Hooker died in 1600, he left the finished version of the other three books in his study; but, as the editor of the second edition lamented in his Preface, 'some evill disposed mindes ... smothered them, and by conveying away the perfect copies, left unto us nothing but certaine olde unperfect and mangled draughts'. A third edition of five books came out in 1611, and other editions followed. But it was not till 1666 that all eight books came out together for the first time, the last three having been elaborated from the rough drafts of Hooker which had been preserved.

398. *Of the Lawes of Ecclesiasticall Politie, Eyght Bookes. By Richard Hooker.* 1593   (STC 13712, GS 14)

399. *Of the Lawes of Ecclesiasticall Politie. The fift Booke. By Richard Hooker.* 1597   (STC 13712, GS 14)

The Puritan reaction to Hooker's formidable criticism was surprisingly weak; though it is less surprising when we reflect that their forces were now in disarray as a result of the Anglican counter-attack led by Whitgift, Bancroft, Cosin, Sutcliffe and others. Only five years later did the first objections appear in print, in the form of an anonymous *Christian Letter*, whose plural authorship may well have been led by Thomas Cartwright. Under a mask of mildness its authors ventured to suggest that Hooker was in fact undermining the very foundation of Christian religion. Not long after its publication Hooker died; and his defence was taken up by his friend, William Covell, who published *A Iust and Temperate Defence* of Hooker's work.

400. *A Christian Letter of certaine English Protestants, unfained favourers of the present state of Religion, authorised and professed in England: unto that Reverend and learned man, Mr. R. Hoo. requiring resolution in certaine matters of doctrine (which seeme to overthrow the foundation of Christian Religion, and of the church among us) expresslie contained in his five books of Ecclesiasticall Pollicie.* 1599 (STC 4707)

401. *A Iust and Temperate Defence of the Five Books of Ecclesiastical Policie: written by M. Richard Hooker: Against an uncharitable Letter of certain English Protestants (as they tearme themselves) craving resolution, in some matters of doctrine, which seeme to overthrow the foundation of religion, and the Church amongst us. Written by William Covel Doctor in Divinitie, and published by authority.* 1603 (STC 5881)

By way of postscript, mention may be made of a Puritan work that appeared just before the end of the reign, Josias Nichols' *Plea of the Innocent*. This was written not against Hooker, but in defence of the maligned Puritans. It was again William Covell who took up his pen to refute the book, in his *Modest and reasonable examination*, which was published in the new reign as a kind of companion volume to his defence of Hooker. But by that time the centre of religious controversy had shifted, once more, from the Puritans to the Catholics.

402. *The Plea of the Innocent: Wherein is averred: That the Ministers & people falslie termed Puritanes, are iniuriouslie slaundered for enemies or troublers of the State. Published for the common good of this Realme of England as a countermure Against all Sycophantising Papists, Statising Priestes, Neutralising Atheistes, and Satanising scorners of all godlinesse, trueth and honestie. Written: By Iosias Nichols, a faithfull Minister of the Ghospell of Christ: and an humble servaunt, of the English Church.* 1602 (STC 18541)

403. *A Modest and reasonable examination, of some things in use in the Church of England, sundrie times heretofore misliked, and now lately, in a Booke called the (Plea of the Innocent:) and an Assertion for true*

and Christian Church policy, made for a full satisfaction to all those, that are of iudgement, and not possessed with a preiudice against this present Church Government, wherein the principall poynts are fully, and peaceably aunswered, which seeme to bee offensive in the Ecclesiasticall State of this Kingdome. By William Covell, Doctor of Divinitie. 1604   (STC 5882)

CHAPTER 5

Appellant Considerations

a) *Discoveries of treason*

IN THE circumstances of the Elizabethan Age religious controversy inevitably entered the field of politics. If the Puritan appeal was to the divine ideal of Scripture, as offering a pattern of Church government, the Catholic appeal was to the reality of past tradition, when Europe had been united in one Christian faith. For this reason many Catholic controversialists, particularly those in the circle of Allen and Persons, took an historical approach to the existing situation and saw in the recent religious changes a Machiavellian plot for the subversion of England. There is a significant series of books proposing such an interpretation, from the early '70s to the mid-'90s; and they were regarded as a serious danger by the English authorities. The first of these books was entitled *A Treatise of Treasons*, possibly by John Leslie, Bishop of Ross, and a staunch supporter of Mary Queen of Scots. Written in reply to a small, anonymous pamphlet attributed to Sir William Cecil (attacking the imprisoned Duke of Norfolk), it presented the whole Elizabethan settlement as a conspiracy of two men, Sir William Cecil and Sir Nicholas Bacon, to gain supreme power in England. It was shortly followed by *A Table* gathered out of the *Treatise*; and this was sent with a dedicatory epistle to Queen Elizabeth. The outcome of these books, however, was a royal proclamation, dated 28 September 1573, against all Catholic 'bookes and libelles', especially those containing 'argumentes of discoveries of treasons'.

404. *Salutem in Christo. Good men and evill delite in contraryes.* 1571 (STC 11504)

   (The pamphlet has no title-page, but is signed 'R. G.' It is generally attributed to Cecil.)

405. *A Treatise of Treasons against Q. Elizabeth, and the Croune of England, divided into two Partes: whereof. The first Parte answereth certaine Treasons pretended, that never were intended: And the second,*

discovereth greater Treasons committed, that are by few perceived: as more largely appeareth in the Page folowing. 1572 (STC 7601, AR 454, ERL 254)

406. *A Table gathered owt of a Booke named A Treatise of treasons against Q. Elizabeth, and the Croune of England. Latelie compiled by a stranger and sent owt of France.* 1573 (Not in STC, AR 806)

407. *By the Queene. Whereas certayne obstinate and irrepentant traytours, after theyr notorious rebellions made against this theyr naturall countrey, have fledde out of the same . . .* 28 September 1573 (STC 8064)

(Particular mention is made of 'certayne seditious bookes and libelles . . . with argumentes of discoveries of treasons'.)

Some 12 years later this *Treatise*, which was also known as 'The Papist's Commonwealth', was followed by another book of like nature, which came to be known as 'Leicester's Commonwealth' or (on account of its cover) 'Greencoat'. The latter purported to be *The Copie of a Leter, wryten by a Master of Arte of Cambridge, to his friend in London*; and it attributed the evils in England not so much to Cecil as to the Earl of Leicester, though its occasion was 'a litle boke, then newlie set forth, conteining A defence of the publique iustyce done of late in Englande, uppon dyvers Pryestes and other Papystes for treason' – namely, Cecil's *Execution of Justice*. Its authorship was widely attributed at the time to Robert Persons, though he would never acknowledge the fact. Both the popular title and the popular attribution appear in title of the second edition of this book in 1641 – in very different political circumstances.

408. *The Copie of a Leter, wryten by a Master of Arte of Cambridge, to his friend in London, concerning some talke past of late between two worshipful and grave men, about the present state, and some procedinges of the Erle of Leycester and his friendes in England. Conceyved, spoken and publyshed, wyth most earnest protestation of al duetyful good wyl and affection, towardes her most excellent Ma. and the Realm, for whose good onely it is made common to many.* 1584 (STC 19399, AR 261, ERL 192)

(The second edition of 1641 bore the title:

Leicester's Commonwealth. Conceived, spoken and published with most earnest protestation of dutifull goodwill and affection towards this Realme. By Robert Parsons Jesuite. Whereunto is added Leicesters Ghost. (Wing L968))

Another book of the same kind, professing to reveal the hidden secrets of an earlier stage of the English Reformation, was the above-mentioned *De*

Origine ac Progressu Schismatis Anglicani (261), which first appeared —
several years after the author's death — in 1585. It looked for the origin of
present evils beyond the reign of Elizabeth to that of her father Henry VIII,
discerning a 'mystery of iniquity' at work behind the outer appearances of
English politics. Persons himself had a hand in the subsequent editions of
this book, which soon became a best-seller in contemporary Europe.
Gradually Allen, too, became involved in these writings, though it was his
policy as President of the English College to keep religion as far removed as
possible from politics. A test-case was provided in 1587 when the Catholic
commander of some English forces, Sir William Stanley, decided to restore
the town of Deventer to the Spanish king as its rightful ruler, and Allen was
asked for his judgment in the matter. In *The Copie of a Letter written by M.
Doctor Allen*, he gave his full approval to Stanley's action. His letter went
into two English editions the same year (with different titles), and was also
published in French translation.

409. *The Copie of a Letter written by M. Doctor Allen: concerning the
     yeelding up, of the citie of Daventrie, unto his Catholike Maiestie, by
     Sir William Stanley Knight. Wherin is shewed both howe lawful,
     honorable, and necessarie that action was: and also that al others,
     especiallie those of the English Nation, that detayne anie townes, or
     other places, in the lowe countries, from the King Catholike, are bound,
     upon paine of damnation, to do the like. Before Which is also prefixed
     a gentlemans letter, that gave occasion, of this discourse.* 1587.   (STC
     370, AR 8, ERL 51)

(The other edition of 1587 was entitled:

*A Copie of a Lettre written by an English Gentleman, out of the campe
of the low countreys, unto the Reverend, Master Doctor Allain,
towching the act of rendring the Towne of Deventer and other places,
unto the Cathol. King: and his answerre and resolution unto the same.*
(Not in STC, AR 9))

410. *Justification pour le Catholique, Noble, Chevalier Anglois, le Sieur
     Guillaume Stanlay, et autres honorables Capitaines, et Gentils-hommes
     Anglois de son regiment, sur la rendition de la ville de Deventer, et
     autres lieux, a l'obeysance de sa Majeste Catholique, qui ont este
     detenuz par la Reyne d'Angleterre, pour support des Heretiques de
     Hollande, et Zelande.* 1588

This work of Allen prompted an anonymous English writer, who signed
himself G. D., to publish an indignant *Briefe Discoverie of Doctor Allens
seditious drifts* in 1588. In more general terms William Lightfoot uttered a
Complaint of England against the treasonable practices of Papists against the
state.

411. *A Briefe Discoverie of Doctor Allens seditious drifts, contrived in a Pamphlet written by him, Concerning the yeelding up of the towne of Deventer, (in Overrissel) unto the King of Spain, by Sir William Stanley. The contentes whereof are particularly set downe in the page following.* 1588   (STC 6166)

412. *The Complaint of England. Wherein it is clearly prooved that the practises of Traitrous Papists against the state of this Realme, and the person of her Maiestie, are in Divinitie unlawfull, odious in Nature, and ridiculous in pollicie. In the which they are reprooved of wilfull blindnes, in that they see not the filthines of the Romish goverment: and convinced of desperate madnesse, in that they feare not the mischiefe of Spanish invasion: The former whereof is exemplified by the Popes practises both here in England, and abroad in other countries: the later by the Spaniards outrages, in his exactions raised upon Naples, and his tyrannies executed in the Indies. Lastly the necessitie, equitie, and benefits of the late proceeding in iustice are set downe; with a friendly warning to seditious Papists for their amendment; and an effectuall consolation to faithfull subiectes for their incouragement.* 1587   (STC 15595)

The political involvement of Allen came to a climax with the expedition of the Spanish Armada against England in 1588. The year before, he had been created Cardinal by Pope Sixtus V; and now he came out with *An Admonition to the Nobility and People of England*, supporting the Spanish enterprise and the Papal decree of excommunication against Elizabeth. His *Admonition* was also compressed into a broadside, to be distributed among the English in the case of a Spanish victory, entitled *A declaration of the sentence and deposition of Elizabeth*. This was later reprinted in 1600 by one of the Appellant clergy under the title of *The Declaration of Sixtus Quintus*, and attributed rather to Persons (under his pseudonym of N. D.) than to Allen. Copies of both the *Admonition* and the *Declaration* came to the notice of the English authorities before they had been distributed; and they were immediately banned by a royal proclamation of July 1588.

413. *An Admonition to the Nobility and People of England concerninge the present warres made for the execution of his Holines Sentence, by the highe and mightie Kinge Catholike of Spaine. By the Cardinal of Englande.* 1588   (STC 368, AR 5, ERL 74)

414. *A declaration of the sentence and deposition of Elizabeth, the usurper and pretensed quene of Englande.* 1588   (STC 22590, AR 770, ERL 370)

The 1600 edition bore the altered title:

The Declaration of Sixtus Quintus his Bull, a new challenge made to N. D.)

415. *By the Queene. A Proclamation against the bringing in, dispersing,*
uttering and keeping of Bulles from the Sea of Rome, and other
Traiterous and sedicious Libels, Bookes, and Pamphlets. 1 July 1588.
(STC 8172)

It was with reference to this general situation, rather than to any particular publication, that Thomas Rogers published his *Historical Dialogue touching Antichrist* in 1589. Similarly, John Swan brought out an English translation of the Huguenot Lambert Daneau's *Tractatus de Antichristo* (1576) in consideration of 'this late cruell attempt of the Spanyards'.

416. *An Historical Dialogue touching Antichrist and Poperie, Drawen and*
published for the common benefit and comfort of our Church in these
dangerous daies, & against the desperate attempts of the vowed
adversaries of Iesus Christ his Gospell, and this florishing State. By
Thomas Rogers. 1589 (STC 21237)

417. *A Treatise Touching Antichrist. Wherein, the Place, the Time, the*
Forme, the workmen, the Uphoulders, the Proceeding; and lastly, the
ruine and overthrow of the Kingdome of Antichrist, is plainly laid open
out of the word of God: where also manie darke, and hard places both
of Daniell and of the Revelation are made manifest. By Lambert
Danaeus. Meete in these dayes to be considered, where-in, the
kingdome of the Beast is by force and trecherie sought to be revived:
And published for the encouragement of those which ioyne in the
intended actions against the Spaniard and otherwise, for the further
overthrow of Antichrist, and the enlarging of Christ his kingdome, with
the pure preaching and sincere government of the same. 1589 (STC
6229)

To counter the various accusations spread abroad in England against the Catholics and the Spaniards occasioned by the Armada, an anonymous *Copy of a Letter* was published in 1589, purporting to have been written by a Spaniard taken prisoner from the Armada and subsequently ransomed. It has been attributed to Richard Verstegan, Persons' intelligencer in the Low Countries.

418. *The Copy of a Letter, lately written by a Spanishe Gentleman, to his*
freind in England: in refutation of sundry calumnies, there falsly
bruited, and spred emonge the people. The originall whereof was
written in Spanish, since the authors being in England, who by reason
of a ship of those that miscaried of the late Armado, was taken, and
there detained prisoner, untill his delivery by ransome. Now newly
translated into Englishe, for the benefite of those (of that nation) that
understand not the Spanishe tounge. 1589 (STC 1038, AR 60, ERL
81)

The consequent escalation of repressive measures taken against the Catholics by the English government came to a head with a royal proclamation dated 18 October 1591. This was aimed particularly against the seminary priests and Jesuits, but it also included an attack on the King of Spain. It evoked a series of pseudonymous protests from English Catholics living abroad, some in Latin and some in English. 'Andreas Philopater' was soon identified as Robert Persons, whose Latin *Responsio* was the most vigorous of all the protests. 'Didymus Veridicus Henfildanus' was recognised as Thomas Stapleton: he undertook to write a Latin *Apologia* for King Philip of Spain. Under the pseudonym of 'Joannes Pernius', Joseph Cresswell conveyed his criticism in the form of a spurious *Exemplar Literarum* supposed to have been sent out of Germany to Lord Burghley. A similar plan was adopted by the anonymous author, variously identified as Richard Verstegan and Joseph Cresswell, of *An Advertisement written to a Secretarie*, though the actual contents are little more than an English summary of the *Philopater*. Perhaps the most remarkable of these writings was one which dispensed with a pseudonym altogether, and has been attributed now to Verstegan, now to Persons himself. Entitled *A Declaration of the True Causes*, it belongs to the tradition of the *Treatise of Treasons* and *Leicester's Commonwealth* in presenting the political developments in England as the outcome of a deep Machiavellian plot engineered by Lord Burghley. None of these books, however, dealing as they did with dangerous affairs of state, elicted any reply from the Protestant side.

419. *By the Queene. A declaration of great troubles pretended against the Realme by a number of Seminarie Priests and Iesuits, sent, and very secretly dispersed in the same, to worke great Treasons under a false pretence of Religion, with a provision very necessary for remedy thereof. Published by this her Maiesties Proclamation.* 18 October 1591 (STC 8207)

420. *Elizabethae, Angliae Reginae Haeresim Calvinianam Propugnantis, saevissimum in Catholicos sui Regni edictum, quod in alios quoque Reipub. Christianae Principes contumelias continet indignissimas: Promulgatum Londini 29. Novemb. 1591. Cum responsione ad singula capita: qua non tantum saevitia, & impietas tam iniqui edicti, sed mendacia quoque, & fraudes ac imposturae deteguntur, & confutantur. Per D. Andream Philopatrum presbyterum ac Theologum Romanum, ex Anglis olim oriundum.* 1592

(Another edition, published in 1593, bore the altered title:

Elizabethae Reginae Angliae Edictum Promulgatum Londini 29 Novemb. Anni MDXCI. Andreae Philopatri ad idem edictum Responsio.

Three more editions in Latin followed, with translations into German and French, but none into English.)

421. *Apologia Pro Rege Catholico Philippo II. Hispaniae, & caet. Rege. Contra varias & falsas accusationes Elisabethae Angliae Reginae. Per edictum suum 18. Octobris Richmondiae datum, & 20 Novembris Londini proclamatum, publicatas & excusas. In qua omnium turbarum & bellorum quibuscum his annis 30. Christiana Respub. conflictatur, fontes aperiuntur, & remedia demonstrantur. Authore Didymo Henfildano.* 1592

422. *Exemplar Literarum, Missarum, e Germania, Ad D. Guilielmum Cecilium, Consiliarium Regium.* 1592

(The Dedication to Lord Burghley is signed Ioannes Pernius.)

423. *An Advertisement written to a Secretarie of my L. Treasurers of Ingland, by an Inglishe Intelligencer as he passed through Germanie towardes Italie. Concerninge An other booke newly written in Latin, and published in diverse languages and countreyes, against her Maiesties late proclamation, for searche and apprehension of Seminary priestes, and their receavers. Also of a letter written by the L. Treasurer in defence of his gentrie, and nobility, intercepted, published, and answered by the papistes.* 1592   (STC 19885, AR 264, ERL 166)

424. *A Declaration of the True Causes of the great troubles, presupposed to be intended against the realme of England. Wherein the indifferent reader shall manifestly perceave, by whome, and by what meanes, the realme is broughte into these pretented perills.* 1592.   (STC 10005, 19400, AR 844, ERL 360)

b) *The* Book of Succession

A further development of this political aspect of the religious controversies took place in connection with the delicate question of succession. The Queen was now growing old, and on the person of her successor would depend the future of the English Church: whether it would continue Protestant, or else revert to its Catholic past, as in Queen Mary's reign. This question had been discussed in a Latin treatise, *De Iusta Reipub. Christianae . . . Authoritate* (1590), with overt reference to the French succession, by William Reynolds of Douai, under the pseudonym of Rossaeus. It was subsequently touched upon in an interesting book entitled *Newes from Spayne and Holland* (1593) which was probably written by the Jesuit, Richard Walpole, with the assistance of Robert Persons. Referring to 'the great variety of bookes both in Inglishe and Latyn, and other languages already come forth, or in the makynge . . . against the laste proclamation of her Maiestie', the author devoted the second part of his book to 'certaine considerations of State', notably the question 'of the Prince that shal follow'. This led up to the highly explosive *Conference about the Next Succession* by R. Doleman, a pseudonym behind which contemporaries generally saw the figure of Persons, though it is probable that others of his party, Allen himself, Verstegan and Sir Francis Englefield, had their several shares in its composition. Drawing much of his argument from Rossaeus, the author treated his subject in an easy, reasonable style, using the form of an Utopian dialogue; but he was treading on dangerous ground, especially when he dedicated his book to the Earl of Essex. The reaction at the English court was naturally violent; but because of the forbidden nature of the subject, no immediate reply was forthcoming in print.

425. *De Iusta Reipub. Christianae in reges impios et haereticos Authoritate: Iustissimaque Catholicorum ad Henricum Navarraeum & quemcumque haereticum a regno Galliae repellendum confoederatione. G. Guilielmo Rossaeo Authore, Liber. Cuius particularia Capita vide post praefationem.* 1590

426. *Newes from Spayne and Holland conteyning. An information of Inglish affayres in Spayne with a conferrence made theruppon in Amsterdame of Holland. Written by a Gentleman travelour borne in the low countryes, and brought up from a child in Ingland, unto a Gentleman his frend and Oste in London.* 1593   (STC 22994, AR 634, ERL 365)

427. *A Conference about the Next Succession to the Crowne of Ingland, divided into two partes. Whereof the first conteyneth the discourse of a civill Lawyer, how and in what manner propinquity of blood is to be preferred. And the second the speech of a Temporall Lawyer, about the particuler titles of all such as do or may pretende within Ingland or without, to the next succession. Where unto is also added a new & perfect arbor or genealogie of the discents of all the kinges and princes of Ingland, from the conquest unto this day, whereby each mans pretence is made more plaine. Directed to the right honorable the earle of Essex of her Maiesties privy councell, & of the noble order of the Garter. Published by R. Doleman.* 1595   (STC 19398, AR 271, ERL 104)

The first Protestant reply to *Doleman*, or the *Conference* (as the book was variously called), was contained in *A Pithie Exhortation* by Peter Wentworth, the Puritan member of Parliament; and it was only published posthumously in 1598, two years after the author's death, from the safety of Edinburgh. This was followed in 1600 by *A Discoverye of a Counterfecte Conference*, published at Cologne by a Catholic opponent of Persons, the sonneteer Henry Constable. A third reply was undertaken by the Scottish jurist, Sir Thomas Craig; but just as he was about to send his manuscript to the press, the Queen died and the publication of his book at that juncture was considered unadvisable. All the same, it was in 1603 that the only answer to be published in England for the time being came from the pen of the English jurist Sir John Hayward, who dedicated his work to 'the Kings most excellent Maiestie'. He also added a Preface 'to R. Doleman', in which he found it necessary to explain the long delay in coming out with a refutation.

428. *A Pithie Exhortation to her Maiestie for establishing her successor to the crowne. Whereunto is added a discourse containing the Authors opinion of the true and lawfull successor to her Maiestie. Both compiled by Peter Wentworth Esquire.* 1598   (STC 25245)

(The discourse that is added has its own title-page:

A Treatise containing M. Wentworths Iudgement concerning the person of the true and lawfull successor to these Realmes of England and Ireland. Wherein the title is briefly and plainelie set down: Dolmans obiections refuted, and inconveniences removed. Made two yeeres before his death, but published a yeere after his death for the publike benefite of this Realme.)

429. *A Discoverye of a Counterfecte Conference helde at a counterfecte place, by counterfecte travellers, for thadvancement of a counterfecte tytle, and invented, printed, and published by one (PERSON) that dare not avowe his name.* 1600   (STC 6913, AR 253, ERL 6)

430. *The Right of Succession to the Kingdom of England, in Two Books; Against the Sophisms of Parsons the Jesuite, Who assum'd the Counterfeit Name of Doleman; By which he endeavours to overthrow not only the Rights of Succession in Kingdoms, but also the Sacred Authority of Kings themselves. Written Originally in Latin above 100 Years since, by the Eminently Learned and Judicious Sir Thomas Craig of Riccartoun, the Celebrated Author of the Jus Foedale, and now faithfully Translated into English, with a large Index of the Contents, and a Preface by the Translator, giving an account of the Author and of his Adversary.* 1703

431. *An Answer to the First Part of a Certaine Conference, concerning Succession, published not long since under the name of R. Dolman.* 1603   (STC 12988)

c) *The Appellant controversy*

It was to some extent this involvement of the English Jesuits, especially Robert Persons, in political affairs (though for the cause of religion) to which a group of seminary priests, known as Appellants, objected in a highly scandalous controversy that broke out in the last two or three years of Elizabeth's reign. The origins of the disaffection between this group of priests and the Jesuits are to be found partly in certain 'stirs' about the year 1595 at Wisbeach Castle in Norfolk, where many Catholic priests were held prisoner, and partly in certain differences between some seminarians at the English College, Rome, and their Jesuit teachers. The proximate occasion of their outburst, however, was the appointment in 1598 of George Blackwell, a seminary priest known as a friend of the Jesuits, as Archpriest over all the Catholic clergy in England. An appeal to Rome against his appointment was drawn up by a number of the disaffected priests at Wisbeach, with the connivance of the English authorities; but it was rejected by the Pope, and the Archpriest went on to treat the Appellants as rebels and schismatics. It was on this occasion that a Jesuit, Thomas Lister, wrote a strongly worded pamphlet against the group, entitling it *Adversus Factiosos in Ecclesia*. But the Appellants took this opportunity to make a further appeal to Rome on 17 November 1600, supported by the signatures of some 33 priests. Two compilations were also made of relevant documents, which were later published in London, one in Latin edited by John Mush, and the other in English edited (as is sometimes thought) by William Bishop. The Latin compilation included a copy of the priests' Appeal to Rome, and mentioned Lister's book as a principal reason for this Appeal. Among the names of the signatories are those of Bluet, Bagshaw, Colleton, Mush, Watson, Clark, Champney and Bennett, each of whom took up his pen against the Jesuits in the course of the subsequent controversy. In addition to this Appeal, as we learn from the *Dialogue* attributed to Mush, Lister's book was answered by Champney, and Lister in turn 'wrot the second time a replie, and divulged it also'. But neither Champney's answer nor Lister's further reply have come down to us, presumably on account of the Pope's order that all such works were to be suppressed.

432. *Adversus Factiosos in Ecclesia.* 1598

> (No copy of this work survives, owing to its suppression by the Pope; but the text is given in full by Bagshaw in his *Relatio Compendiosa Turbarum* (436), pp. 37–47.)

433. *Declaratio Motuum ac Turbationum quae ex controversiis inter Iesuitas iisque in omnibus faventem D. Georg. Blackwellum Archipresbyterum, & Sacerdotes Seminariorum in Anglia, ab obitu illmi Cardlis Alani piae memoriae, ad annum usque 1601. Ad S.D.N. Clementem octavum exhibita ab ipsis sacerdotibus qui schismatis, aliorumque criminum sunt insimulati.* 1601   (STC 3102, AR 552, ERL 39)

434. *The Copies of certaine discourses, which were extorted from divers, as their friends desired them, or their adversaries drove them to purge themselves of the most greevous crimes of schisme, sedition, rebellion, faction, and such like, most uniustly laid against them for not subscribing to the late authoritie at the first sending thereof into England: In which discourses are also many things discovered*

concerning the proceedings in this matter abroad. 1601   (STC 5724,
AR 254, ERL 84)

The two compilations of the Appellants were strongly criticised by
Blackwell in a letter of 23 June 1601. But this only elicited two more books
from the priests – one by John Bennett, entitled *The Hope of Peace*,
directly answering the Archpriest (with his letter presented in full); and the
other in Latin by Christopher Bagshaw, entitled *Relatio Compendiosa
Turbarum*, narrating the events that had led up to the confrontation between
the Seminary Priests and the Jesuits.

435. *The Hope of Peace. By laying open such doubts and manifest untruthes
as are divulged by the Arch-priest in his Letter or Answere to the
Bookes which were published by the Priestes*. 1601   (STC 1041, 1884,
AR 103, ERL 82)

436. *Relatio Compendiosa Turbarum quas Iesuitae Angli, una cum D.
Georgio Blackwello Archipresbytero, Sacerdotibus Seminariorum
populoque Catholico concivere ob schismatis & aliorum criminum
invidiam illis iniuriose impactam sacro sanctae inquisitionis officio
exhibita, ut rerum veritate cognita ab integerrimis eiusdem iudicibus
lites & causae discutiantur & terminentur.* 1601   (STC 3106, AR 63,
ERL 71)

These books of the Appellant Priests were all published in London, with
the connivance of the authorities, though they tried to disguise the fact
under false imprints. Thus the *Declaratio Motuum* has the imprint,
'Rhotomagi Apud Iacobum Molaeum, sub signo Phenicis'; *The Copies of
certaine discourses*, 'Imprinted at Roane, by the heires of Ia. Walker'; *The
Hope of Peace*, 'Imprinted at Franckford by the heires of D. Turner'; and the
Relatio Compendiosa Turbarum, 'Rothomagi, per Iacobum Molaeum sub
signo Phaenicis' – though the names of the London printers can be
identified in each case. In his replies to the priests Persons (the only Jesuit to
represent his brethren in the course of this controversy) naturally made
much of this fact, and presented the priests as renegades and traitors to the
Catholic cause. He came forward with *A Briefe Apologie*, in which he gave a
clear historical account of the whole matter from the Jesuit viewpoint, and
went on to deal with 'two late bookes or libels set forth by our discontented
brethren', the *Declaration* and the *Copies*. A month or two later, early in
1602, he added *An Appendix to the Apologie* in refutation of the other two
books by Bennet and Bagshaw – the latter of whom had been his enemy
long ago at Balliol College, Oxford.

437. *A Briefe Apologie, or Defence of the Catholike Ecclesiastical
Hierarchie, & subordination in England, erected these later yeares by
our holy Father Pope Clement the eyght: and impugned by certayne
libels printed & published of late both in Latyn & English: by some*

*unquiet persons under the name of Priests of the Seminaries. Written
and set forth for the true information and stay of all good Catholikes,
by Priests united in the subordination to the Right Reverend
Arch-priest, and other their Superiors.* 1601   (STC 4832, 19392, AR
614, ERL 273 [= AR 613])

438. *An Appendix to the Apologie, lately set forth, for defence of the
Hierarchie, and subordination of the English Catholike Church,
inpugned by certaine discontented Priestes. Wherin two other bookes or
libels of the impugners, the one in English the other in Latin, no lesse
intemperate than the former, are examined, and considered, By the
Priestes that remaine in due obedience to their lawful Superior.* 1602
(Not in STC, AR 612, ERL 273)

Meanwhile, further books were coming from the London presses against
the Jesuits in rapid succession and with increasing virulence. To Bagshaw is
attributed the anonymous *True relation of the faction begun at Wisbich*,
which gave the priests' version of the 'Wisbeach stirs'. Even more actively
involved in the task of publication was William Watson, whom Persons
described as 'their secretary', though he was the certain author of only one
book. At least, he arranged for the publication of the next three books, to
each of which he gave a Preface signed with his initials. These were
Important Considerations, *A Sparing Discoverie of our English Iesuits* and *A
Dialogue betwixt a Secular Priest and a Lay Gentleman*, of which the
authors were identified by a contemporary Jesuit, Anthony Rivers (writing
to Persons in July 1602), as respectively Thomas Bluet, Christopher
Bagshaw and John Mush. Watson's own book followed shortly afterwards, the
rather eccentric *Decacordon of Ten Quodlibeticall Questions*, usually
known as the *Quodlibets*, which became the most notorious of all these
writings. Another work of this kind came from the pen of Anthony Copley,
entitled *An Answere to a Letter of a Iesuited Gentleman*, justifying the
priests' recourse to printed books 'for their publike defence'.

439. *A True relation of the faction begun at Wisbich, by Fa. Edmonds, alias
Weston, a Iesuite, 1595. and continued since by Fa. Walley, alias
Garnet, the Provinciall of the Iesuits in England, and by Fa. Parsons in
Rome, with their adherents: Against us the Secular Priests their
brethren and fellow Prisoners, that disliked of novelties, and thought it
dishonourable to the auncient Ecclesiasticall Discipline of the
Catholicke Church, that Secular Priests should be governed by Iesuits.*
1601   (STC 1188, AR 65, ERL 24)

440. *Important Considerations, which ought to move all true and sound
Catholikes, who are not wholly Iesuited, to acknowledge without all
equivocations, ambiguities, or shiftings, that the proceedings of her
Maiesty, and of the State with them, since the beginning of her*

*Highnesse raigne, have bene both mild and mercifull. Published by
sundry of us the secular Priests, in dislike of many treatises, letters, and
reports, which have bene written and made in diverse places to the
contrarie: together with our opinions of a better course hereafter, for
the premoting of the Catholike faith in England.* 1601   (STC 25125,
AR 122, ERL 31)

441. *A Sparing Discoverie of our English Iesuits, and of Fa. Parsons
proceedings under pretence of promoting the Catholike faith in
England: For a caveat to all true Catholiks our very loving brethren and
friends, how they embrace such very uncatholike, though Iesuiticall
deseignments.* 1601   (STC 25126, AR 64, ERL 39)

442. *A Dialogue betwixt a Secular Priest, and a Lay Gentleman. Being an
abstract of the most important matters that are in controversie betwixt
the priests and the Spanish or Iesuiticall faction.* 1601   (STC 25124,
AR 553)

(Another edition, published in the same year, is entitled:

*A Dialogue betwixt a Secular Priest, and a Lay Gentleman. Concerning
some points obiected by the Iesuiticall faction against such Secular
Priests, as have shewed their dislike of M. Blackwell and the Iesuits
proceedings.* 1601   (Not in STC, AR 554, ERL 39)

443. *A Decacordon of Ten Quodlibeticall Questions concerning Religion
and State: Wherein the Author framing himself a Quilibet to every
Quodlibet, decides an hundred crosse Interrogatorie doubts, about the
generall contentions betwixt the Seminarie Priests and Iesuits at this
present.* 1602   (STC 25123, AR 883, ERL 197)

444. *An Answere to a Letter of a Iesuited Gentleman, by his Cosin, Maister
A.C. Concerning the Appeale; State, Iesuits.* 1601   (STC 5735, AR
257, ERL 31)

These additional books were all dealt with by Persons in his next
contribution to this controversy, *A Manifestation of the Great Folly*, which
came out in 1602. His original aim was to refute the *True relation* and
Important Considerations while adding 'a brief confutation of a fond
pamphlet set forth in answere to the book of succession', the above
mentioned *Discoverye of a Counterfecte Conference* (429). But before he
could complete his task, five more books had appeared against the Jesuits;
and so he added a seventh chapter dealing with them — complaining that
'every day there come forth and appeare new bookes from them, the later
ever worse and more intollerable then the former'. One of these five is not
listed above, as it has not come down to us in printed form: this was Robert
Fisher's *Memorial against the Jesuits*, itself an attack on Persons' unpublished *Memorial ffor the reformation of Englande*, which was much criticised

by the Appellants under the name of the 'high Counsell of Reformation'. After existing a century in manuscript, Persons' work was published by the Anglican, Dr. Edward Gee, soon after the flight of James II, in 1688, to show his fellow-countrymen the fate from which they had just been delivered.

445. *A Manifestation of the Great Folly and bad spirit of certayne in England calling themselves secular priestes. Who set forth dayly most infamous and contumelious libels against worthy men of their owne religion, and divers of them their lawful Superiors, of which libels sundry are heer examined and refuted. By priestes lyving in obedience.* 1602   (STC 19411, AR 633, ERL 169)

446. *A Memoriall ffor the reformation of Englande Conteyninge Certayne notes and Advertisements wch seeme might be proposed in the first Parliament and National Councell of our country after God of his mercie shall restore it to the Catholique faith for the better establishment and preservation of the said religion. Gathered and set downe by R. P.* 1596   (MS)

(The 1690 edition of Dr. Edward Gee has the following title:

The Jesuit's Memorial, for the Intended Reformation of England, Under their first Popish Prince. Published from the Copy that was presented to the Late King James II. With an Introduction, and some Animadversions, By Edward Gee, Rector of St. Benedict Paul's-Wharf, and Chaplain in Ordinary to Their Majesties. (Wing P 569))

Apart from the books of Persons, only two others appeared in defence of the Jesuits and in protest against the slanders of the Appellants. To his *Relation of Sixtene Martyrs*, published in 1601, the president of Douai, Thomas Worthington, added a declaration 'that English Catholiques suffer for the Catholique Religion, and that the Seminarie Priests agree with the Iesuites' — reserving special words of praise for Persons, who in his short stay in England 'did more good in two yeares, then I think anie of his emulators have donne in twentie'. Also in 1601 appeared *The Copie of a Letter* with the initials S. N., expressing grief at the 'scandalous dissention' and indignation at the 'notorious ingratitude' shown by the priests towards Father Persons for all his indefatigable labours on behalf of the English Mission.

447. *A Relation of Sixtene Martyrs: glorified in England in twelve monethes. With a declaration. That English Catholiques suffer for the Catholique Religion. And That the Seminarie Priests agree with the Iesuites. In answer to our Adversaries calumniations, touching these two points.* 1601   (Not in STC, AR 917, ERL 350)

448. *The Copie of a Letter written to a very worshipful Catholike Gentleman in England, of greif conceaved about some scandalous*

dissention, and bookes set forth, tending to the disgracing one of another, by such as labour in the same cause. By S.N. that dearely loveth them all. 1601 (Not in STC, AR 565, ERL 80)

The replies of Persons, however, only served to provoke further publications from the disaffected priests. Their case was now put forward with notable skill by John Colleton in *A Iust Defence*, which he completed in 1602 shortly after the publication of the *Apologie* and the *Appendix* of Persons – though he was not writing in answer to either of these books. It was from the pen of Dr. Humphrey Ely that an authoritative answer came in the form of *Certaine Briefe Notes*, to which others of the Appellants added their several answers to imputations made against them by Persons. The next year one A. P. (Andreas Philalethes, commonly identified as Robert Charnock) brought out his fuller *Reply to a Notorious Libell* (i.e. the *Apologie*); and to this John Bennett added his reply to the *Appendix*. Under the same pseudonym Charnock had previously published an *Answere* to a letter by Blackwell supporting the Jesuits.

449. *A Iust Defence of the Slandered Priestes: Wherein the reasons of their bearing off to receive Maister Blackwell to their Superiour before the arrivall of his Holines Breve are layed down, and the imputation of disobedience, ambition, contention, scandall, &c., is by able arguments and authorities removed, the obiection of the adverse part sufficiently answered, and the Popes sentence in the controversie truly related. By Iohn Colleton.* 1602 (STC 5557, AR 246, ERL 317)

450. *Certaine Briefe Notes upon a Briefe Apologie set out under the name of the Priestes united to the Archpriest. Drawne by an unpassionate secular Prieste friend to both partyes, but more frend to the truth. Wherunto is added a severall answeare unto the particularites obiected against certaine Persons.* 1602 (STC 7628, AR 291, ERL 171)

(The following pamphlets were added to Ely's *Notes*:

a) *An Answeare unto the particulars obiected in the Apology against Master Doctor Byshope.*
b) *An Answere made by me Charles Paget Esquier, to certayne untruthes and falsityes, tochinge my selfe, contayned in a booke, intitled a briefe Apologie or defence, of the Catholicke Hierarchie & subordination in Englande, & cet.*
c) *An Answear of M. Doctor Bagshaw to certayne poyntes of a libell called, An Apologie of the subordination in England.*)

451. *A Reply to a Notorious Libell, Intituled A Briefe Apologie, or defence of the Ecclesiastical Hierarchie, &c. Wherein sufficient matter is discovered to give all men satisfaction, who lend both their eares to the question in controversie betweene the Iesuits and their adherents on the*

one part, and the Saecular Priests defamed by them on the other part.
Whereunto is also adioyned an answere to the Appendix. 1603 (STC
19056, AR 236, ERL 90)

(The Preface is signed A. P.; and the 'Answere to the Appendix' is
signed J. B.)

452. *An Answere made by one of our brethren, a secular Priest, now in*
prison, to a fraudulent Letter of M. George Blackwels, written to
Cardinall Caietane, 1596, in commendation of the Iesuits in England.
1602 (STC 19830 AR 235, ERL 112)

(The book is signed at the end Andreas Philalethes.)

In response to Persons' *Manifestation* Anthony Copley published two
more of his *Letters* in 1602. In the following year another of the Appellants,
writing under the initials W. C. (probably William Clarke), set forth *A Replie*
unto a certaine Libell (i.e. the *Manifestation*.).

453. *Another Letter of Mr. A. C. to his dis-iesuited kinseman, concerning the*
Appeale, State, Iesuites. Also a third Letter of his, Apologeticall for
himselfe against the calumnies contained against him in a certaine
Iesuiticall libell, intituled, A manifestation of folly and bad spirit, &c.
1602 (STC 5736, AR 258, ERL 100)

454. *A Replie unto a certaine Libell, latelie set foorth by Fa: Parsons, in the*
name of united Priests, intituled, A manifestation of the great folly and
bad spirit, of certaine in England, calling themselves seculer Priestes.
With an addition of a Table of such uncharitable words and phrases, as
by him are uttered in the said Treatise, aswell against our parsons, as
our bookes, actions, and proceedings. 1603 (STC 4321, AR 241, ERL
115)

The Appellants found additional support for their writings in the
neighbouring land of France, where there was considerable animosity against
the Jesuits, not only among the Protestant Huguenots, but also among the
Gallican Catholics. The latter were represented by two eminent lawyers and
members of the Parlement of Paris, Etienne Pasquier and Antoine Arnauld.
Already in 1594 they had both written against the Jesuits, and their books
had immediately been translated into English. Now in 1602 they both
returned to the attack, Pasquier with his *Catechisme des jesuites*, and
Arnauld with his *Franc et Veritable Discours*; and again they were
immediately translated into English, this time through the agency of William
Watson.

455. *The Iesuite displayed. Containing the Original and proceedings of the*
Iesuites, togither with the fruites of their doctrine. Openly discoursed
in an Oration against them made in the Parliament house of Paris, by

> one *Maister Pasquier in that action advocate for the Universitie there, against the Iesuites plaintifes in that Court. Faithfully translated out of French, by E. A.* 1594   (STC 19448)

(The initials are those of Edward Aggas.)

456. *The arrainment of the whole Society of Iesuits in France, holden in the honourable Court of Parliament in Paris, the 12 and 13 of Iuly. 1594. wherein is laied open to the world, that, howsoever this new Sect pretendeth matter of Religion, yet their whole travailes, endevours, and bent, is but to set up the kingdome of Spaine, and to make him the onely Monarch of all the West. Translated, out of the French copie imprinted at Paris by the Kings Printer.* 1594   (STC 779)

457. *The Iesuites Catechisme. Or Examination of their doctrine. Published in French this present yeere 1602. and nowe translated into English. With a Table at the end, of all the maine poynts that are disputed and handled therein.* 1602   (STC 19449, AR 596, ERL 264)

458. *Le franc Discours. A Discourse, presented of late to the French King, in aunswer of sundry requests made unto him, for the restoring of the Iesuits into Fraunce, as well by theyr friends abroad, & at home, as by themselves in divers Petitionarie Bookes. Written in French this present yeere, 1602. and faithfully Englished.* 1602   (STC 780, AR 42, ERL 237)

d) *Protestant reactions*

Meanwhile, the English Protestants were somewhat bewildered by this unusual altercation between the secular priests and the Jesuits, and their reactions were mixed. There were those, on the one hand, who interpreted the whole controversy as a sinister plot of the Papists to obtain toleration for themselves and so to regain their lost strength in the realm. This feeling was first expressed in the anonymous *Humble Motives*, attributed to the Puritan William Bradshaw, and published 'as an antidote against the pestilent treatises of secular Priests'. Two other Puritan pamphlets took issue with Watson's *Quodlibets*, from which they derived their titles: *An Antiquodlibet* and *Let Quilibet Beware of Quodlibet* – the latter being in effect an appendix to the former. The contents of the *Anitiquodlibet* were arranged under four headings, of which the third states 'that the contention betwixt the Iesuit and Secular Priest, being of such nature, and in such degree as is pretended, is a colour and pretext onely'. In his *Catholicon* the Puritan author Andrew Willet likewise saw 'the scope & end of these popish books' as an attempt on the part of the adversaries 'to insinuate themselves to the State, and to perswade a toleration of religion'.

459. *Humble Motives for Association to Maintaine Religion Established.*

Published as an antidote against the pestilent treatises of secular Priests.
Virtus unita valet. 1601   (STC 3518)

460. *An Antiquodlibet, or An Advertisement to beware of Secular Priests.*
1602   (STC 10765 — where the book is impossibly attributed to
Dudley Fenner, who had died long since in 1587.)

461. *Let Quilibet Beware of Quodlibet.* 1602   (STC 20562)

462. *A Catholicon, that is, A generall preservative or remedie against the*
Pseudocatholike religion, gathered out of the Catholike epistle of S.
Iude, briefly expounded, and aptly, according to the time, applied to
more then halfe an hundreth of popish errours, and as many
corruptions of manners. With a Preface serving as a preparative to the
Catholicon, and a dyet prescribed after. 1602 ,   (STC 25673)

The only one of these pamphlets to elicit an answer from the Catholics
was the *Humble Motives.* It was partially answered by Thomas Fitzherbert in
his *Defence of the Catholyke Cause* in 1602, and more fully by an
anonymous author (probably a Jesuit) in *A Briefe Censure* in 1603.

463. [=526] *A Defence of the Catholyke Cause, contayning a Treatise in*
confutation of sundry untruthes and slanders, published by the
heretykes, as wel in infamous lybels as otherwyse, against all english
Catholyks in general, & some in particular, not only concerning matter
of state, but also matter of religion: by occasion whereof divers poynts
of the Catholyke faith now in controversy, are debated and discussed.
Written by T. F. With an Apology, or Defence, of his innocency in a
fayned conspiracy against her Maiesties person, for the which one
Edward Squyre was wrongfully condemned and executed in November
in the yeare of our Lord 1598, wherewith the author and other
Catholykes were also falsly charged. Written by him the yeare
folowing, and not published until now, for the reasons declared in the
preface of this Treatyse. 1602   (STC 11016, AR 310, ERL 146)

(The other controversy in which this book was involved will be dealt
with in the next chapter.)

464. *A Briefe Censure upon the Puritane Pamphlet: Entituled, (Humble*
Motyves, for association to maintayne Religion established.)
Reprooving it of so many Untruthes, as there be leaves in the same.
1603.   (STC 3519, AR 141, ERL 47)

On the other hand, those Protestants who understood the reality of the
situation, such as the renegade priest, Thomas Bell, were filled with glee. In
his *Anatomie of Popish Tyrannie*, published in 1603 as a postscript to the
whole affair, he gave expression to 'that rare conceived ioy, which hath
environed me on everie side'; and he stated his aim 'to couch in a small

volume and portable manuall, the summe & effect of all their bookes, pamphelets, libells, edicts, and letters'. The list of the books he used in this compilation is instructive:

> The Relation; the Sparing discoverie; the Important considerations; the Hope of peace; the Copies of discourses; the Quodlibets; the Dialogue; the answer to the Iesuited gentleman; the Letters of A. C.; the Apologie; the reply to the libell of Parsons the Iesuite; the aunswer to the Apologie, compiled by Master D. Ely; M. Colletons defence; the manifestation of folly; the Replie to the Apologie; the Franke discourse; the Iesuites catechisme.

465. *The Anatomie of Popish Tyrannie: Wherein is conteyned a plaine declaration and Christian censure, of all the principall parts, of the Libels, Letters, Edictes, Pamphlets, and Bookes, lately published by the Secular-priests and English hispanized Iesuites, with their Iesuited Arch-priest; both pleasant and profitable, to all well affected readers.*
   1603   (STC 1814)

That year, however, Queen Elizabeth died; and this strange controversy ended as suddenly as it had begun. Ironically, her last proclamation, dated 5 November 1602, was directed as well against the secular priests, for all their professions of loyalty to her, as against the Jesuits.

466. *By the Queene. A Proclamation for proceeding against Iesuites and Secular Priestes, their Receivers, Relievers, and Maintainers.*
   5 November 1602   (STC 8295)

> (Particular reference is made to the recent 'contention and controversy . . . betwixt the Iesuits and the secular priests combined with them on the one part, and certain of the secular priests dissenting from them in divers points on the other part'.)

CHAPTER 6

Protestant v. Papist

a) *Protestant attacks*

WITH the growing number of seminary priests and Jesuits coming over to England during the '90s there was a corresponding increase both in the numerical strength of English Catholics and in the official persecution against them. There was also an increase in the number of books and pamphlets written by the Protestants against them; but these were mainly left unanswered. The Catholics for the most part relied on the apologetic which had been developed in the past by Harding and Allen, Bristow and Campion, while the priests were trained abroad on the Latin controversial writings of Sanders, Stapleton and Bellarmine, as well as the English notes to the Rheims Testament. For the time being they worked and suffered in silence; but towards the end of the decade they began to give answer to the Protestants. The main theme of the sporadic controversies during this period was the question of the true Church and its four marks – unity, sanctity, universality (or catholicity), and apostolicity. These had notably been claimed by Bristow and others for the Church of Rome; but the Protestants now became increasingly loud in their counter-claim: that they alone were truly Catholic, and that the Papists were heretics. This counter-claim had already been made by Robert Crowley in the '80s. In his *Briefe discourse* (which arose out of a talk with the seminary priest, Everard Hanse, in Newgate) he remarked that the priests 'prevaile by nothing more, then by applying to their schisme, the true notes of the right and true Catholique Church'. Later, in his *Deliberat Answere made to a rash offer*, he aimed at proving 'that the papists that doo nowe call themselves Catholiques are indeed Antichristian schismatiks: and that the religious protestants, are in deed the right Catholiques'. This is also the contention of the anonymous author of *A Letter written by a true christian Catholike*, in which he refutes two Papist propositions: 'the one, that the principles of your doctrine, are grounded firmlie upon the Catholike Church, which antiquitie, universalitie, and consent doe plainelie make manifest unto you. The other, that the signes

given of a true Church by them of the reformed religion . . . are no true
signes of a true Church.'

467. [=165] *A briefe discourse, concerning those foure usuall notes,
whereby Christes Catholique Church is knowen: wherein it appeareth
manifestly, that the Romish Church that nowe is, and that hath bene
almost a thousand yeeres last past, is not, neither hath bene Catholique,
but Schismaticall.* 1581   (STC 6081)

468. [=157] *A Deliberat Answere made to a rash offer, which a popish
Antichristian Catholique, made to a learned protestant (as he saieth)
and caused to be publyshed in printe: Anno Do. 1575. Wherein the
Protestant hath plainly & substantially prooved, that the papists that
doo nowe call themselves Catholiques are in deed Antichristian
schismatiks: and that the religious protestants, are in deed the right
Catholiques: Written by Robert Crowley: in the yeere, 1587.* 1588
(STC 6084)

469. *A Letter written by a true Christian Catholike, to a Romaine pretended
Catholike. Wherein uppon occasion of controversie touching the
Catholike Church the 12. 13. and 14. chap. of the Revelations are
breifly and trulie expounded. Which conteine the true estate thereof,
from the birth of Christ, to the end of the world.* 1586   (STC 15526)

About the same time, there appeared several testimonials to the Protestant
religion from former Catholics who had recanted. Thus William Chauncy
published in 1587 his *Conversion of a Gentleman long tyme misled in
Poperie* – though his conversion was not, in fact, of recent occurrence,
seeing that seven years before he had published *The rooting out of the
Romish Supremacie* against the Pope of Rome. Also in 1588 two priests,
William Tedder and Anthony Tyrrell, pronounced formal recantations of
Romish doctrine at Paul's Cross; though this was not without physical and
moral pressure from the side of their captors.

470. *The Conversion of a Gentleman long tyme misled in Poperie, to the
sincere and true profession of the Gospell of Christ Iesus. Wherunto is
annexed a short repetition of the whole, and an Exhortation to his
good Countrymen in England or elswhere, to embrace this trueth with
all the heavenly doctrine of Christes Religion. Written with his owne
hand as an evident witnesse of his undoubted Resolution, W. C.
Esquire.* 1587   (STC 5102)

471. *The rooting out of the Romish Supremacie. Wherein is declared, that
the authoritie which the Pope of Rome doth challenge to himselfe over
all Christian Bishops and Churches, is unlawfully usurped: contrarie to
the expresse word and institution of our Saviour Iesu Christ: who did
give equall power and authoritie to all the Apostles, Bishops, and*

Ministers of his Church, whereof he is the true corner-stone, and only heade. Set foorth by William Chauncie, Esq. 1580   (STC 5103)

472. *The Recantations as they were severallie pronounced by Wylliam Tedder and Anthony Tyrrell: (sometime two Seminarie Priests of the English Colledge in Rome, and nowe by the great mercie of almightie God converted, unto the profession of the Gospell of Iesus Christ) at Paules Crosse, the day and yeere as is mentioned in their several Tytles of theyr Recantations. With an Epistle dedicatorie unto her Maiestie, and their severall Prefaces unto the Reader, contayning the causes that mooved them to the same.* 1588   (STC 23859)

(The separate recantations have separate titles, as follows:

a) *The Recantation made at Paules Crosse, by William Tedder Seminarie Priest, the first of December, Anno. 1588. Whereunto is adioyned: The recantation or abiuration of Anthonie Tyrell, sometime Prieste of the English Colledge in Rome,) pronounced by himselfe at Paules Crosse the next Sunday following, in the same yeare.*

b) *The Recantation or abiuration of Anthonie Tyrrell: (sometime Priest of the Englishe Colledge in Rome, but nowe by the great mercie of God converted, and become a true professor of his word.) Pronounced by himselfe at Paules Crosse, after the Sermon made by M. Pownall Preacher: the eight of December. 1588.*)

In the aftermath of the Armada the same concern to prove their religion to be the true Church of Christ is apparent in a number of Protestant writings. In 1590 Christopher Shute brought out his *Briefe resolution of a right Religion,* considering how 'great controversie hath long bin betweene the Papistes and Protestantes (as they are commonly tearmed) whether of them be the true church, for it is agreed of both sides, that Extra Ecclesiam non est salus'. In the same year Robert Finch published his *Knowledge or appearance of the Church,* in which he proposed the evident notes of the true Church (of the Protestants) and the false Church (of the Papists).

The next year there appeared a translation from the Latin of a certain Hungarian treatise entitled *The Triall of Trueth,* which proposed a similar means of discriminating between the true and the false.

473. *A Briefe resolution of a right Religion. Touching the controversies, that are nowe in England. Written by C. S.* 1590   (STC 21482)

474. *The knowledge or appearance of the Church, gathered out of the holy Scriptures, declaring and plainly shewing, both the Church that cannot but erre, and also the Church that cannot erre. With so evident notes and manifest signes of either of them, that no man reading it, needeth be in doubt which he should beleve. Written by R. Phinch, and now published in this yeare 1590. for the benefite of all such as desire the truth concerning the church.* 1590   (STC 10878)

475. *The Triall of Trueth or A Treatise wherein is declared who should be Iudge betwene the Reformed Churches, and the Romish: In which is shewed that neither the Pope, nor Councels, nor Fathers, nor Traditions, nor Succession, nor consent, nor antiquitie of Custome: But the onely written worde of God, ought to determine the controversies of religion: wherin also is declared which is the true religion, and Catholick Church. Written for the pleasure of the Popes, Cardinalles, Prelates, Abbats, Monkes, and speciallie the Iesuites, which of late were driven out of Transylvania, by the States there. Published in Latine by a certaine Hungarian, a favourer of the trueth: and translated into English by Richard Smith.* 1591   (STC 24274)

During this time the only book appearing on the Catholic side in this controversy was a translation of a French book by Jean de Caumont, *Du firmament des Catholiques contre l'Abisme des heretiques* (1587). A remark of the author explains the silence of the Catholics: 'There neede not so much disputing, nor so much making of bookes, to confounde the heretikes. Men doe in a manner defile themselves when they examin their doctrine'. He then goes on to give 'Twelve Marckes of the true Church'.

476. *The Firme Foundation of Catholike Religion Against the Bottomlles pitt of heresies, wherein is shewed that onlye Catholikes shalbe saved, and that all heretikes of what sect soever are excluded from the kingdome of heaven. Compyled by Iohn Caumont of Champanye, and translated out of Frenche into Englishe by Iohn Paunchfoot the elder Esquire in the tyme of his banishment.* 1590   (STC 4868, AR 212, ERL 50)

A popular anti-Papist book of this time was Andrew Willet's *Synopsis Papismi*, in which he professed to have 'set downe the bodie and summe of all Popish opinions whatsoever, wherein we dissent from them, and they from the truth'. Following the method of his master, William Whitaker, the great Protestant controversialist at Cambridge, he took for his main target of attack the *Controversies* of Robert Bellarmine, the great Jesuit theologian of the age (560). After first publishing his book in 1592, Willet produced increasingly larger editions in 1594 and 1600. He followed it up with a second volume in 1593, entitled *Tetrastylon Papisticum*, in which he aimed at showing up the contradictions inherent (as he maintained) in Popery. This also went into two more editions during that decade.

477. *Synopsis Papismi, that is, A Generall Viewe of Papistry: wherein the whole mysterie of iniquitie, and summe of Antichristian doctrine is set downe, which is maintained this day by the Synagogue of Rome, against the Church of Christ, together with An Antithesis of the true Christian faith, and an Antidotum or counter-poyson out of the*

Scriptures, against the whore of Babylons filthy cuppe of abominations: Devided into three bookes or Centuries, that is, so many hundreds of Popish heresies and errors. Collected by Andrew Willet Bachelor of Divinity. 1592, 1594, 1600   (STC 25696–98)

478. *Tetrastylon Papisticum, That is, The Foure Principal Pillers of Papistrie, the first conteyning their raylings, slanders, forgeries, untruthes: the second their blasphemies, flat contradictions to scripture, heresies, absurdities: the third their loose arguments, weake solutions, subtill distinctions: the fourth and last the repugnant opinions of New Papisters With the old; of the newe one with another; of the same writers with themselves: yea of Popish religion with and in it selfe. Compiled as a necessarie supplement or fit appertinance to the Authors former worke, intituled Synopsis Papismi: To the glorie of God for the dissuading of light-minded men from trusting to the sandie foundation of poperie, and to exhort good Christians stedfastlie to hold the rockie foundation of faith in the Gospell.* 1593, 1596, 1599   (STC 25701–3)

(The third edition is entitled *Tetrastylon Papismi,* and is said to be 'reviewed againe by the former Author, and inlargd throughout'.)

Other anti-Papist books published in 1593 were John Napier's *Plaine Discovery of the whole Revelation of Saint John*, professedly undertaken 'for preventing the apparant danger of Papistrie within this Iland', and Thomas Bell's *Motives* for abandoning the 'Romish Faith and Religion' after having laboured for ten years as a seminary priest in England. Another seminary priest who recanted in this year was Thomas Clarke, whose *Recantation* was published in 1594.

479. *A Plaine Discovery of the whole Revelation of Saint Iohn: set downe in two treatises: The one searching and proving the true interpretation thereof: The other applying the same paraphrastically and Historically to the text. Set foorth by Iohn Napier L. of Marchistoun younger. Whereunto are annexed certaine Oracles of Sibylla, agreeing with the Revelation and other places of Scriptures.* 1593   (STC 18354)

480. *Thomas Bels Motives: concerning Romish Faith and Religion.* 1593 (STC 1830)

481. *The Recantation of Thomas Clarke (sometime a Seminarie Priest of the English Colledge in Rhemes; and nowe by the great mercie of of God converted unto the profession of the Gospell of Iesus Christ) made at Paules Crosse after the Sermon made by Master Buckeridge Preacher, the first of Iuly, 1593. Whereunto is annexed a former Recantation made also by him in a publique assembly on Easter day, being the 15 of April, 1593.* 1594   (STC 5366)

b) *Catholic responses*

It may have been on the occasion of Bell's lapse from Rome in 1592 that Henry Garnet, superior of the Jesuits in England, returned to the question of attendance at Anglican services. A 'lapsed Catholike', probably Bell, had written a 'Defence of schisme' (in manuscript) to a friend of his; and to this Garnet responded with his *Apology against the Defence of schisme* in 1593. He also dealt with this topic in his *Treatise of Christian Renunciation*, published about this time, adding a special discourse: 'Whether it be lawfull for Catholikes to go to hereticall Churches with a Protestation that they come not for liking which they have of the Religion there professed'. To this *Treatise* was added a *Declaration of the Councell of Trent* on the same subject, as a separate item.

482. *An Apology against the Defence of schisme. Lately written by an English Divine at Doway, for answere to a letter of a lapsed Catholicke in England to his frend: who having in the late Commission gone to the Church, defended his fall. wherin is plainly declared, and manifestly proved, the generall doctrine of the Divines, & of the Church of Christ, which hitherto hath bene taught and followed in England, concerning this pointe.* 1593 (STC 711, AR 353, ERL 167)

483. *A Treatise of Christian Renunciation. Compiled of excellent sentences & as it were diverse homelies of Ancient Fathers: wherin is shewed how far it is lawfull or necessary for the love of Christ to forsake Father, Mother, wife and children, and all other worldly creatures. Against the enemies of the Crosse of Christ, who by temporall respects of obedience or other earthlye bonds, withdraw themselves or others from the confession of their faith and Religion. Whereunto is added a short discourse against going to Hereticall Churches with a Protestation.* 1593 (STC 5189, AR 357, ERL 47)

484. *The Declaration of the Fathers of the Councell of Trent, concerning the going unto Churches, at such time as hereticall service is saied, or heresy preached.* 1593 (STC 24264, AR 357, ERL 47)

Garnet's reasons, derived in large part from Bellarmine's writings, were in turn countered by Francis Bunny, in a book entitled *Truth and Falshood* (1595), with special reference to the situation 'in these North parts' of England. In the same year, the same author went on to draw *A Comparison betweene the auncient fayth of the Romans, and the new Romish Religion*.

485. *Truth and Falshood; Or, A Comparison betweene the Truth now taught in England, and the Doctrine of the Romish Church, with a briefe Confutation of that Popish doctrine. Hereunto is added an Answere to such reasons as the popish Recusants alledge, why they will not come to our Churches. By Francis Bunny, sometime fellow of Magdalen College in Oxford.* 1595 (STC 4102)

486. *A Comparison betweene the auncient fayth of the Romans, and the new Romish Religion. Set foorth by Frauncis Bunny, sometime fellowe of Magdalen College in Oxforde.* 1595   (STC 4098)

About this time a Scottish attack on the Catholics, in the form of *Sermons upon the Sacrament of the Lords Supper*, by Robert Bruce, which had been published in 1590, was answered by William Reynolds of Douai in his *Treatise* on the Eucharist. Subsequently, Reynolds was in turn answered by another Scotsman, Alexander Hume, who wrote his *Diduction* in 1602 both against Reynolds' book and against two *Treatises* on the same subject by his former teacher, John Hamilton.

487. *Sermons upon the Sacrament of the Lords Supper: Preached in the Kirk of Edinburgh be M. Robert Bruce, Minister of Christes Evangel there: at the time of the celebration of the Supper, as they were receaved from his mouth.* 1590   (STC 3924)

488. *A Treatise conteyning the true Catholike and Apostolike Faith of the Holy Sacrifice and Sacrament ordeyned by Christ at his last Supper: With a declaration of the Berengarian heresie renewed in our age: and an Answere to certain Sermons made by M. Robert Bruce Minister of Edinburgh concerning this matter. By William Reynolde Priest.* 1593 (STC 20633, AR 703, ERL 27)

489. *Ane Catholik and Facile Traictise, drauin out of the halie scriptures, treulie exponit be the ancient doctores, to confirme the real and corporall praesence of chrystis pretious bodie and blude in the sacrament of the alter. Dedicat. To his souverane Marie the quenes maiestie of scotland. Be Iohne Hamilton student in theologie, and regent in philosophie to the maist excellent and catholik prince Charles of Bourbon in the royal college of Navarre.* 1581   (STC 12729, AR 370, ERL 61)

490. *A Facile Traictise, Contenand, first, ane infallible reul to discerne trew from fals religion: Nixt, a declaration of the Nature, Numbre, Vertew & effects of the sacrament togider with certaine Prayeres of devotion, Dedicat to his Soverain Prince, the Kings Maiestie of Scotland. King Iames the Saxt. Be Maister Ihone Hamilton Doctor in Theologie.* 1600 (STC 12730, AR 371, ERL 43)

491. *A Diduction of the True and Catholik meaning of our Saviour his words, this is my bodie, in the institution of his laste Supper through the ages of the Church from Christ to our owne dayis. Whereunto is annexed a reply to M. William Reynolds in defence of M. Robert Bruce his arguments in this subject: and displaying of M. Iohn Hamiltons ignorance and contradictions: with sundry absurdities following upon the Romane interpretation of these words. Compiled by Alexander Hume Maister of the high Schoole of Edinburgh.* 1602   (STC 13945)

A minor controversy about this time took place at Worcester between Robert Abbot, who later became Bishop of Salisbury, and Paul Spence, a seminary priest imprisoned in the castle there. Abbot had shown Spence two 'places of Chrysostome and Gelasius' that seemed to tell against the Papist position; and Spence had made an 'Answere to those two places', eliciting a 'Reply against the former answere' from Abbot. Then Spence procured a 'secret cavilling Papist' to write a pamphlet on the Eucharist and Justification in answer to Abbot's Reply, drawing on authorities not available to himself in prison. It was against this pamphlet (which is not otherwise known) that Abbot published his *Mirrour of Popish Subtilties* in 1594, as 'A Defense of the Authorities alleaged in the Replie against the answere of P. Spence'.

492. *A Mirrour of Popish Subtilties: Discovering sundry wretched and miserable evasions and shifts which a secret cavilling Papist in the behalfe of one Paul Spence Priest, yet living and lately prisoner in the Castle of Worcester, hath gathered out of Sanders, Bellarmine, and others, for the avoyding and discrediting of sundrie allegations of scriptures and Fathers, against the doctrine of the Church of Rome, concerning Sacraments, the sacrifice of the Masse, Transubstantiation, Iustification, &c. Written by Rob. Abbot, Minister of the word of God in the Citie of Worcester.* 1594 (STC 52)

c) *More Protestant attacks*

In 1596 Thomas Bell again appeared in print, with a *Survey of Popery*, in which he expressed his disappointment that his earlier *Motives* had been met with silence; but the outcome of this book, too, was the same. Once more, in 1598, he returned to his attack on the Pope in *The Hunting of the Romish Foxe* (a title borrowed from William Turner's *The Hunting of the Romish Wolf*), with a rehash of the arguments of his *Survey* 'for the helpe of the simple vulgar sort'. A similar purpose is apparent in a book that appeared two years later, using a similar metaphor, *A Toile for Two-Legged Foxes* by John Baxter, which was aimed against 'all Popish practises'.

493. *The survey of Popery Wherein the reader may cleerely behold, not onely the originall and daily incrementes of Papistrie, with an evident Confutation of the same; but also a succinct and profitable enarration of the state of Gods Church from Adam untill Christs ascension, contained in the first and second Part thereof: and throughout the third Part Poperie is turned up-side downe.* 1596 (STC 1829)

494. *The Hunting of the Romish Foxe. Presented to the popes holines, with the kisse of his disholy foote, as an odoriferous & redolent posie verie fit for his gravitie, so often as he walketh right stately, in his goodly Pallace Bel-videre.* 1598 (STC 1823)

495. *A Toile for Two-Legged Foxes: Wherein their noisome properties; their*
   hunting and unkenelling, with the duties of the principall hunters and
   guardians of the spirituall vineyard is livelie discovered, for the comfort
   of all her Highnes trustie and true-hearted subiects, and their
   encouragement against all Popish practises. By I. B. Preacher of the
   word of God. 1600   (STC 1596)

The year 1598 was particularly prolific in anti-Papist books; but still no
printed defence was forthcoming from the Catholic side. In addition to Bell's
Hunting of the Romish Foxe, John Racster came out with *A Booke of the*
Seven Planets against the *Seven Motives* of the Catholic poet, William
Alabaster — apparently an exposition of his Catholic faith that was circulat-
ing in manuscipt, but is otherwise unknown. The Puritan, Thomas Wilcox,
also published his *Discourse touching the Doctrine of Doubting*, a book he
had written many years before against 'the darke doctrine of poperie'
concerning justification. On a larger scale, another Puritan, Thomas
Stoughton, 'seeing [as he says] religion everywhere to decay', brought out *A*
Generall Treatise against Poperie. It was also in this year that the Cambridge
Puritan, William Perkins, produced his *Reformed Catholicke*. This was highly
regarded, not only by his fellow-Protestants, but also by his Catholic
adversary in the following reign, William Bishop, who remarked of it: 'I have
not seene any booke of like quantity, published by a Protestant, to contayne
either more matter, or delivered in better method' (Preface to his
Reformation of a Catholike Deformed, 1604). The controversy aroused by
this pamphlet, however, belongs to the reign of James I. For the time being
the Catholics maintained their policy of silence. Finally, mention may here
be made of George Gifford's popular *Country Divinitie*, which had first
appeared in 1581 and 1582, and was now brought out in a third edition for
the common counter-attack against the Papists.

496. *A Booke of the Seven Planets, or Seven wandering Motives, of William*
   Alablasters wit, (Aut mentiuntur papistae,) Retrograded or removed, by
   John Racster. 1598   (STC 20601)

   (Another title-page at the end of the book bears the simpler title:

   William Alablasters Seven Motives, Removed and confuted by John
   Racster.)

497. [= 585] *A Discourse touching the Doctrine of Doubting. In which not*
   onely the principall arguments, that our popish adversaries use, for the
   establishing of that discomfortable opinion, are plainely and truely
   aunswered: But also sundrie suggestions of Sathan tending to the
   maintenance of that in the mindes of the faithfull fully satisfied, and
   that with singuler comfort also. Written long since by T. W. and now
   published for the profit of the people of God. 1598   (STC 25621)

(The context of the composition and publication of this book is obscure; but it may have been published as a defence of orthodox Calvinist doctrine against attacks from within the Anglican Church.)

498. *A Reformed Catholicke; or A Declaration shewing how neere we may come to the present Church of Rome in sundrie points of Religion; and wherein we must for ever depart from them: with an Advertisement to all favourers of the Romane religion, shewing that the said religion is against the Catholike principles and grounds of the Catechisme.* 1598 (STC 19736)

499. *A Briefe discourse of certaine points of the religion, which is among the common sort of Christians, which may be termed the Country Divinitie. With a manifest confutation of the same, after the order of a Dialogue. Compiled by George Gifforde.* 1581, 1582, 1598 (STC 11845–7)

In the following year Gifford published the second edition of his *Dialogue betweene a Papist and a Protestant* (first published 1582), though with less success than his *Country Divinitie*. From the pen of Francis Dillingham came *A Disswasive from Poperie*, listing twelve reasons for rejecting Popery and calling on 'all English Papists whatsoever' to answer his challenge – but he remained unanswered. Also in 1599 Francis Trigge published *A Touchstone*, derived from the Epistle of St. Jude, and claiming the true name of Catholic for the Church of England.

500. *A Dialogue betweene a Papist and a Protestant, applied to the capacity of the unlearned. Made by G. Gifford, Preacher in the Towne of Maldon.* 1582, 1599 (STC 11849)

501. *A Disswasive from Poperie, containing twelve effectual reasons, by which every Papist, not wilfully blinded, may be brought to the truth, and every Protestant confirmed in the same: written by Francis Dillingham Master of Arts, and fellow of Christs Colledge in Cambridge, necessarie for all men in these times.* 1599 (STC 6883)

502. *A Touchstone, whereby may easelie be discerned, which is the true Catholike faith, of all them that professe the name of Catholiques in the Church of Englande, that they bee not deceived: Taken out of the Catholike Epistle of S. Iude.* 1599 (STC 24281)

The turn of the century likewise brought in its quota of anti-Papist books; and they were likewise met with silence by the Catholics. A more conciliatory mood appears in Francis Savage's *Conference betwixt a Mother and her Sonne* – as the intimate relationship between the disputants must have indicated; also in John Dove's *Perswasion to the English Recusants*, published two years later. The latter, indeed, utters a fear lest it seem 'as if I dealt too favourably with the Papists'. He gives an interesting list of the books read by the latter, which partly explains the reason for their silence. There was no need to answer books they were unlikely to read!

> They are contented to buy Campion alone, and Gregory Martine his Preface, with the notes of the Seminaries of Rhemes, upon the New Testament, and now and then to reade them. But as for Doctor Whitaker his answere, many of them suffer it not to be in their studies . . . And as for doctor Fulkes answere to Gregorie Martines Preface, and the notes of the Seminaries . . . they are contented to give more mony for the Rhemish Testament alone, then for the same booke with Doctor Fulkes answer ioyned with it.

503. *A Conference betwixt a Mother a devout recusant, and her Sonne a zealous protestant, seeking by humble and dutifull satisfaction to winne her unto the trueth, and publike worship of god established nowe in England. Gathered by him whose hearts desire is, that all may come to the knowledge of God, and be saved.* 1600   (STC 21781)

(The Dedication is signed Francis Savage.)

504. *A Perswasion to the English Recusants, to Reconcile themselves to the Church of England. Written for the better satisfaction of those which be ignorant. By Iohn Dove Doctor of Divinitie.* 1602   (STC 7084)

Other books published at this time were, however, less conciliatory. In his *Triall of Truth* (1600) John Terry provided what he called 'a preservative for the simple against the poisoned doctrine of the Romish Antichrist'; and he followed this up with a *Second Part* in 1602. Also in 1602 John Rhodes published *An Answer to a Romish Rime*, taking the occasion of 'a Toy in Rime, entituled A proper new Ballad, wherein are certaine Catholike questions (for so he termeth them) to the Protestant' (a work otherwise unknown), to attack 'the doctrine of Antichrist the Pope of Rome'. In the conclusion he refers his readers 'for further satisfaction in this poynt, to M. Crowly his booke, which is an answere in prose to the like questions, printed 1587' (cf. 157, 468). Other anti-Papist books published in 1602 were: Henoch Clapham's *The Catholike Pardon*, a revision and adaptation of an old translation from the French by William Hayward; and Josias Nichols' *Abrahams Faith*, which proposed the paradox that it is the Roman religion which is new and the Protestant which is old.

505. *The Triall of Truth: Containing A Plaine and Short Discovery of the chiefest pointes of the Doctrine of the great Antichrist, and of his adherentes the false Teachers and Heretikes of these last times.* 1600 (STC 23913)

506. *The Second Part of the Trial of Truth: Wherein is set downe the proper fountaine or foundation of all good works, & the fowre principal motives which the spirit of God so often useth in the sacred scriptures*

to perswade thereunto: togither with the contrarietie of the doctrine of the Church of Rome to the same: wherein also are opened not only the causes of all true piety and godlines, but also of all heresie and Idolatry, which is and hath beene among Gentiles and Iewes, and us likewise that are called Christians. By Iohn Terry. 1602   (STC 23913)

(A third part, entitled *Theologicall Logicke: or The Third Part of the Tryall of Truth,* came out many years later in 1625, with no explanation of this long gap in time.)

507. *An Answere to a Romish Rime lately printed: Wherein are contayned Catholike questions to the Protestant. The which Rime was put forth without date or day, name of Authour or Printer, Libell-like, scattered and sent abroad, to withdraw the simple from the fayth of Christ, unto the doctrine of Antichrist the Pope of Rome. Written by that Protestant Catholike, I. R.* 1602   (STC 20959) (See Note below, p. 156)

508. *The Catholike Pardon: given first in Paradise, and sithence newly confirmed by our almightie Father, with many large Privileges, Graunts, and Bulles graunted for ever: As it is to be seene heereafter. Drawne out of French, into English, by William Hayward: and now revised and enlarged, by Henoch Clapham.* 1602   (STC 13013)

(The original version of 1560 was entitled:

The General Pardon, geven long agone, and sythe newly confyrmed by our Almightie Father, with many large Privileges, Grauntes, and Bulles graunted for ever, As it is to be seen hereafter: Drawne out of Frenche into English. By Wyllyam Hayward.   (STC 13012))

509. *Abrahams Faith: that is, The olde Religion. Wherein is taught, that the Religion now publikely taught and defended by order in the Church of England, is the onely true Catholicke, auncient, and unchangeable faith of Gods elect. And the pretensed religion of the Sea of Rome is a false, bastard, new, upstart, hereticall and variable superstitious devise of man. Published by Iosias Nicholls, an humble servant and minister of the gospell in the Church.* 1602   (STC 18538)

d) *The* Watchword *controversy*

In contrast to the silence that greeted all these books from the Catholic side, a vigorous controversy followed on the publication in 1598 of a book entitled *A Watchword to all religious, and true hearted English-men,* by the Puritan knight, Sir Francis Hastings. The author directed his attack not so much against Popish doctrine as against the Papists, emphasising the danger to true Englishmen from 'the raging hearts of Rome and Spaine'. This challenge provoked a strong reply from Robert Persons, who published his

Ward-word in the following year in the form of eight 'encounters' with his adversary. In return, Sir Francis offered another eight 'resistances' in his *Apologie* of 1600. (Here he also refers with satisfaction to 'a booke written by one Iohn Bishop a Recusant Papist, proving that the Pope cannot depose her Maiestie'. This was a posthumous book, which had been published under Protestant auspices against its author's declared will in 1598. It was also used by the Appellants in their controversy with the Jesuits.)

510. *A Watchword to all religious, and true hearted English-men. By Sir Francis Hastings, Knight.* 1598   (STC 12927)

511. *A Temperate Ward-word, to the turbulent and seditious Wach-word of Sir Francis Hastinges knight, who indevoreth to slaunder the whole Catholique cause, & all professors therof, both at home and abrode. Reduced into eight several encounters, with a particuler speeche directed to the Lordes of her Maiesties most honorable Councel. To whome the arbitrement of the whole is remitted. By N. D.* 1599   (STC 19415, AR 639, ERL 31)

512. *An Apologie or Defence of the Watch-word, against the virulent and seditious Ward-word published by an English-Spaniard, lurking under the title of N. D. Devided into eight severall Resistances according to his so many encounters, written by Sir Francis Hastings Knight.* 1600 (STC 12928)

513. *A Courteous Conference with the English Catholickes Romane, about the six Articles ministred unto the Seminarie priestes, wherein it is apparently proved by their owne divinitie, and the principles of their owne religion, that the Pope cannot depose her Maiestie, or release her subiectes of their allegeance unto her. And finally that the Bull of Pius Quintus pronounced against her Maiestie is of no force eyther in lawe or conscience, all Catholicke scruples to the contrarie beeing throughly and perfectly cleared and resolved, and many memoriall matters exactly discussed, which have not beene handled by any man heeretofore. Written by Iohn Bishop a recusant papist.* 1598   (STC 3092)

The Dean of Exeter, Matthew Sutcliffe, now turned from his controversial writings against the Puritans to deal with Persons in *A Briefe Replie*, which he published in 1600 under the disguised initials of O. E. – so as to show up his adversary, N. D., as a 'Noddie'. To this *Replie* Sutcliffe added two other works: *A New Challenge*, including five more encounters with Persons; and *A Briefe Refutation* of another recent book of Persons relating an important conference held in 1600 before the French king between the Huguenot champion, Philip de Mornay, and the Catholic Bishop of Evreux, Jacques du Perron. This conference had originated from the former's treatise on the institution of the Eucharist, as challenged by the latter; and it entered into the English controversy, as Persons gave it as an example of what the Jesuits in England had long been demanding — a public disputation on equal terms between the Catholics and the Protestants. This was, in effect, what Persons and Sutcliffe were now to conduct between themselves, at least in print. In addition to Persons' *Relation*, of which only the second edition of 1604 has survived, another Catholic account of the conference, entitled *A trew discourse*, was published about the same time — translated from the French *Discours veritable de l'ordre et forme* which was attributed to the Bishop of Evreux himself. Also, in addition to Sutcliffe's *Refutation* there appeared *A Discourse of the Conference*, also translated from the French and attributed to the Huguenot champion, de Mornay. At the same time, the latter's treatise on the Eucharist was also published in English translation.

514. *A Briefe Replie to a certaine odious and slanderous libel, lately published by a seditious Jesuite, calling himselfe N. D. in defence both of publike enemies, and disloyall subiects, and entitled A temperate ward-word, to Sir Francis Hastings turbulent watchword: Wherein not only the honest, and religious intention, and zeale of that good Knight is defended, but also the cause of true catholicke religion, and the iustice of her Maiesties proceedings against Popish malcontents and traitors, from divers malitious imputations and slanders cleered, and our adversaries glorious declamation answered, and refuted by O. E. defendant in the Challenge, and encounters of N. D. Hereunto is also added a certaine new Challenge made to N. D. in five encounters, concerning the fundamentall pointes of his former whole discourse: Together with a briefe refutation of a certaine calumnious relation of the conference of Monsieur Plessis and Monsieur d'Evreux before the French king, lately sent from Rome into England; and an answer to the fond collections, and demands of the relator.* 1600 (STC 23453)

(The two additions have separate title-pages with separate pagination, and may therefore be treated separately.)

515. *A New Challenge made to N. D. Wherein O. E. offereth to iustifie, that popish religion is not catholike or apostolike; secondly that it is compounded of divers novelties and haeresies; thirdly that the church of Rome, is not the true church of Christ Iesus. Lastly that such as have died in the popes quarrell, were rather false traitors, then Christian martyrs.* 1600 (Bound with 514 — STC 23453)

516. *A Briefe Refutation of a certaine calumnious relation of the conference passed betwixt the Lord of Plessis Marli, and I. Peron, calling himselfe bishop of Evreux, the fourth of May last, sent from Rome into England, and devised by some idle Iesuite to the slaunder of that noble and vertuous Gentleman, and of true religion, which he professeth. Therein also the relators cogging glosses and commentaries are*

examined, and his petition is answered. 1600   (Bound with 514 – STC 23453)

517. *A Relation of the Triall Made before the King of France, upon the yeare 1600 between the Bishop of Evreux, and the L. Plessis Mornay. About Certayne pointes of corrupting and falsifying authors, wherof the said Plessis was openly convicted. By N. D.* 1600

(The second edition, which alone survives, and which was published in 1604 as an appendix to Vol. II of Persons' *Treatise of Three Conversions*, bears the following addition to the above title: *Newly revewed, and sett forth againe, with a defence therof, against the impugnations both of the L. Plessis in France, and of O. E. in England.*   (STC 19416, AR 637; see ERL 305))

518. *A trew discourse of the order observed in the assemble & meeting made by the leave of the king at Fontainebleau: for the effectuating of the dispute agreed upon, betwixt the Lord Bishoppe of Evreux, and the Sr. of Plessis Mornay, upon Thursday being the 4. of May Anno Domini 1600. In the presence of the Kinges Maiestie, of many Prelates, Princes, Lords, Gentlemen, and other persons of divers qualities; Concerning the falsehoodes which the aforesaid Lord of Evreux had marked in 500 places, cited by the aforesaid Sr. of Plessis in a booke which he lately made & imprinted against the most Blessed Sarcrament of the Alter. Translated out of French.* 1600   (Not in STC, AR 831, ERL 374)

(The French original, dated 1600, is entitled: *Discours veritable de l'ordre et forme qui a esté gardée en l'assemblée faicte a Fontainebleau par le congé du Roy, pour l'effect de la conference accordée entre M. l'evesque d'Evreux et le sieur Du Plessis Mornay.*)

519. *A Discourse of the Conference holden before the French King at Fontain-bleau, betweene the L. Bishop of Evreux, and Mounsieur du Plessis L. of Mornay, the 4. of May 1600. Concerning certaine pretended corruptions of Authors, cyted by the sayd Munsieur du Plessis in his booke against the Masse. Faithfully translated out of the French.* 1600   (STC 6381)

(The French original, attributed by Persons to 'Monsieur Plessis and his Hugonote Ministers' and criticised by him in his second edition of the *Relation*, is entitled: *Discours veritable de la conference tenue à Fontainebleau le quatriesme de may, 1600.*)

520. *Fowre Bookes of the Institution, Use and Doctrine of the Holy Sacrament of the Eucharist in the old Church. As likewise, how, when, And by what Degrees the Masse is brought in, in place thereof. By my Lord Philip of Mornai, Lord of Plessis-Marli; Councellour to the King in his Councell of Estate, Captaine of fiftie men at armes at the Kings*

*paie, Governour of his towne and Castle of Saumur, Overseer of his
house and Crowne of Navarre.* 1600   (STC 18142)

(The French original, published in 1598, is entitled: *De l'institution,
usage et doctrine du sainct sacrament de l'Eucharistie en l'Eglise
ancienne.* A revised edition came out in 1604, and a Latin translation in
1606. In addition to Du Perron, the Jesuit Louis Richeome subjected it
to detailed criticism in his *La saincte messe déclarée et défendue* in
1600.)

Persons now published his reply to Sir Francis' *Apologie* in 1602, entitling
it *The Warn-word to Sir Francis Hastinges Wast-word*; and at the same time
he attacked the 'vaunting minister masked with the letters O. E.' Another
reply to O. E., entitled *A Detection of divers notable untruthes*, came out in
the same year under the opposite initials E. O., in which Sutcliffe recognised
the hand of the seminary priest, Philip Woodward. This book was a Catholic
reply, not only to Sutcliffe's *New Challenge*, but also to Willet's earlier
books, *Synopsis Papismi* and *Tetrastylon Papisticum* (477, 478), each of
which had recently appeared in a third edition. This led to replies both from
Sutcliffe, who issued another *Challenge concerning the Romish Church* that
year, annexing an answer 'to a certeine worthlesse Pamphlet lately set out by
some poore disciple of Antichrist'; and from Willet, who published *A
Retection, or Discoverie of a False Detection* the following year. Another
Catholic response to Sutcliffe's *New Challenge*, entitled *A Brief and Cleere
Confutation*, came out in 1603 under the initials W. R., identified by
Sutcliffe as belonging to 'Walpoole, the ruler of the kitchin or porredge pot
of the colledge of yong English popish traitors in Rome' – i.e. Richard
Walpole, the Minister of the English College under Persons as Rector. At the
end of his book Walpole added 'An Advertisement' on Sutcliffe's further
Challenge concerning the Romish Church, which had only reached him when
his book was 'almost all drawne from the presse'. The continuation of this
controversy, however, belongs to the next reign – and the next volume.

521. *The Warn-word to Sir Francis Hastinges Wast-word: Conteyning the
issue of three former Treatises, the Watch-word, the Ward-word and the
Wast-word (intituled by Sir Francis, an Apologie or Defence of his
Watch-word) togeather with certaine admonitions & warnings to the
said knight and his followers. Wherunto is adioyned a breif reiection of
an insolent, and vaunting minister masked with the letters O. E. who
hath taken upon him to wryte of the same argument in supply of the
knight. There go also foure several Tables, one of the chapters, another
of the controversies, the third of the cheif shiftes, and deceits, the
fourth of the particular matters conteyned in the whole book. By N. D.
author of the Ward-word.* 1602   (STC 19418, AR 642, ERL 302)

522. *A Detection, of divers notable untruthes, contradictions, corruptions,*

*and falsifications. Fathered out of Mr Sutcliffes Newe Challenge, and
Mr. Willets Synopsis Papismi, and Tetrastylon Papisticum. According to
the Platforme of that conference, which passed betwixt the R.
Bishoppe of Evreux, and the Lorde of Plessis, in the presence of the
French King. 1602* (STC 18754, AR 906, ERL 106)

(The Preface is signed with the initials E. O.)

523. *A Challenge concerning the Romish Church, her doctrine & practises,
published first against Rob. Parsons and now againe reviewed, enlarged,
and fortified, and directed to him, to Frier Garnet, to the Archpriest
Blackewell and all their adhaerents, By Matth. Sutcliffe. Thereunto also
is annexed an answere unto certeine vaine, and frivolous exceptions,
taken to his former challenge, and to a certeine worthlesse Pamphlet
lately set out by some poore disciple of Antichrist, and entituled A
detection of divers notable untrueths, contradictions, corruptions, and
falsifications gathered out of M. Sutcliffes new Challenge, &c. 1602*
(STC 23454)

(Each part of the *Challenge* has an inner title of its own:

a) 'A Challenge concerning the malignant church of Antichrist, and
false doctrine, and lewd practises of Papists, Directed to Rob.
Parsons, Frier Garnet, G. Blackwell the Archpriest, and all their
adhaerents.'

b) 'An answere first unto such exceptions, as by a certaine namelesse,
and worthlesse fellow are taken to the Challenge precedent: and next
unto the same parties most idle observations. Thereto also is added a
briefe of certaine notorious falsifications and untruthes of the
Papists.')

524. *A Retection, or Discoverie of a False Detection: Containing a true
defence of two bookes, intituled, Synopsis Papismi, and Tetrastylon
Papisticum, together with the author of them, against divers pretended
untruths, contradictions, falsifications of authors, corruptions of
Scripture, obiected against the said bookes in a certain Libell lately
published. Wherein the uniust accusations of the Libeller, his
sophisticall cavils, and uncharitable slaunders are displayed. 1603*
(STC 25694)

525. *A Brief, and Cleere Confutation, of a new, vaine, and vaunting
Challenge, made by O. E. Minister, unto N. D. Author of the
Ward-word. Wherin Yssue is ioyned upon the five several pointes,
proposed by the Chalenger: and his egregious ignorance, falshood, and
folly, discovered in them all. By W. R. 1603* (STC 19391, AR 874,
ERL 243)

A few more items connected with this controversy appeared before the end of the reign. On the Catholic side, Thomas Fitzherbert published *A Defence of the Catholyke Cause* in 1602 against the accusations of O. E. and of Thomas Diggs (i.e. the *Humble Motives* of William Bradshaw (459)). To it he added an earlier, unpublished work of his, entitled *An Apology*, denying his involvement in the pretended Squire conspiracy of 1598. This *Apology* had been mainly directed against 'a certayne pamphlet printed in England', entitled *A Letter written out of England*, and attributed by some to Sir Francis Bacon. Another Catholic book written on the same occasion was Martin Aray's *Discoverie and Confutation of a Tragical Fiction*, in which reference is also made to the above *Letter*.

526. [=463] *A Defence of the Catholyke Cause, contayning a Treatise in confutation of sundry untruthes and slanders, published by the heretykes, as wel in infamous lybels as otherwyse, against all english Catholyks in general, & some in particular, not only concerning matter of state, but also matter of religion: by occasion whereof divers poynts of the Catholyke faith now in controversy, are debated and discussed. Written by T. F. With an Apology, or Defence, of his innocency in a fayned conspiracy against her Maiesties person, for the which one Edward Squyre was wrongfully condemned and executed in November in the yeare of our Lord 1598. wherewith the author and other Catholykes were also falsly charged. Written by him the yeare folowing, and not published until now, for the reasons declared in the preface of this Treatyse.* 1602   (STC 11016, AR 310, ERL 146)

527. *An Apology of T. F. in defence of himself and other Catholyks, falsly charged with a fained conspiracy agaynst her Maiesties person, for the which one Edward Squyre was wrongfully condemned and executed in the yeare of our Lord 1598. wherein are discovered the wicked, and malicious practises of some inferior persons to whose examination the causes of Catholykes are commonly committed, and their iniurious manner of proceding, not only against the sayd Squyre but also agaynst many Catholykes that have ben uniustly condemned for lyke fayned conspiracies, against her maiesty and the state. Written in the yeare of our Lord 1599. and dedicated to the right honorable the Lords of her mayesties privie councel.* 1602   (STC 11016, AR 310, ERL 146)

(This book is bound with 526, but with separate title-page and pagination.)

528. *A Letter written out of England to an English Gentleman remaining at Padua, containing a true Report of a strange Conspiracie, contrived betweene Edward Squire, lately executed for the same treason as Actor, and Richard Wallpoole a Iesuite, as Deviser and Suborner against the person of the Queenes Maiestie.* 1599   (STC 10017)

529. *The Discoverie and Confutation of a Tragical Fiction, devysed and*

*played by Edward Squyer yeoman soldier, hanged at Tyburne the 23.
of Novemb. 1598. Wherein the argument and fable is, that he should be
sent from Spaine by William Walpole Iesuit, to poyson the Queene and
the Earle of Essex, but the meaning and moralization therof was, to
make odious the Iesuites, and by them all Catholiques. Written for the
only love and zeale of truth against forgerie, by M. A. Preest, that knew
and dealt with Squyer in Spayne.* 1599   (STC 9, AR 35, ERL 71)

On the Protestant side, John Hull published his *Unmasking of the
Politique Atheist* in 1602 as a general attack on the Papists and particularly
on 'Parsons that Iugling Iesuite', and also as a defence of 'the workes of Sir
Francis Hastings and D. Sutlive'. In the following year Thomas Bell again
appeared in print, with two books in one volume: *The Golden Ballance of
Tryall*, which largely repeated the ideas of *The Triall of Trueth* (475); and *A
Counterblast*, in which he takes E. O. to task for the *Detection*. In his
Preface Woodward had confessed his original intention 'to have adioyned, a
reformed brother of theirs, one Thomas Bell', but had decided that Bell's
writings were not worth refuting.

530. *The Unmasking of the Politique Atheist. By I. H. Batcheler of Divinitie.*
1602   (STC 13934)

531. *The Golden Ballance of Tryall. Wherein the Reader shall plainly and
briefely behold, as in a Glasse of Crystall; aswell by what rule all
controversies in Religion, are to be examined, as also who is, and of
what right ought to be the upright Iudge in that behalfe. Whereunto is
also annexed a Counterblast against a masked Companion, terming
himselfe E. O. but supposed to be Robert Parsons the trayterous
Iesuite.* 1603   (STC 1822)

532. *A Counterblast: against the vaine blast of a masked Companion, who
termeth himselfe, E. O. but thought to be Robert Parsons, that
trayterous Iesuite.* 1603   (Bound with 531 – STC 1822)

e) *Calvino-Turcism v. Turco-Papism*

Persons was not, in fact, the first to break the long silence of the Catholics
with his *Ward-word*, since already in 1597 a strong criticism of the
Protestant position, in Latin, had been published in Cologne by William
Reynolds under the provocative title of *Calvino-Turcismus*. His comparison
of the Protestants to the Turks, in retaliation for similar treatment of
Catholics by Protestant authors, had been suggested in an earlier Latin
treatise by Thomas Stapleton, *Speculum Pravitatis Haereticae*, which had
denied any real religion in heretics. In reply, Matthew Sutcliffe cast this
comparison back into the teeth of his adversaries in his *De Turcopapismo* – with special reference to William Gifford, who had merely
completed and edited the work of his colleague (d. 1594).

533. *Speculum Pravitatis Haereticae Per orationes quodlibeticas sex ad oculum demonstratae. Authore Thoma Stapletono Anglo S. Theologiae Doctore & in Alma universitate Duacena Controversiarum Professore Regio & Ordinario.* 1580

(The six theses of Stapleton are as follows:

a) 'Utrum Ecclesiae Romanae religio ab illis hodie reformata fuerit, qui se Ecclesiae reformatores vel Ecclesiam reformatam hodie vocant.'
b) 'Utra sit magis christiana & ecclesiastica liturgiae forma, missa Catholica, an Protestantum quae vocatur Coena dominica.'
c) 'Utrum maior sit in haereticis nostri temporis Nequitia quam Astutia.'
d) 'Utrum horum temporum haereses proximam Antichristo viam parent.'
e) 'Utrum ulla sit in haereticis horum temporum certa & constans doctrina.'
f) 'Utrum ulla prorsus sit in haereticis hodie Religio.')

534. *Calvino-Turcismus, id est, Calvinisticae Perfidiae, cum Mahumetana Collatio, et dilucida utriusque sectae confutatio: Quatuor libris explicata. Ad stabiliendam, S. Romanae Ecclesiae, contra omnes omnium haereses, fidem orthodoxam, accommodatissima. Authore Gulielmo Reginaldo Anglo, sacrae Theologiae quondam in collegio Pontificio Anglorum apud Rhemenses professore.* 1597.

(The Preface is signed Gulielmus Giffordus Anglus.)

535. *De Turcopapismo, Hoc est, De Turcarum & Papistarum adversus Christi ecclesiam & fidem coniuratione, eorumque in religione & moribus consensione & similitudine, Liber unus. Eidem praeterea adiuncti sunt, de Turcopapistarum maledictis & calumniis, adversus Gulielmi Giffordi famosi Pontificum Rom. & Iebusitarum supparasitas trivolumen illud contumeliosissimum, quod ille Calvinoturcismus inscripsit, Libri quatuor. In quibus non tantum huius hominis levissimi, sed etiam aliorum importunissimorum scurrarum adversus orthodoxam Christi ecclesiam continenter latrantium, malitia & petulantia reprimitur, hominumque piorum fama ab eorum calumniis vindicatur.* 1599   (STC 23460)

(The appendix has a separate title-page, which reads:

De Turcopapistarum Maledictis, & Calumniis, adversus Gulielmi Giffordi Calvinoturcismum, libri quatuor.)

The ideas of Reynolds evidently inspired the Catholic priest Thomas Wright in composing his *Certaine Articles or Forcible Reasons*, which was published in two editions in 1600 and a third in 1605, under the initials

'H. T.' Following the syllogistical method advocated many years ago by William Fulke in his *Retentive* (1580) (47, 154) Wright set out to prove five articles: that the Protestants have no faith nor religion; that the learned Protestants are infidels; that all Protestants ignorant of the Greek and Latin tongues are infidels; that the Protestants know not what they believe; and that the Protestants have no means to determine controversies, and abolish heresies. He naturally roused strong indignation among his adversaries, three of whom published replies to him in the next five years. William Barlow, later bishop of Lincoln, came first with his *Defence* in 1601, in which he accused this 'vernacular penman' of having taken the 'pestiferous libels' of Reynolds and Gifford, translated them into English, and 'abbreviated them into a portible libell'. Edward Bulkeley followed with his *Apologie for Religion* in 1602, in which he identified H. T. as Thomas Wright, 'with whose spirit I had been acquainted'. Finally, in response to the third edition of 1605, Anthony Wotton brought out his *Answere to a popish Pamphlet*.

536. *Certaine Articles or Forcible Reasons. Discovering the palpable absurdities, and most notorious and intricate errors of the Protestants Religion.* 1600, 1605   (STC 23618, AR 920–2, ERL 301)

537. *A Defence of the Articles of the Protestants Religion, in aunsweare to a libell lately cast abroad, intituled Certaine Articles, or forcible reasons, discovering the palpable absurdities, and most intricate errours of the Protestantes Religion.* 1601   (STC 1449)

538. *An Apologie for Religion, Or An Answere to an unlearned and slanderous Pamphlet intituled: Certaine Articles, or forcible Reasons discovering the palpable absurdities, and most notorious errors of the Protestants religion, pretended to be printed at Antwerpe 1600. By Edward Bulkley Doctor of Divinitie.* 1602   (STC 4025)

539. *An Answere to a popish Pamphlet, of late newly forbished, and the second time Printed, Entituled: Certaine articles, or forcible reasons discovering the palpable absurdities, and most notorious errors of the Protestants religion. By Anthony Wotton.* 1605   (STC 26002)

f) *More* Reasons *refuted*

The mention of 'articles' and 'reasons' recalls the writings of Bristow, which were in fact reissued about this time: the *Demands* about 1597, and the *Motives* in 1599. Persons' *Briefe Discourse*, with its 'reasons, Why Catholiques refuse to goe to Church', was also reissued in 1599, and again in 1601. Moreover, a new book of the same kind, *A Quartron of Reasons* (where 'quartron' means the fourth part or quarter of hundred), was published in 1600 by Thomas Hill, a seminary priest who later became a Benedictine. This was answered, after a lapse of time, by two Protestant divines – Francis Dillingham of Cambridge, who claimed to have 'unquartered' the *Quartron*, and George Abbot of Oxford, later Archbishop of Canterbury, who claimed to have 'unmasked' Hill's *Reasons*. The latter in particular noted that 'in the yeare 1599 some body thought good to revise their olde trinkets, and for lacke of richer stuffe, out were put these Motives againe printed at Antwerpe', but that 'this honest friend D. Hill, thought he would not leave it so, but the very next yeare after . . . sendeth this script unto us, as if it were some new excellent booke', whereas all is 'taken out of Bristow'.

540. *A Quartron of Reasons of Catholike Religion, with as many briefe reasons of refusall: By Tho. Hill.* 1600   (STC 13470, AR 400, ERL 98)

541. *A Quartron of Reasons, composed by Doctor Hill, unquartered, and prooved a quartron of follies: by Francis Dillingham, Bachelour of Divinitie.* 1603   (STC 6889)

542. *The Reasons which Doctour Hill hath brought, for the upholding of Papistry, which is falselie termed the Catholike Religion: Unmasked, and shewed to be very weake, and upon examination most insufficient for that purpose: By George Abbot Doctor of Divinity & Deane of the Cathedrall Church in Winchester. The first part.* 1604   (STC 37)

(The second part never appeared.)

g) *Latin controversies with Stapleton*

Behind the English controversies others on a more scholarly level, though not without scurrility, were taking place in Latin: notably those between Thomas Stapleton, Professor of Controversy at Douai, and the two Cambridge scholars, William Fulke and William Whitaker; and subsequently those between Robert Bellarmine, the eminent Jesuit theologian in Rome who was created Cardinal in 1599, and almost all the leading Protestant divines in England from 1590 onwards. The first and most outstanding work of Stapleton in these controversies was his *Principiorum Fidei Doctrinalium Demonstratio Methodica*, which came out in many editions from 1578 onwards, and which in turn looks back to Sanders' monumental *De Visibili Monarchia Ecclesiae* (50). To this massive work there was no complete Protestant reply; but in 1579 Fulke published a criticism of two chapters in Book IV, where Stapleton had attacked his *Two Treatises* (1577) (58, 151) containing his reply to Rishton. Stapleton answered Fulke in his 1582 edition of the *Principiorum*, adding a thirteenth book to the original twelve. In reply, Fulke published his treatise *De Successione Ecclesiastica* in 1584.

543. *Principiorum Fidei Doctrinalium Demonstratio Methodica, Per Controversias septem in Libris duodecim tradita. In quibus ad omnes de*

Religione controversias diiudicandas sola & certissima Norma, & ad
easdem semel finiendas sola & Suprema in terris Authoritas, Via & Ratio
demonstrantur. Opus saluberrimum. Authore Thoma Stapletono Anglo,
S. Theologiae Doctore, & in Academia Duacena, Controversiarum
Professore Regio & Ordinario. 1578

544. *Ad Thomae Stapletoni Professoris Regii & Ordinarii in Academia*
Duacena, controversiarum cavillationes & calumnias in sua principiorum
doctrinalium demonstratione methodica, contra satisfactionem ad
Rishtoni postulata quaedam, lib. 4. cap. 10 & 11. adhibitas, Guilielmi
Fulconis Angli Aulae Pembrochianae in Cantabrigiensi Academia
praefecti Responsio. 1579   (STC 11418)

545. *Successionis Ecclesiasticae Defensio Amplior, et Fugitivae ac Latentis*
Protestantum Ecclesiae Confutatio Copiosior. Contra Guilielmi
Fulconis Angli inanes cavillationes, adversus huius operis libri 4. cap. 10
& 11. editas. Liber decimus tertius. 1582

(Book XIII of Stapleton's *Principiorum Fidei Doctrinalium*, added to
the 1582 edition.)

546. *De Successione Ecclesiastica et Latente ab Antichristi tyrannide*
Ecclesia, Liber contra Thomae Stapletoni principiorum fidei
doctrinalium librum decimum tertium: Authore Guilielmo Fulcone
Anglo, Aulae Pembrochianae in Cantabrigiensi Academia Praefecto.
1584   (STC 11429)

It was also partly in answer to Stapleton's work, particularly where it
dealt with the respective authority of Holy Scripture and the Church, that
John Reynolds of Oxford published his *Sex Theses* in 1580. This aim, which
was only implicit in that first edition, became explicit in the titles both of the
English version of 1584, *Six Conclusions . . . With a defense of such thinges*
as Thomas Stapleton and Gregorie Martin have carped at therein, and of the
second Latin edition of 1602, to which is added an 'apologia contra
Pontificios', including Stapleton by name. But there was no controversy
between Stapleton and Reynolds, as there was with Fulke and Whitaker.
(cf. 169–70) It was the latter, William Whitaker, Regius Professor of
Divinity at Cambridge, who now took on Stapleton together with Bellarmine
in his *Disputatio de Sacra Scriptura*, published in 1588. From Stapleton's
work he selected one question, the third Question of the first Controversy,
'De Scripturae authoritate', as a fundamental point at issue between the
Catholics and the Protestants. Stapleton replied in 1592 with his
Authoritatis Ecclesiasticae circa S. Scripturarum approbationem, referring to
Whitaker with respect as an adversary 'neutiquam etiam a nobis negligendus
aut despectui habendus'. Whitaker responded two years later in 1594 with a
Duplicatio; and Stapleton had his answer ready after another two-year

interval, in the form of an appendix to a *Relectio* of his earlier work, entitled *Triplicatio Inchoata adversus Gulielmi Whitakeri . . . Duplicationem.*

547. *Disputatio de Sacra Scriptura, contra huius temporis Papistas, in primis Robertum Bellarminum Iesuitam, Pontificium in Collegio Romano, & Thomam Stapletonum, Regium in Schola Duacena Controversiarum Professorem: Sex Quaestionibus proposita et tractata a Guilielmo Whitakero Theologiae Doctore, ac Professore Regio, & Collegii D. Ioannis in Cantabrigiensi Academia magistro.* 1588 (STC 25366)

548. *Authoritatis Ecclesiasticae circa S. Scripturarum approbationem, adeoque in universum, luculenta & accurata Defensio Libris III digesta. Contra Disputationem de Scriptura Sacra Guilielmi Whitakeri Anglocalvinistae in Academia Cantabrig. Professoris Regii. Authore D. Thoma Stapletono Anglo S. Theologiae Doctore & in Academia Lovaniensi S. Script. Professore Regio.* 1592

549. *Adversus Thomae Stapletoni Anglopapistae in Academia Lovaniensi Theologiae Professoris Regii Defensionem Ecclesiasticae authoritatis, quam ipse luculentam & accuratam inscripsit, tribusque libris digessit, Duplicatio, Pro authoritate atque* αὐτοπιστία *S. Scripturae. Authore Guilielmo Whitakero, S. Theologiae in Academia Cantabrigiensi Doctore ac Professore Regio; & Collegii D. Ioannis Evangelistae in eadem Academia Praefecto.* 1594 (STC 25363)

550. *Triplicatio inchoata adversus Gulielmi Whitakeri Anglo-calvinistae Duplicationem, Pro Ecclesiae Authoritate, Relectioni Principiorum fidei doctrinalium per modum Appendicis adiuncta: Authore Thoma Stapletono, Anglo, S. Theol. Doctore, & in Academia Lovaniensi Professore Regio.* 1596.

   (This was published as an Appendix (with a separate title-page and pagination) to the revised edition of the *Principiorum Fidei doctrinalium*, which bears the altered title:

   Principiorum Fidei doctrinalium Relectio Scholastica & compendiaria. Per Controversias, Quaestiones et Articulos tradita. Accessit per modum Appendicis Triplicatio Inchoata adversus Gulielmum Whitakerum Anglo-calvinistam pro Authoritate Ecclesiae. Opus adversus omnes hereses saluberrimum. Authore Thomae Stapletono Anglo, S. Theol. Doct. et S. Script. in Academia Lovaniensi Professore Regio.)

This controversy was brought to an end by Whitaker's death in 1595; and he was shortly followed by Stapleton in 1598. Subsequently, however, a posthumous work of Whitaker was edited by his disciple John Allenson and published in 1600, a treatise in three books *De Peccato Originali*, attacking an earlier work of Stapleton, *De Universa Iustificationis Doctrina*, which had been published at Paris in 1582.

551. *De Universa Iustificationis Doctrina hodie controversa. Libri duodecim. In quibus Christi gratia, & hoc ipsum quo Christiani sumus (Iustitia nostra) contra varias horum temporum haereses solide defenditur, & Ordine explicatur. Authore Thoma Stapletono, S. Theologiae Doctore, & in Academia Duacena, Controversiarum Professore Regio & Ordinario.* 1582

(The first three chapters, attacked by Whitaker, are as follows:

I. 'De Peccato originali in se.'
II. 'De Corruptione naturae per peccatum originale invecta.'
III. 'De Concupiscentia, seu relicta corruptione, in Renatis.')

552. *Tractatus Doctissimi Viri Guilielmi Whitakeri, nuper Sacrae Theologiae in Academia Cantabrigiensi Doctoris & Professoris Regii, & Collegii Scti Ioannis Evangelistae in eadem Academia Praefecti, De Peccato Originali. In tres libros distributus, adversus tres primos libros Thomae Stapletoni de universa Iustificationis doctrina hodie controversa. Editus opera et cura Ioannis Allenson Sacrae Theologiae Baccalaurei & Collegii praedicti socii.* 1600   (STC 25370)

Stapleton was also prolific in other Latin writings directed more generally against the heresies of the age. These consisted for the most part of a series of commentaries on the Epistles and Gospels, variously entitled *Promptuaria* and *Antidota*, for the different seasons of the liturgical year, with a view to preparing priests to deal with the heresies of the time in their sermons. Since they were not aimed against any Protestant author in particular, they elicited no work in refutation of them.

553. *Promptuarium Morale super Evangelia Dominicalia Totius Anni. Ad Instructionem Concionatorum, Reformationem Peccatorum, Consolationem Piorum. Ex Sacris Scripturis, SS Patribus, & optimis quibusque authoribus studiose collectum: Authore Thoma Stapletono, Anglo. S. Theol. Doctore & Regio Professore Lovanii. Pars Hyemalis.* 1591. *Pars Aestivalis* 1591.

554. *Thomae Stapletoni Angli, S. Theologiae Doctoris, et Professoris Regii Lovanii. Promptuarium Catholicum. Ad instructionem Concionatorum contra haereticos nostri temporis. Super omnia evangelia totius anni tam dominicalia quam de festis. In quo inveniet concionator, unde ex litera Evangelica, vel plerasque haereses apte refutet, vel contra haereticorum hodie fraudes & mendacia fidem Catholicam praetextu Evangelii plausibiliter ab illis impugnatam solide defendat.* 1592

(To this were also added:

a) *Promptuarii Catholici super Evangelia de Festis Sanctorum totius anni. Pars secunda.* 1592

b) *Promptuarium Catholicum, Super Evangelia Ferialia in totam Quadragesimam. 1594)*

555. *Antidota Evangelica contra horum temporum haereses. In quibus Quatuor Evangeliorum illi textus explicantur, quibus vel haeretici hodie (maxime Calvinus et Beza) ad sua dogmata propugnanda uti solent, vel ad haereticorum dogmata impugnanda Catholici uti possunt. Authore Thoma Stapletono Anglo, S. Theolog. Doctore, et S. Scripturarum in Academia Lovaniensi professore Regio. 1595*

556. *Antidota Apostolica contra nostri temporis haereses: In quibus loca illa explicantur, quae haeretici hodie (maxime Calvinus & Beza) vel ad sua placita stabilienda, vel ad Catholicae Ecclesiae dogmata infirmanda, callide & impie depravarunt. In Acta Apostolorum: Tomus I. 1595*

   In Epistolam B. Pauli ad Romanos: Tomus II. 1595
   In duas B. Pauli Epistolas ad Corinth. Tomus III. 1598
   Authore Thoma Stapletono Anglo, S. Theol. Doctore, & in Academia Lovaniensi S. Scripturarum Professore regio.

Mention should also be made of Stapleton's biographical work on the *Tres Thomae* (St. Thomas the Apostle, St. Thomas of Canterbury and Sir Thomas More); for this, too, had an essentially controversial aim. Finally, after his death he left a posthumous work, *Vere Admiranda*, on the greatness of the Roman Church, as a continuation of his *Antidota Apostolica*: it was published in 1599. Later on, his works were gathered together and published in his *Opera omnia* at Paris in 1620.

557. *Tres Thomae seu De S. Thomae Apostoli rebus gestis. De S. Thoma Archiepiscopo Cantuariensi & Martyre. D. Thomae Mori Angliae quondam Cancellarii Vita. His adiecta Oratio Funebris in laudem R. P. Arnolde de Ganthois Abbatis Marchennensis. Authore Thoma Stapletono Anglo S. Theolog. Doctore. 1588*

558. *Vere Admiranda, seu De Magnitudine Romanae Ecclesiae Libri duo. Auctore Thoma Stapletono Anglo, S. Scripturarum nuper in Academia Lovaniensi Professore Regio ac Primario. 1599*

559. [= 93] *Thomae Stapletoni Angli, Sacrae Theologiae Doctoris, et Professoris Regii, Duaci primo, deinde Lovanii Opera quae extant omnia, nonnulla auctius et emendatius, quaedam iam antea Anglice scripta, nunc primum studio & diligentia Doctorum virorum Anglorum Latine reddita. In quatuor tomos distributa, quorum Elenchum Pagina decima-nona indicabit. 1620*

h) *Latin controversies with Bellarmine*

Even more influential than Stapleton's controversial writings were those of the great Jesuit theologian, Robert Bellarmine, who had held the chair of controversial theology at the Gregorian University in Rome since 1576. The lectures which he gave there on almost every aspect of the controversies of the time were eventually published in three large tomes in 1586, and reissued at the rate of almost a new edition every year over the next decade at Ingolstadt, Lyons and Paris. These *Disputationes De Controversiis Christianae Fidei* at once became a target for attack by Protestant scholars in many countries, including England.

560. *Disputationes Roberti Bellarmini Politiani, Societatis Iesu, De Controversiis Christianae Fidei, adversus huius temporis haereticos, Tribus Tomis comprehensae.* 1586

(The contents of each volume are as follows:
'Tomus Primus. Controversia prima, De Verbo Dei scripto, et non scripto.
II. De Christo capite totius Ecclesiae.
III. De summo Pontifice capite militantis Ecclesiae.
IV. De Ecclesia militante, tum in Conciliis congregata, tum sparsa toto orbe terrarum.
V. De membris Ecclesiae militantis, Clericis, Monachis, Laicis.
VI. De Ecclesia quae est in Purgatorio.
VII. De Ecclesia quae triumphat in coelis.
Tomi Secundi Controversiae generales quinque.
I. De Sacramentis in genere.
II. De Baptismo.
III. De Eucharistia.
IV. De Poenitentia.
V. De Sacramentis ceteris.
Tomi Tertii Controversiae generales tres.
I. De gratia primi hominis, & statu innocentiae.
II. De gratiae amissione, & statu peccati.
III. De gratiae reparatione, & statu iustificatorum per Christum.)

The most pertinacious of Bellarmine's opponents in England was Matthew Sutcliffe, who wrote successive treatises *De Purgatorio* in 1590, *De Catholica Ecclesia* in 1592, *De Pontifice Romano* in 1599, *De Vera Christi Ecclesia*, *De Conciliis* and *De Monachis* in 1600 and *De missa papistica* in 1603.

561. *Matthaei Sutlivii adversus Roberti Bellarmini de Purgatorio disputationem, Liber unus.* 1590   (STC 23449)

562. *Matthaei Sutlivii De Catholica, Orthodoxa, et Vera Christi Ecclesia, Libri duo: In quorum primo pseudoecclesiae Romanae speciosa ecclesiae Catholicae persona, qua multos miseros mortales multos iam annos ludificata est, detrahitur: in secundo orthodoxa per Angliam, Germaniam, Scotiam, Galliam, & alios regiones in una fide consentiens ecclesia a Bellarmini, Sanderi, Rossaei, Alani, Ulenbergii, Bozii, Rescii,*

Verstegani & reliquorum Pontificiae ecclesiae propugnatorum calumniis vindicatur: In utroque omnis illa Bellarmini de notis ecclesiae disputatio, eiusdemque, & reliquorum contumeliosissima, & mendacissima in ecclesiam nostram, ecclesiaeque nostrae nonnullos claros viros scripta, imagines, & convitia varie sparsa refelluntur. 1592 (STC 23455)

563. *Matthaei Sutlivii De Pontifice Romano, eiusque iniustissima in Ecclesia dominatione, adversus Robertum Bellarminum, & universum Iebusitarum sodalitium, libri quinque.* 1599 (STC 23457)

564. *Matthaei Sutlivii De Vera Christi Ecclesia adversus Rob. Bellarminum, aliosque sectae Iebusiticae sodales, eorumque errores & haereses, Liber unus.* 1600 (STC 23462)

565. *Matthaei Sutlivii De Conciliis, & eorum authoritate, adversus Robertum Bellarminum, & bellos eiusdem sodales Libri duo.* 1600 (Bound with 564 − STC 23462)

566. *Matthaei Sutlivii de Monachis, eorumque institutis & moribus, adversus Robertum Bellarminum, universamque monachorum & mendicantium fratrum colluviem disputatio.* 1600 (Bound with 564 − STC 23462)

567. *Matthaei Sutlivii De missa papistica, variisque synagogae Rom. circa Eucharistiae sacramentum erroribus & corruptelis. Adversus Robertum Bellarminum, & universum Iebusaeorum & Cananaeorum sodalitium. Libri quinque: Quorum primus de reali praesentia, secundus de transubstantiatione, tertius de sacrificio missae, quartus de missis privatis & communione sub una specie, ultimus de missae caerimoniis & partibus controversias tractat.* 1603 (STC 23456)

More scholarly, and more highly respected by Bellarmine himself, were the lectures of Whitaker at Cambridge, which were published after his death by the care of John Allenson: *De Ecclesia* in 1599, and *De Conciliis* in 1600. To these may be added the above-mentioned *Disputatio de Sacra Scriptura*, which was primarily written against Bellarmine and was the first book of its kind to be published in England. In his Dedication Whitaker expressed his own admiration of Bellarmine, as 'virum sane doctum, ingenio faelice, iudicio subtili, lectione multiplici praeditum, qui soleret etiam apertius ac simplicius agere quam reliqui consueverunt Papistae, & argumentum pressius urgeret, & arctius ad causam adhaeresceret'.

568. [= 586] *Praelectiones Doctissimi Viri Guilielmi Whitakeri, nuper Sacrae Theologiae in Academia Cantabrigiensi Doctoris et Professoris Regii, et Collegii S. Ioannis Evangelistae in eadem Academia Praefecti. In quibus tractatur Controversia de Ecclesia contra Pontificios, imprimis Robertum Bellarminum Jesuitam, in septem Quaestiones distributa, quas sequens pagina indicabit. Exceptae primum ab ore authoris, deinde cum aliis exemplaribus collectae, & post eius mortem ad breves illius*

Annotatiunculas examinatae. Opera et cura Ioannis Allenson, Sacrae Theologiae Baccalaurei, et Collegii praedicti socii. His accessit eiusdem Doct. Whitakeri ultima concio ad Clerum, una cum descriptione vitae & mortis, Authore Abdia Assheton Lancastrensi, sacrae Theologiae Baccalaureo, & eiusdem Collegii Socio, quam sequuntur carmina funebria. 1599 (STC 25368)

569. *Praelectiones Doctissimi Viri Guiliemi Whitakeri nuper Sacrae Theologiae in Academia Cantabrigiensi Doctoris & Professoris Regii, & Collegii S. Ioannis Evangelistae in eadem Academia Praefecti. In quibus tractatur Controversia de Conciliis contra Pontificios, imprimis Robertum Bellarminum Iesuitam, in sex Quaestiones distributa, quas pagina sequens indicabit. Editae opera & cura Ioannis Alenson sacrae Theologiae Baccalaurei & Collegii praedicti Socii. His adiecta est in fine alia eiusdem Praelectio alterius argumenti, coram multis Nobilissimis viris, & plurimis Generosis habita.* 1600 (STC 25367)

Another eminent English theologian to cross swords with Bellarmine at this time was the Puritan scholar, John Reynolds, President of Corpus Christi College, Oxford. In 1596 he published his *De Romanae Ecclesiae Idololatria* against the Jesuit theologians, Robert Bellarmine and Gregory of Valencia. This was in some measure answered by Edward Weston, a professor at Douai, in his *De Triplici Hominis Officio* in 1602. From Cambridge Francis Dillingham attacked Bellarmine with his *Disputatio Brevis* in 1602, and his *Tractatus Brevis* in 1603. Also in 1603 Robert Abbot directed the argument of his widely admired *Antichristi Demonstratio* chiefly against Bellarmine. During these years two books attacking Bellarmine in English were: Francis Bunny's *Survey of the Pope's Supremacie* in 1595; and George Downham's *Treatise concerning Antichrist* in 1603.

570. *Johannis Rainoldi, De Romanae Ecclesiae Idololatria, in cultu sanctorum, reliquiarum, imaginum, aquae, salis, olei, aliarumque rerum consecratarum, & sacramenti Eucharistiae, operis inchoati Libri duo. In quibus cum alia multa variorum Papismi patronorum errata patefiunt: tum imprimis Bellarmini, Gregoriique de Valentia, calumniae in Calvinum ac ceteros Protestantes, argutiaeque pro Papistico idolorum cultu discutiuntur & ventilantur.* 1596 (STC 20606)

571. *De Triplici Hominis Officio, ex notione ipsius Naturali, Morali, ac Theologica; Institutiones orthodoxae, contra Atheos, Politicos, Sectarios. Authore Odovardo Westono Anglo, S.T.D. et in collegio Anglorum Duaci Professore.* 1602

572. *Disputatio Brevis et Succincta de Duabus Quaestionibus, viz. De Limbo Patrum, et De Comparatione Petri cum Paulo adversus Robertum Bellarminum: Per Franciscum Dillinghamum Baccalaureum in Theologia.* 1602 (STC 6081)

573. *Tractatus Brevis, in quo ex praecipuorum Papistarum, imprimis ipsius Bellarmini Confessione, multa Protestantium dogmata, iustissima esse concluduntur. Per Franciscum Dillinghamum Baccalaureum in Theologia. In calce huius operis reperies lector tractatum de Iohanna Papissa adversus Bellarmini sophismata conscriptum.* 1603   (STC 6892)

574. *Antichristi Demonstratio, contra Fabulas Pontificias, & ineptam Roberti Bellarmini de Antichristo disputationem. Authore Roberto Abbotto, Oxoniensi, olim a Collegio Baliolensi, sacrae Theologiae professore.* 1603   (STC 43)

575. *A Survey of the Popes Supremacie: Wherein is a triall of his title, and a proofe of his practises: and in it are examined the chiefe arguments that M. Bellarmine hath for defence of the said supremacie, in his bookes of the bishop of Rome. By Francis Bunny sometime fellow of Magdalene Colledge in Oxford.* 1595   (STC 4101)

576. *A Treatise concerning Antichrist, divided into two bookes, the former, proving that the Pope is Antichrist: the latter, maintaining the same assertion, against all the obiections of Robert Bellarmine, Iesuit and Cardinall of the Church of Rome. By George Downame, Doctor of Divinitie, and lately reader of the Divinity Lecture in Paules.* 1603 (STC 7120)

The principal controversy involving Bellarmine with English divines, however, was yet to come — in the reign of James I, who himself took a leading part in it.

NOTE

The *Romish Rime* criticized by John Rhodes (507) may have been that appended to the second edition of Gregory Martin's *Love of the soule*, which was published about this time (undated):

> *The love of the soule Made by G. Mar. Whereunto are annexed certaine Catholike questions to the Protestants.* [1602?]   (STC 17505, AR 527, ERL 363 [= AR 530])

These questions are presented in verse form, and are probably not by Martin himself.

CHAPTER 7

Puritan v. Protestant

a) *Predestination v. Free-will*

DURING the reign of Queen Elizabeth the name of 'Puritan' was associated rather with liturgical and political than with doctrinal issues. The Puritans (as they came to be called in the '70s, out of the Whitgift–Cartwright controversy) differed from the other Protestants in England by reason of their increasing demand, first, for purer forms of worship than those prescribed in the *Book of Common Prayer*, and second, for a purer form of Church government than that accepted in the religious settlement of 1559. The official doctrine of the Anglican Church, as stated in the Thirty-Nine Articles of 1562 and explained in the two volumes of *Homilies* published in 1547 and 1563, was received no less by the Puritans than by the other Protestants. Moreover, the theology of Calvin, as distinct from his ecclesiastical polity in Geneva, was received no less by the other Protestants than by the Puritans. There were, indeed, some things, if not in the Thirty-Nine Articles, at least in the *Homilies*, especially the obligation to read them in church instead of preaching a free sermon (without special licence), to which the Puritans took strong exception. They were also characterised by their enthusiastic and uncritical support for the theological ideas of Calvin; whereas other Protestant theologians came to subject not only the polity, but also the theology of Geneva – both of Calvin himself and of his successor, Theodore Beza – to criticism. The main point on which this theology was most open to criticism, and on which the Calvinists had already come into opposition not only with Catholics, but also with Lutherans, was Calvin's emphasis on absolute predestination by God, without respect to human merit. Under the guidance of Puritan theologians, such as William Whitaker and Laurence Chaderton at Cambridge, Laurence Humphrey and John Reynolds at Oxford, this doctrine came to be generally accepted as the orthodox teaching of the Elizabethan Church. So when it was eventually challenged at Cambridge by William Barrett in 1595, it was authoritatively formulated in the *Lambeth Articles* of that year, as drawn up by William Whitaker and other Cambridge divines, and accepted with modifications by John Whitgift, Archbishop of Canterbury. But the Queen refused to impose such points of abstract theology on the acceptance of her subjects; and so the *Articles* remained a dead letter. Instead, they came to represent the high-water mark of Calvinist orthodoxy in England, from which the tide of Anglican theological opinion swiftly receded in favour of an increasingly humanistic, or Arminian, interpretation of Scripture, allowing for a measure of human cooperation in the work of divine salvation. The existence of a controversy on this subject within the Elizabethan Church appears however, as early as 1566, when Robert Crowley published his *Apologie* for the doctrine of predestination against an otherwise unknown work 'set abroade by one that hath no name'. The title of this work – whether by a Protestant or a Catholic is uncertain – is given by Crowley as follows:

> *The copie of an Aunswere, made unto a certaine letter: wherein the Aunswerer purgeth himselfe and other, from Pelagius errours, and from the errour of free will or iustification of workes: wherewithall he semeth to be charged, by the sayde letter: And further he sheweth, wherin he differeth in iudgement, from certaine English writers and Preachers, whome he chargeth with the teaching of false doctrine, under the name of Predestination.*

Crowley himself subscribed his name to the *Apologie*, which appeared in two editions in the same year; though he significantly refrained from doing so in his (presumed) challenge to Archbishop Parker, published in the same year under the title of *A briefe discourse* (98).

577. *An Apologie, or Defence, of those Englishe Writers & Preachers which Cerberus the three headed Dog of Hell, chargeth with false doctrine, under the name of Predestination. Written by Robert Crowley Clerke, and Vicare of Sainct Giles without Creplegate in London.* 1566 (STC 6076–7)

The first open opposition to Calvinist orthodoxy came, however, many years later, towards the end of the '70s, from a Frenchman at Cambridge, Peter Baro, who had come to England from Geneva and had been appointed Lady Margaret Professor of Divinity in 1574 – a chair that had but recently been filled by Thomas Cartwright. He maintained the thesis that 'Gods purpose and decree taketh not away the libertie of mans corrupt will'; and this was published in 1579, as an Appendix to his *Praelectiones in Ionam Prophetam*. An English translation was published several years later by John Ludham, as an Appendix to Andreas Gerardus' *Treatise of Gods Providence*. In 1580 he published similar ideas in his treatise *De Fide*, which was the substance of a lecture given at Cambridge on *Romans* 3. 28. His editor, Osmund Lake, admits that it may seem to depart from the officially received opinion, but maintains that this is not really the case: 'Cui si vulgo recepta opinio primo aspectu visa sit reclamare: re tamen propius animadversa, nihil hic proponi intelligant omnes, quod vel a recepta sententia dissideat, vel Christianam pietatem non maxime promoveat'. At the time, his thesis was opposed by Laurence Chaderton; but no published answer appeared till 1592, when a book with the same title, *De Fide*, came out against Baro under the initials 'E. H.' The author laments the fruit of unsound doctrine, whose seeds he says were sown by Baro twelve years before: 'En tibi Baro vociferationis tuae fructum, cuius tu semina abhinc duodecennium ... sparsisti'.

578. *Petri Baronis Stempani, Sacrae Theologiae in Academia Cantabrigiensi Doctoris ac Professoris, in Ionam Prophetam Praelectiones 39. In quibus multa pie docteque disseruntur & explicantur. Adiecta sunt etiam, & alia quaedam eiusdem Authoris, quae sequens Pagina indicabit. Opera et studio Osmundi Laki Cantabrigiensis, e Regio Collegio Ministri, & ab Authore ipso recognita.* 1579   (STC 1492)

(The contents of the Appendix are as follows:

'3 Conciones ad Clerum Cantabrigiensem habitae, in Templo D. Mariae. 1. in Psalmum 233 integrum, 2. in Psalmum 15 integrum, 3. in Jacob cap. 2, a versu 14 ad finem 17. 2 Theses, publice in Scholis peroratae & disputatae. 1. Dei Decretum non tollit pravae Voluntatis libertatem. 2. Nostra cum Christo Coniunctio tota est Spiritualis. 2 Precationes, quibus usus est Author in suis Praelectionibus inchoandis & finiendis Item, alius doctissimi cuiusdam viri Tractatus adversus Missam & Transubstantiationem Papistarum.')

579. *A speciall Treatise of Gods Providence, and of comforts against all kinde of crosses & calamities to be fetched from the same. With an exposition of the 107. Psalme. Heerunto is added an appendix of certaine Sermons & Questions, (conteining sweet & comfortable doctrine) as they were uttered and disputed ad Clerum in Cambridge. By P. Baro, D. in Divi. Englished by I. L. Vicar of Wethers-fielde.* [1588?]   (STC 11760)

(The Appendix is introduced by a separate title-page:

Fower Sermons and two Questions. As they were uttered and disputed ad Clerum in S. Maries Church and Schooles in Cambridge. By that learned Frencheman P. B. D. of Divinitye. And Englished by I. L.

The Questions are also introduced by a title-page of their own:

Two Theames or Questions, handled and disputed openly in the schooles at Cambridge, in the Latin tung, by P. Baro, Doctor of Divinitye and Englished by I. L.)

580. *De Fide, Eiusque Ortu, & Natura, plana ac dilucida Explicatio. (ceu) P. Baronis Stempani sacrae Theologiae in Academia Cantab. Doctoris ac Professoris, Praelectio, in Cap. 3. ad Rom. vers. 28. Adiecta sunt alia quaedam eiusdem Authoris, de eodem Argumento, quae sequens Pagina indicabit.* 1580   (STC 1489)

581. *De Fide, Eiusque Ortu et Natura. Contra P. Baronis Stempani, Theologiae in Academia Cantab. professoris, praelectionem. In Cap. 3 ad Rom. vers. 28. Per E. H. servum Domini Iesu Christi.* 1592   (STC 12563)

Baro's fullest statement on the subject of Predestination appeared in a treatise *De Praedestinatione,* which was completed in 1594, but not published till 1613 – when it was printed by his adversaries in conjunction with the contrary opinions of such eminent Calvinist divines as Junius, Piscator and Whitaker. It was also on this occasion that the *Lambeth Articles* were published for the first time, though they had been drawn up long before in 1595. In that year a disciple of Baro, William Barrett, had preached a controversial sermon at St. Mary's Church in Cambridge on the certainty of salvation – with strong criticism of the doctrine of Calvin and Beza on this point. After his sermon (on 29 April) he found himself opposed by Whitaker and Chaderton, who made him recant his statements on 10 May. He was, however, supported not only by Baro himself, but also by Lancelot Andrewes, Master of Pembroke, and John Overall, soon to become Regius Professor of Divinity in succession to Whitaker (who died later that year). It was as a result of this controversy that the *Lambeth Articles* were drawn up and approved by Whitgift; but because the Queen refused to give them her royal sanction, they remained unpublished till 1613. Subsequently, they were again published in a very different context, with the addition of comments by both Andrewes and Overall, and an introductory history of the *Articles* attributed to John Cosin.

582. *Petri Baronis Summa Trium de Praedestinatione Sententiarum. Cum Clarissimorum Theologorum, D. Iohannis Piscatoris ad eam Notis et D. Francisci Iunii ad eandem disquisitione ac denique D. Guilihelmi Whitakeri Praelectione adversus universalem gratiam: & Concione de Praedestinatione, divinae gratiae Constantia ac certitudine salutis. Quibus accedunt Assertiones orthodoxae seu Articuli Lambethani: approbati ab Archiepiscopis aliisque Angliae Episcopis Anno 1595.* 1613

583. *Articuli Lambethani: Id est, I. Articulorum Lambethae exhibitorum Historia. II. Articuli de Praedestinatione, & annexis capitibus a D. Whitakero Lambethae propositi. III. Iidem prout ab Episcopis Theologisque concepti & admissi. IV. Lanceloti Andrewes Wintoniensis Episcopi, de Synodo oblatis Articulis Judicium; una cum ejusdem*

Censura Censurae D. Barreti, de Certitudine Salutis. Quibus annexa est
V. Sententia D. Overal Theologiae in Academia Cantabrigiensi
Professoris olim Regii, de Praedestinatione. 1651   (STC 15183, Wing L
3890)

In spite of the *Lambeth Articles*, Baro went on to preach a university
sermon on 12 January 1596, on the subject of grace and reprobation; and in
letters he sent shortly afterwards to Lord Burleigh and Archbishop Whitgift,
he explained his sermon, distinguishing between the antecedent or condi-
tional will and the consequent will of God with regard to salvation. This
distinction had already been made by Richard Hooker in an important
sermon he had preached at Paul's Cross in 1581 at the invitation of John
Aylmer, Bishop of London; and it was soon after repeated in the same place
by Samuel Harsnet in 1584. The former sermon has only come down to us
indirectly in an account by Izaak Walton in his *Life of Hooker*; but the latter
was published many years later as an Appendix to *Three sermons* of Richard
Stuart in 1656. It was of Hooker's sermon in 1581 that Travers reported in
his *Supplication made to the Privy Counsel* in 1586 (published in 1612) that
his rival 'had taught certain things concerning predestination otherwise than
the word of God doth, as it is understood by all churches professing the
gospel' (396). Hooker gave a fuller explanation of his position on this matter
in his *Fragments of an Answer to the Letter of certain English Protestants*
(i.e. the anonymous *Christian Letter*), which were not published till 1836.
At the end of these *Fragments* he gives his own version of the *Lambeth*
Articles, from which he significantly omits that on the individual's certainty
of his salvation. As for Baro, he was supported in his position by Overall,
who had just succeeded Whitaker as Regius Professor, and now came to lead
the counter-attack on Calvinism at Cambridge. Barrett, however, left England
for the continent in 1597, where he became a Catholic. It was probably as a
contribution to this controversy that Wilcox's *Discourse touching the*
Doctrine of Doubting, written long since against the Papists, was now
published in 1598. In the following year – the year of Baro's death in
London, whither he had retired from Cambridge – Whitaker's final oration
as Regius Professor, in which he had particularly dwelt on the subject of
Predestination, was published under the title of *Cygnea Cantio*, together
with his lectures *De Ecclesia* against Robert Bellarmine.

584. *A sermon preached at S. Pauls Cross in London, the 27. day of*
     October, Anno Reginae Elizabethae 26. by Samuel Harsnet then Fellow
     of Pembroke Hall in Cambridg, but afterwards Lord Arch-Bishop of
     Yorke. 1656

(Published as Appendix to:

Three sermons Preached by the Reverend, and Learned, Dr. Richard
Stuart, Dean of St. Pauls, afterwards Dean of Westminster, and Clerk of

161

the Closset to the late King Charles. To which is aded, A fourth
sermon, Preached by the Right Reverend Father in God, Samuel
Harsnett, Lord Arch-Bishop of Yorke. (Wing S 5526))

585. [= 497] *A Discourse touching the Doctrine of Doubting. In which not
onely the principall arguments, that our popish adversaries use, for the
establishing of that discomfortable opinion, are plainely and truely
aunswered: But also sundrie suggestions of Sathan tending to the
maintenance of that in the mindes of the faithfull fully satisfied, and
that with singuler comfort also. Written long since by T. W. and now
published for the profit of the people of God. 1598.* (STC 25621)

586. [= 568] *Cyngea Cantio Guilielmi Whitakeri, hoc est, ultima illius
concio ad clerum habita Cantabrigiae in templo Beatae Mariae, paulo
ante mortem. Octob. 9. Dom. 1595.* 1599

(Published as Appendix to:

*Praelectiones Doctissimi Viri Guilielmi Whitakeri, nuper Sacrae
Theologiae in Academia Cantabrigiensi Doctoris et Professoris Regii,
et Collegii S. Ioannis Evangelistae in eadem Academia Praefecti. In
quibus tractatur Controversia de Ecclesia contra Pontificios, imprimis
Robertum Bellarminum Jesuitam, in septem Quaestiones distributa,
quas sequens pagina indicabit. Exceptae primum ab ore authoris,
deinde cum aliis exemplaribus collatae, & post eius mortem ad breves
illius Annotatiunculas examinatae. Opera et cura Ioannis Allenson,
Sacrae Theologiae Baccalaurei, et Collegii praedicti socii. His accessit
eiusdem Doct. Whitakeri ultima concio ad Clerum, una cum
descriptione vitae & mortis, Authore Abdia Assheton Lancastrensi,
sacrae Theologiae Baccalaureo, & eiusdem Collegii Socio, quam
sequuntur carmina funebria. 1599* (STC 25368))

Meanwhile, another champion of Calvinist orthodoxy had appeared in the
person of Whitaker's disciple, William Perkins. In his earliest book, the
Armilla Aurea (which went into two Latin editions in 1590 and 1591, before
being translated into English by Robert Hill as *A Golden Chaine*), he dealt
with 'the order of the causes of Salvation and Damnation'. Also in the
Epistle prefixed to the English translation he denounced the 'newe
Pelagians', who 'place the cause of Gods Predestination in man: in that they
hold, that God did ordeine men either to life or death, according as he did
foresee, that they would by their naturall free will, either reject or receive
grace offered'. Later, in 1596, he preached a sermon at St. Mary's Church in
Cambridge against the opinions of Baro and Overall; and in 1598 he
developed his ideas in a Latin treatise, *De Praedestinationis Modo et Ordine*,
which was translated into English in 1606. This was subsequently attacked
by Arminius himself; and Perkins (now dead) was defended by his disciple,
John Yates. The rest of this controversy belongs to the Arminian

controversy, which spread from the Low Countries to England particularly subsequent to the Council of Dort in 1618.

587. *Armilla Aurea, id est, miranda series causarum et salutis & Damnationis iuxta verbum Dei: Eius Synopsin continet annexa Tabula.* 1590   (STC 19655)

588. *A Golden Chaine, or The Description of Theologie, containing the order of the causes of Salvation and Damnation, according to Gods woord. A view of the order wherof, is to be seene in the Table annexed. Written in Latin by William Perkins, and Translated by an other. Hereunto is adioyned the Order which M. Theodore Beza used in comforting troubled consciences.* 1591   (STC 19657)

589. *De Praedestinationis Modo et Ordine: et de Amplitudine Gratiae Divinae Christiana & perspicua disceptatio.* 1598   (STC 19682)

590. *A Christian and plaine treatise of the manner and order of Predestination, and of the largenes of Gods grace. First written in Latine by that Reverend and faithfull servant of God, Master William Perkins, late Preacher of the Word in Cambridge. And carefully translated into English by Francis Cacot, and Thomas Tuke.* 1606 (STC 19683)

591. *Iacobi Arminii Veteraquinatis Batavi, S. Theologiae Doctoris eximii, Examen Modestum Libelli, quam D. Gulielmus Perkinsius apprime doctus Theologus, edidit ante aliquot annos De Praedestinationis modo & ordine, itemque de Amplitudine gratiae divinae. Addita est propter argumenti convenientiam Analysis Cap. IX ad Roman. ante multos annos ab eodem ipso D. Arminio delineata. Cum indice rerum contentarum.* 1612

592. *Gods Arraignement of Hypocrites: with an Inlargement concerning Gods decree in ordering sinne. As likewise a Defence of Mr. Calvine against Bellarmine; and of Mr Perkins against Arminius.* 1615   (STC 26081)

b) *The Article of Christ's descent*

Another point of doctrinal difference that emerged in the '90s between Protestant and Puritan concerned the article in the Apostles' Creed about Christ's descent into hell. On this point Calvin had taught that the literal interpretation which had prevailed in the Middle Ages was altogether unnecessary, and that a figurative interpretation was required: namely, that in his soul Christ had suffered the pains of hell while hanging on the cross; in his body he was buried in the earth (or hell) after having been taken down from the cross. As early as 1552 this thesis had been publicly defended at

Cambridge by Christopher Carlile. Ten years later, in 1562, it was criticised – with special reference to Calvin and Carlile – by the Catholic theologian Richard Smith, from his place of exile in Louvain. Carlile eventually published his thesis in 1582, under the title of *A Discourse, Concerning two divine Positions*. In the same year there appeared the second edition of John Northbrooke's *Breefe and pithie summe of the christian faith*, which had first been published in 1571. In this book he had undertaken to prove that 'all the souls of the righteous, that died before Christes commyng in the fleshe, were in heaven, and not in any Purgatorie, Limbo, or Hell. That christes soule should not neede to goe downe thither to fetch them out . . . that his soule (departyng from his bodie) wente straight into heaven, and not into hell, the place of the dampned'. But as he had been widely criticised for his apparent denial of an article of the Creed, he altered the Preface in his second edition and devoted it to 'an apologie or defence' of his position, as explained in the 4th, 5th and 6th chapters of his book.

593. [= 89] 'Refutatio luculentae, crassae, & exitiosae, haeresis Ioannis Calvini, & Christophori Carlili, Angli, qua astruunt Christum non descendisse ad inferos alios, quam ad infernum infimum, qui est locus damnatorum perpetuus, aut ad sepulchrum.' In *Confutatio eorum, quae Philippus Melanchthon obijcit contra Missae sacrificium propitiatorium. Autore Ricardo Smythaeo Wigorniensi, Anglo, Sacrae Theologiae Professore, Lovanii. Cui accessit & repulsio calumniarum Ioannis Calvini, & Musculi, & Ioannis Iuelli, contra Missam, eius canonem, & Purgatorium, denuo excusa.* 1562

594. *A Discourse, Concerning two divine Positions. The first effectually concluding, that the soules of the faithfull fathers, deceased before Christ, went immediately to heaven. The second sufficientlye setting foorth unto us Christians, what we are to conceive, touching the descension of our Saviour Christ into Hell: Publiquely disputed at a Commencement in Cambridge, Anno Domini 1552. Purposely written at the first by way of a confutation, against a Booke of Richard Smith of Oxford, D. of Divinity, entituled a Refutation imprinted 1562. & published against Iohn Calvin, & C. Carlile: the title wherof appeareth in the B page. And now first published by the said Christopher Carlile, 1582.* 1582   (STC 4654)

595. *Spiritus est Vicarius Dei in terra. A breefe and pithie summe of the christian faith, made in fourme of a confession, with a confutation of the papistes obiections and argumentes in sundry points of religion, repugnaunt to the christian faith: made by Iohn Northbrooke, Minister and Preacher of the worde of God.* 1571, 1582   (STC 18663–4)

(Ch. 4: 'Of Christs burial, and the profite we have gotten thereby.'
Ch. 5: 'How many waies this worde [hell] is taken in Scripture, and after what maner Christe descended into hell.'

Ch. 6: 'Reasons and argumentes of those that holde, that Christ went
downe to hell in his soule: Answered.')

It was not, however, till the early '90s that this became a subject of
controversy within the Anglican Church. On 28 February 1590, an Oxford
divine, Adam Hill, preached a sermon at Chippenham in Wiltshire on the
article of Christ's descent into hell; and he was taken up in a private letter by
a Scottish schoolmaster, Alexander Hume. Thereupon Hill published his
Defence of the Article in 1592, dedicating it to the Archbishop of
Canterbury with a complaint that 'divers Ministers ... very often preach
against the true interpretation of this branche of our Creed', and that they
'do upon this occasion strive more bitterly one against another, than either
of both do against our common adversary'. The following year Hume
published his *Reioynder*, printing his original letter, together with the text of
Hill's reply, and upholding Calvin's teaching that after his death on the cross
Christ went straight to heaven in his soul.

596. *The Defence of the Article: Christ descended into Hell. With*
Arguments obiected against the truth of the same doctrine: of one
Alexander Humes. All which reasons are confuted, and the same
doctrine cleerely defended. By Adam Hyll, D. of Divinity. 1592 (STC
13466)

597. *A Reioynder to Doctor Hil concerning the Descense of Christ into Hell.*
Wherein the Answere to his Sermon is iustlie defended, and the roust of
his reply scraped from those arguments as cleanlie, as if they had never
bene touched with that canker. By Alexander Hume, Maister of Artes.
Heere, besides the Reioynder, thou hast his Paralogismes: that is, his
fallacies and deceits in reason pointed out, and numbered in the
margin: amounting to the nomber of 600, and above; and yet not half
reckoned. 1593 (STC 13948)

The next development in this protracted controversy came with some
sermons preached by Thomas Bilson, newly made Bishop of Winchester, at
Paul's Cross and elsewhere in London, defending the Patristic teaching on
Christ's descent into hell. The substance of these sermons he later published
in 1599, under the title *The effect of certaine Sermons touching The Full*
Redemption of mankind. Here he complained of 'some conceited and too
much addicted to novelties, who spared not in their Catechisings and
readings, to urge the suffering of the verie paines of Hell in the soul of Christ
on the crosse, as the chiefest part, and maine ground of our Redemption by
Christ'. But before his book was published, he found his sermons refuted by
a Puritan minister, Henry Jacob, in *A Treatise of the Sufferings and Victory*
of Christ, which appeared in 1598. On his side, Jacob complained that 'of
late great iniury hath bene done by no meane Prelate, to this poinct of
christian veritie, in such wise as no Protestant hath ever done the like

heretofore, neither hath brought more offence to the godly, or disquietnes to the Churches in England'. This led Bilson to add his criticisms of Jacob's *Treatise*, both to his Preface 'to the Christian Reader' and in a lengthy 'Conclusion to the Reader, for the cleering of certaine obiections made against the doctrine before handled', which took up 140 pages. To 'this new doctrine sprung up from Winchester' (as he called it) Jacob replied in 1600 with *A Defence of a Treatise*, maintaining that Bilson's teaching had been 'never heard of before in England (but only in the dayes of Popery)'. Bilson's answer did not appear till four years later, in the beginning of the new reign, under the title of *The Survey of Christs Sufferings*.

598. *The effect of certaine Sermons touching The Full Redemption of mankind by the death and bloud of Christ Iesus: wherein Besides the merite of Christs suffering, the manner of his offering, the power of his death, the comfort of his Crosse, the glorie of his resurrection, Are handled, What paines Christ suffered in his soule on the Crosse: Together, With the place and purpose of his descent to hel after death: Preached at Paules Crosse and else where in London, by the right Reverend Father Thomas Bilson Bishop of Winchester. With a conclusion to the Reader for the cleering of certaine obiections made against the said doctrine.* 1599   (STC 3064)

599. *A Treatise of the Sufferings and Victory of Christ, in the work of our redemption: Declaring by the Scripturs these two questions: That Christ suffered for us the wrath of God, which we may well terme the paynes of Hell, or Hellish sorrowes. That Christ after his death on the crosse, went not into Hell in his Soule. Contrarie to certaine errours in these points publiklie preached in London: Anno 1597.* 1598   (STC 14340)

(The book is signed H. I.)

600. *A Defence of a Treatise touching the Sufferings and Victorie of Christ in the Worke of our Redemption. Wherein is confirmed, 1. That Christ suffered for us, not only Bodily griefe, but also in his Soule an impression of the proper wrath of God, which may be called the paines of Hell. 2. That after his death on the Crosse he went not downe into Hell. For Answere to the late writings of Mr. Bilson, L. Bishop of Winchester, which he initleth, The effect of certaine sermons, &c. Wherein he striveth mightily against the doctrine aforesaid. By Henry Iacob, Minister of the worde of God.* 1600   (STC 14333)

601. *The Survey of Christs Sufferings for Mans redemption: and of his Descent to Hades or Hel for our deliverance: By Thomas Bilson Bishop of Winchester. Perused and allowed by publike Authoritie.* 1604   (STC 3070)

Jacob was further supported in his defence of Calvin by two well-known Puritan scholars of the time. Already in 1595 William Perkins had presented his interpretation of 'the descension of Christ' in his *Exposition of the Symbole or Creed of the Apostles*, where he expressed the view as 'very likely', that 'Christ Iesus when he was dying upon the crosse, felt and suffered the pangs of hell and the full wrath of God seazing upon his soule'. Subsequently, he was taken to task by John Higgins who published *An Answere to Master William Perkins* on this point.

602. *An Exposition of the Symbole or Creed of the Apostles, according to the Tenour of the Scriptures, and the consent of Orthodoxe Fathers of the Church: By William Perkins.* 1595   (STC 19703)

603. *An Answere to Master William Perkins, concerning Christs Descension into Hell: By John Higins.* 1602   (STC 13442)

The other scholar was the eccentric Hugh Broughton, who now came out with a series of learned disquisitions on the precise significance of the Hebrew Sheol, the Greek Hades and the English Hell. He directed his writings in particular to Archbishop Whitgift, who had encouraged Bilson in his sermons and books on the subject, blaming him 'for turning the Q. auctority against her owne faith' in an elaborate *Explication of the Article* which only survives in its second edition of 1605. He was answered in 1599 by an anonymous writer, who accused Broughton of 'the fume of envie, and the fome of vanitie', for having chosen 'the most Reverend father the L. Archbishop of Canterbury to launce and cut' with his sharp style. The same writer also speaks of 'Doctor Andrewes having, in a Sermon upon that article, strongly out of Scripture and Fathers confirmed the descent'; and of 'that great controversie twixt D. R. [Doctor Reynolds, of Oxford] and your selfe'. The latter controversy was a very one-sided affair, in which Reynolds remained silent, while Broughton brought out a series of highly eccentric pamphlets on the computation of time in the Old Testament, before becoming involved in the controversy over Christ's descent into hell. He now went on to address two more criticisms of Bilson to the Archbishop, though in more deferential terms: a *Declaration of generall corruption of Religion* (which had, in his opinion, been brought about by Bilson's sermon), and *Two little workes defensive of our Redemption*, dedicated 'to the aged Sir, Iohn of Canterb. Archbishop' – in the very year of his death, 1604. Subsequently, on the publication of Bilson's *Survey*, he returned to the subject of the word Hades in two more pamphlets, one directly replying to 'the r. R. F. Th. Winton', and the other generally appealing to 'the BB. of England.

604. *An Explication of the Article* κατῆλθεν εἰς ᾅδου, *of our Lordes soules going from his body to Paradise; touched by the Greek, generally* ᾅδου, *The world of Soules; termed Hel by the old Saxon, & by all our*

translations: with a defence of the Q. of Englands religion: To, &
against the Archb. of Canterbury: who is blamed for turning the Q.
auctority against her owne faith. Sundry Epistles are prefixed &
affixed. by H. Br. The second edition, wherein the Typographicall falts
of the former are amended. 1605   (STC 3863)

605. *Master Broughtons Letters, Especially his last Pamphlet to and against
the Lord Archbishop of Canterbury, about Sheol and Hades, for the
descent into Hell, answered in their kind. 1599   (STC 3864)*

606. *Declaration of generall corruption of Religion, Scripture and all
learning; wrought by D. Bilson. While he breedeth a new opinion, that
our Lord went from Paradise to Gehenna, to triumph over the Devills.
To the most reverend Father in God Iohn Wh. Doct. in Divinitie, and
Metropolitan of England. By Hugh Broughton. 1603   (STC 3855)*

607. *Two little workes defensive of our Redemption, That our Lord went
through the veile of his flesh into Heaven, to appeare before God for us.
Which iourney a Talmudist, as the Gospell, would terme, a going up to
Paradise: But heathen Greeke, a going down to Hades, and Latin,
Descendere ad inferos. Wherein the unlearned barbarous anger God and
man, saying, That Iesus descended to Hell: and yeelde unto the
blasphemous Iewes by sure consequence upon their words, That he
should not be the Holy one of God. By Hugh Broughton. 1604   (STC
3892)*

608. *A Replie upon the r. R. F. Th. Winton for heads of his divinity in his
Sermon and Survey: How he taught a perfect truth, that our Lord went
hence to Paradise: But adding that he went thence to Hades, & striving
to prove that, he injurieth all learning & Christianitie. To the most
noble Henry Prince of Great Britany. 1605   (STC 3881)*

609. *Positions of the Word Hades: That it is the generall place of Soules: and
holdeth as well the Godly which are in Paradise, as the wicked that are
in Tartarus. With a Catalogue of our heresies, from which one word
handled by a right Grecian would have saved us. To the BB. of England.
By Hugh Broughton. 1605   (STC 3879)*

c) *Possession and exorcism*

Another controversy, of a more practical and sensational nature, which arose
between some Puritans and the established Church towards the end of the
century, was over the question of possession and dispossession by devils. A
Puritan preacher in Nottingham, John Darrell, claimed to have successfully
exorcised certain individuals possessed by the devil through the power of
God's word. He further narrated the manner of his exorcisms in *A Breife
Narration*, published in 1598. This led to widespread controversy as to

whether the cases described by him were genuine cases of possession or not; since the general Protestant opinion, in opposition to that of the Catholics (who had also claimed success in exorcising devils earlier, in the '80s), was that 'miracles are ceased'. Darrell was therefore summoned to Lambeth, and subjected to cross-examination and trial. Out of this situation he produced two more books in 1599: one, an account of his trial, with his answer to the various allegations made against him, and dedicated to the Lord Chief Justice, Sir John Popham; and the other, *A brief apologie*, dedicated to 'the most reverend Iudges of the Common Lawes of Englande'. There is another, undated pamphlet by Darrell, entitled *An Apologie*, which deals with the same subject-matter as the preceding: namely, the particular case of the possession of William Somers in Nottingham, which was the main point at issue in the trial.

610. *A Breife Narration of the possession, dispossession, and, repossession of William Sommers; and of some proceedings against Mr. John Dorrell preacher, with aunsweres to such obiections as are made to probe the pretended counterfeiting of the said Sommers. Together with certaine depositions taken at Nottingham concerning the said matter.* 1598 (STC 6281)

611. *The Triall of Maist. Dorrell, or A Collection of Defences against Allegations not yet suffered to receive convenient answere. Tending to cleare him from the Imputation of teaching Sommers and others to counterfeit possession of Divells. That the mist of pretended counterfetting being dispelled, the glory of Christ his royal power in casting out Divels, at the prayer and fasting of his people, may evidently appeare.* 1599   (STC 6287)

612. *A brief apologie proving the possession of William Sommers. Written by Iohn Dorrell, a faithfull Minister of the Gospell: but published without his knowledge. With a Dedicatorie Epistle, disclosing some disordered procedings against the saide Iohn Dorrell. Quod in religionem committitur, in omnium fertur iniuriam.* 1599   (STC 6282)

613. *An Apologie, or defence of the possession of William Sommers, a yong man of the towne of Nottingham. Wherein this worke of God is cleared from the evil name of counterfaytinge; and thereupon also it is shewed that in these dayes men may be possessed with Devils, and that being so, by prayer and fasting the uncleane spirit may be cast out. By John Darrell Minister of Christ Jesus.* [1599?]   (Not in STC; but in British Library, shelfmark: 8632. bbb. 49)

The champion of Anglican orthodoxy against Darrell's claims was Samuel Harsnet, chaplain to the Bishop of London, and later to become Archbishop of York. He now published *A Discovery of the Fraudulent practises of Iohn*

Darrell in 1599. In the following year Darrell replied with his *Detection*, in which he remarks that 'the name & sound of Darrell, or his imprisonment, and the cause therof, hath in a manner possessed & overspread the whole land'. Also in 1600 he went on to give *A True Narration* of his experiences; and to this he joined a theoretical justification of *The Doctrine of the Possession and Dispossession of Demoniakes*, which is often referred to as a separate work — it has separate pagination, but no separate title-page.

614. *A Discovery of the Fraudulent practises of Iohn Darrell Bacheler of Artes, in his proceedings Concerning the pretended possession and dispossession of William Somers at Nottingham: of Thomas Darling, the boy of Burton at Caldwell: and of Katherine Wright at Mansfield, & Whittington: and of his dealings with one Mary Couper at Nottingham, detecting in some sort the deceitfull trade in these latter dayes of casting out Devils.* 1599   (STC 12883)

615. *A Detection of that sinnful, shamful, lying, and ridiculous discours, of Samuel Harshnet, entituled: A Discoverie of the Frawdulent Practises of Iohn Darrell. Wherein is manifestly and apparantly shewed in the eyes of the world, not only the unlikelihoode, but the flate impossibilitie of the pretended counterfayting of William Somers, Thomas Darling, Kath. Wright, and Mary Couper, togeather with the other 7. in Lancashire, and the supposed teaching of them by the saide Iohn Darrell.* 1600   (STC 6283)

616. *A True Narration. Of the strange and grevous vexation by the devil, of 7. persons in Lancashire, and of William Somers of Nottingham. Wherein the doctrine of possession and dispossession of demoniakes out of the word of God is particularly applyed unto Somers, and the rest of the persons controverted: togeather with the use we are to make of these workes of God.* 1600   (STC 6288)

In the following year, 1601, there appeared two more books against Darrell by joint authors, John Walker and John Deacon. In the first they dealt more generally with the 'late-bred broyles not long since brewed & broached at Nottingham' as publicly reported in print, in the form of *Dialogicall Discourses*. In the second they gave *A Summarie Answere* to Darrell's books, with special reference to the *Doctrine* and the *Detection*. To each of these books Darrell published his reply in the following year: in *A Survey of Certaine Dialogical Discourses*, and in *The Replie of Iohn Darrell*. He thus succeeded in having the last word in this controversy; and it was not till 1617 that he again took up his pen, this time in defence of the English Church against the separatists.

617. *Dialogicall Discourses of Spirits and Divels. Declaring their proper essence, natures, dispositions, and operations: their possessions, and dispossessions: with other the appendantes, peculiarly appertaining to*

those speciall points. Verie conducent, and pertinent to the timely procuring of some Christian conformitie in iudgement; for the peaceable compounding of the late sprong controversies concerning all such intricate and difficult doubts. By Iohn Deacon, Iohn Walker. Preachers. 1601   (STC 6439)

618. *A Summarie Answere to al the material points in any of Master Darel his bookes. More especiallie to that one booke of his, intituled, the Doctrine of the Possession and Dispossession of Demoniaks out of the word of God. By Iohn Deacon. Iohn Walker. Preachers.* 1601   (STC 6440)

619. *A Survey of Certaine Dialogical Discourses: written by Iohn Deacon, and Iohn Walker, concerning the doctrine of Possession and Dispossession of Divels. Wherein is manifested the palpable ignorance and dangerous errors of the Discoursers, and what according to proportion of God his truth, every Christian is to hold in these poyntes. Puplished by Iohn Darrell minister of the gospell.* 1602   (STC 6285)

620. *The Replie of Iohn Darrell, to the Answer of Iohn Deacon, and Iohn Walker, concerning the doctrine of the Possession and Dispossession of Demoniakes.* 1602   (STC 6284)

By way of postscript to this controversy, Harsnet went on to turn his criticisms against the Papists, in connection with a similar controversy over the exorcisms practised by a group of Jesuits and seminary priests in the '80s. These had been recorded in an unpublished *Book of Miracles*, compiled by their leader, William Weston or Edmonds; but the controversy had not emerged in print – save (perhaps) indirectly in a book mentioned above (474), Robert Finch's *Knowledge or appearance of the Church* (1590). The *Book of Miracles* had recently been discovered by the authorities, in the course of a search made in the house of 'one Ma. Barnes a Popish recusant'. This was now the occasion of Harsnet's *Declaration of egregious Popish Impostures*, which produced no reaction from the Catholic side, though it provided Shakespeare with material for his characterisation of Edgar as a mad beggar in *King Lear*.

621. *A Declaration of egregious Popish Impostures, to with-draw the harts of her Maiesties Subiects from their allegeance, and from the truth of Christian Religion professed in England, under the pretence of casting out devils. Practised by Edmunds, alias Weston a Iesuit, and divers Romish Priests his wicked associates. Where-unto are annexed the Copies of the Confessions, and Examinations of the parties themselves, which were pretended to be possessed, and dispossessed, taken upon oath before her Maiesties Commissioners, for causes Ecclesiasticall.* 1603   (STC 12880)

(The Dedication 'to the Seduced Catholiques of England' is signed 'S. H.')

d) *The later Brownists*

In spite of their disapproval of many aspects of the established Church, the majority of Puritans remained substantially within her communion. This was the consistent policy of Cartwright, as he had expressed it in his *Letter* to Harrison in the early '80s (143). There had always been a few – Browne and Harrison on that occasion, Barrow and Greenwood in the early '90s and now Francis Johnson in the late '90s – who had chosen the path of separation and exile from home or imprisonment. But they had found no less opposition from among their fellow-Puritans (who took this opportunity of demonstrating their loyalty) than from the Anglican bishops. An adherent of Barrow and Greenwood, Johnson had been expelled from Cambridge in 1589 for his presbyterian tendencies; and after spending several years in exile, he had returned to London, only to be imprisoned on several occasions. In 1595 his fundamental cleavage of opinion from the main body of English Puritans appeared in an exchange of letters between him and Arthur Hildersham, which he published under the title of *A Treatise of the Ministery of the Church of England*. In the following year he drew up a manifesto of the separatist position with the help of his colleague Henry Ainsworth, calling it *A True Confession of the Faith*. From 1597 onwards he held the position of separatist pastor at Amsterdam; and from there he continued to publish his writings till well on into the reign of James I.

622. *A Treatise of the Ministery of the Church of England. Wherein is handled this question, Whether it be to be separated from, or ioyned unto. Which is discussed in two letters, the one written for it, the other against it. Wherunto is annexed, after the preface, A brief declaration of the ordinary officers of the Church of Christ. And, a few positions. Also in the end of the treatise, Some notes touching the Lordes prayer. Seven Questions. A table of some principal thinges conteyned in this treatise.* 1595   (STC 13464)

623. *A True Confession of the Faith, and Humble Acknowledgment of the Alegeance, which wee hir Maiesties Subjects, falsely called Brownists, doo hould towards God, and yeild to hir Majestie and all other that are over us in the Lord. Set down in Articles or Positions, for the better & more easie understanding of those that shall read yt : And published for the cleering of our selves from those unchristian slanders of heresie, schisme, pryde, obstinacie, disloyaltie, sedicion, &c. which by our adversaries are in all places given out against us.* 1596   (STC 237)

(This book is attributed to Ainsworth by the STC, but Ainsworth himself attributed it to Johnson.)

From the beginning the more extreme ideas of Johnson were opposed by Henry Jacob, who had himself taken the path of exile into Holland, but who was unwilling to reject the validity of the Anglican ministry. In 1599 he published *A Defence of the Churches and Ministery of Englande* in two treatises: one proving 'that the Churches of England are the true Churches of God', and the other upholding 'the truenes of a Pastorall Calling in Pastors made by Prelates'. This prompted Johnson to bring out *An Answer* in the following year.

624. *A Defence of the Churches and Ministery of Englande. Written in two Treatises, against the Reasons and Obiections of Maister Francis Iohnson, and others of the separation commonly called Brownists. Published, especially, for the benefitt of those in these partes of the lowe Countries.* 1599   (STC 14335)

(The two treatises have separate titles, as follows:

a) 'An Argument proving that the Churches of Englande are the true Churches of God.'
b) 'A Short Treatise concerning the truenes of a Pastorall Calling in Pastors made by Prelates.'

The author's name is given in a note 'to the Christian Reader'.)

625. *An Answer to Maister H. Iacob his Defence of the Churches and Ministery of England. By Francis Iohnson an exile of Iesus Christ.* 1600   (STC 14658)

Another adversary who emerged from among the separatists, and who went on to profess his reconversion to the Anglican Church, was Henoch Clapham. While remaining faithful (as he considered) to the memory of Barrow and Greenwood, he criticised the separatists for their sin of schism in a series of pamphlets from 1598 to 1600. His first publication, in 1598, was entitled *The Syn against the Holy Ghoste* — with reference to the separatists. In the following year he came out with *The Discription of a True Visible Christian*, adapting the title of Barrow's *True Description of the Visible Church*, which had been reprinted (as Clapham complains) by the separatists in 1597 to make it seem 'as if he had bene of theyr mind'. Thirdly, he published an *Antidoton* in 1600, dedicating it 'to all such specially, as whose soules distressed with our ages controversies, doe desire resolution drawen from reason and experience', and declaring his own 'conversion from schism'. None of these writings, however, drew any response from his adversaries, as he complained later in 1608. 'Search all the bookes that I have writ,' he says in *Errour on the Left Hand*, 'and that is from Anno Dom. 1595, hitherto, and consider if still I provoked not all the Factious, specially on the right hand [i.e. those who show 'preposterous zeale'], howsoever hitherto unanswered of any.'

626. *The Syn, against the Holy Ghoste: Made manifest from those grounds of Faith, which have bene taught & received by the Faithfull in England, & that for those 40. y. togither under the prosperous raigne of my Soveraigne Lady & Quene Elishabet. Which may serve for a rayning in of the heady, & yet for a spur to slouthfull Spirits: By Henoch Clapham.* 1598   (STC 5345)

627. *The Discription of a True Visible Christian: right confortable & profitable for all such as are distressed in sowle about present controversies in the Churche. Drawen by He. Cl. but published by occasion (as will appeare in the Epistle) by Io. I.* 1599   (STC 5337)

(In his Epistle the publisher, John Joope, presents this as the third chapter of a larger book containing 26 chapters; but this was apparently never published.)

628. *Antidoton: or A Soveraigne Remedie against Schisme and Heresie: Gathered to Analogie and proportion of Faith, from that Parable of Tares.* 1600   (STC 5330)

(Nine sermons on the Parable of the Tares, now drawn into one sermon.)

For the time being, the separatists with Francis Johnson were troubled with other problems. For one thing, Johnson had sent a copy of his *Confession of Faith* to the Dutch theologian, Francis Junius, only to receive a cold, non-committal answer; but he published the correspondence between them in 1602. For another, the domestic broils that had been taking place within the separatist community in Amsterdam were brought out into the open by Francis Johnson's brother George, who published *A discourse of some troubles* in 1603, recalling the similar troubles that had taken place among the English exiles in Frankfurt during Mary's reign (cf. 125). Addressing his brother, George declared: 'I hope thorow Gods grace never to be intangled by you agayne'. The further history of the separatists, involving separation within separation, belongs to the reign of James I.

629. *Certayne Letters/ translated into English/ being first written in Latine. Two, by the reverend and learned Mr. Francis Iunius, Divinitie Reader at Leyden in Holland. The other, by the exiled English Church, abiding for the present at Amsterdam in Holland. Together with the Confession of Faith prefixed: where upon the said letters were first written.* 1602 (STC 7298)

630. *A discourse of some troubles/ and excommunications in the banished English Church at Amsterdam. Published for sundry causes declared in the preface to the Pastour of the sayd Church.* 1603   (STC 14664)

INDEX

(References are to bibliographical items in the text.)

b) TITLES